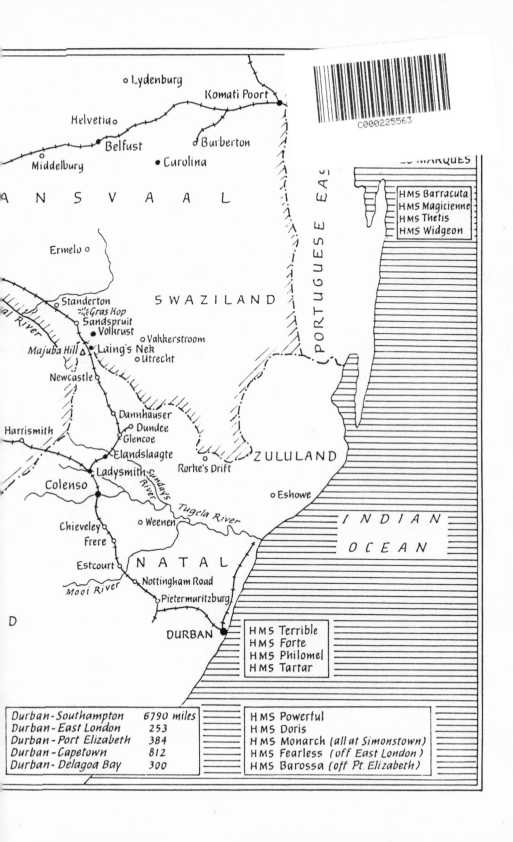

FIELD GUN JACK
VERSUS THE BOERS

FIELD GUN JACK VERSUS THE BOERS

The Royal Navy in South Africa
1899–1900

by

TONY BRIDGLAND

with a Foreword by
ADMIRAL OF THE FLEET LORD LEWIN
KG, GCB, LVO, DSC

LEO COOPER

First published in Great Britain in 1998 by
LEO COOPER
an imprint of
Pen & Sword Books Ltd
47 Church Street
Barnsley
South Yorkshire
S70 2AS

ISBN 0 85052 580.2

A catalogue record for this book is
available from the British Library

Typeset by SetSystems Ltd, Saffron Walden, Essex
Printed in England by Redwood Books, Trowbridge, Wiltshire

TO THE EVER-PRESENT MEMORY OF MY FATHER,
BORN 21 DECEMBER 1899, WHILST
LADYSMITH, KIMBERLEY AND MAFEKING WERE ALL
UNDER SIEGE,
AND LATER
ORDINARY SEAMAN
LZ 8269
HMS *PEEL CASTLE*
FIRST WORLD WAR

CONTENTS

————

Foreword   ix
Acknowledgments   xi

1. Powerful and Terrible   1
2. Scott to the Rescue   5
3. Delagoa Bay   10
4. 'Goodbye Dolly Gray'   13
5. In the Nick of Time   15
6. 'Take that Kopje and be Hanged to it!'   26
7. 'Not much Brass Band and Glory'   40
8. Up the Line   49
9. A Hat-trick of Victories   53
10. Black Week   57
11. Christmas with Jack   73
12. Slaughter at Spion Kop   88
13. Grant's Guns go Ashore   98
14. Stalemate at Vaal Krantz   100
15. Jack Races to Paardeberg   107
16. 'Lollies ere Long'   123
17. Powerfuls in Pompey and Windsor   138
18. The Others   148
19. That Old Pig at Bloemfontein   151
20. To the Foot of Majuba   161
21. Travelling Light to Viljoen's Drift   168
22. Majuba Taken   176
23. Many Miles from Salt Water   183

24. De Wet goes on the Rampage 187

25. Lonely Tartars and Philomels 189

26. A Tablecloth in Pretoria 191

27. Grant's Guns chase De Wet 197

28. Squeezing the Lemon 201

29. Windswept and Watching 209

30. Time to Go Home. 212

Postscript 221

Appendices 223

Bibliography 235

Index 237

FOREWORD
by Admiral of the Fleet Lord Lewin KG, GCB, LVO, DSC.

It was Lord Grey who said, 'The British Army should be a projectile to be fired by the British Navy'. An eminent politician at the turn of the last century, he spoke perhaps with an awareness that during the preceding eighty years the Royal Navy's warlike operations had been conducted almost entirely on shore, establishing the Pax Britannica. Wherever there was trouble, on every continent and in every ocean, the Navy was there. Often first to arrive, sailors and marines were landed to restore order. If the Army was in difficulty, the Navy was always on hand. There are examples without number; to take just two: in the Crimea, besides bombarding enemy positions, naval batteries were set up with heavy guns landed from the ships and a naval brigade five thousand strong helped to relieve the hard-pressed soldiers; not long after, a brigade landed with the guns from HMS *Shannon* played a magnificent part in the relief of Lucknow in the Indian Mutiny.

So it came as no surprise when, at the end of the century, the Army, finding itself out-gunned by the well-armed Boers in South Africa, called on the Navy for help that the response was immediate. Although the scene of action was hundreds of miles from the sea-ship's guns, from twelve pounders to six inch, on improvised mountings and manned by their sailor crews, were soon engaged and later played a vital part in both the siege and relief of Ladysmith and Kimberley.

Tony Bridgland's thorough research into a wide variety of official and personal sources has enabled him to bring Navy's part in operations throughout the Boer War to vivid life. The dangers, trials and tribulations were a great test of character and names which became familiar for their leadership and brave deeds in both world wars sprinkle the pages. Notice particularly the sixteen-year-old Midshipman Cunningham, who later became one of the great sea-going Admirals in the Second World War. Left on board his ship in Simonstown and itching for excitement, he braved 'his ogre of a Captain' to seek permission to go to the front.

The Navy's very considerable part in the Boer War has been largely ignored by military historians. In this book Tony Bridgland redresses the balance and makes a major contribution to Naval History.

ACKNOWLEDGEMENTS

It has been said many times that the writer's lot is a lonely one. That may be so, but I have to say that the writing of this book provided me with many hours of enjoyable browsing through old books, documents and newspapers. In that sense, it was indeed lonely. All the same, when the browsing was over, and the time came to get down to the task of producing a readable story, I needed to call on the help and patience of many people. Without them, I could never have written it.

My sincere gratitude to Admiral of the Fleet Lord Lewin, KG, GCB, LVO, DSC and to the late Captain John Wells, CBE, DSC, (who sadly died as the final manuscript was being prepared) for their ready words of encouragement and technical guidance; to Stephen Sharp and John Wood for their kind provision of access to private family records, and indeed their generous hospitality; to the staffs of Rye and Hastings Public Libraries and the Public Record Office; to Tom Fowle for the long and patient loan of vital books of reference; to Reg Jenkins for his drawing skills; to Amanda de Jongh of the Chief Directorate of Surveys and Land Information, Cape Town, for her prompt and willing help with research of old maps; to the Ladysmith Historical Society and Maureen Richards of the Siege Museum, Ladysmith, for their suggestions of possible sources of information, which proved to be most fruitful, to Carole Clements for her guidance through the labyrinthine mysteries of desk-top technology and to Gian-Maria Bridgland for her thorough work on the index.

Once the bug had bitten, and I had become a Boer War addict, I neglected my wife and family most shamefully and my thanks are due to Maria and our children for their patience and forbearance in that regard.

I hope that all these people will consider that the end product is worthy of their contribution to the writing of this book.

Tony Bridgland
Rye, East Sussex, 1998

GLOSSARY

Burgher — An enfranchised Boer.
Donga — A dried-up river bed.
Dhoolie — A curtained couch carried on poles by two servants.
Drift — A ford.
Kloof — A ravine.
Kopje (or Kop) — A hill.
Kraal — A native village or cattle enclosure.
Krantz — A valley or cleft between two hills.
Laager — A Boer encampment.
Landrost — A District Magistrate.
Mealies — Indian corn.
Nek — A saddle connecting two hills.
Pont — A ferry. Usually a raft, hauled back and forth by chains.
Poort — A pass between two hills.
Rooinek — Red neck. Boer nickname for Englishmen.
Schantz — An improvised rampart, usually built of rocks or sandbags.
Sangar — A stone breastwork.
Spruit — A small river or stream.
Veldt — Open plain country
Vlei — A pond or small lake.
Vrau (or Vrouw) — A Boer housewife.
Zarp — A Boer policeman (*Zuid Afrikaansche Republiek Politie*).

CHAPTER 1

POWERFUL AND TERRIBLE

By 1897 the seventy-eight-year-old Queen Victoria had reigned for sixty years and the celebration of her Diamond Jubilee was to be of unprecedented splendour. Her birthday was on 24 May and a month later, on Saturday, 26 June, the Spithead Naval Review was to take place. One hundred and sixty-five ships of the Royal Navy were to assemble off Portsmouth, stretched in five lines, in all over thirty miles long, and manned by forty thousand sailors.

It was planned for the Queen herself to review her Fleet from the Royal Yacht *Victoria and Albert* as she steamed slowly along the lines, although on the day Victoria was indisposed and sent her son, the Prince of Wales, in her place. Many foreign Powers had been invited to send representative ships to take part in the Review and among those accepting were Germany, France, Italy, Japan, Norway, the United States of America and Russia. The Russian ship was the *Rossiya*, at 12,200 tons, the biggest that country had ever built.

The *Rossiya*'s presence was significant and timely. Great Britain had long been aware of the need to preserve her naval superiority against a combination of jealous rivals on the world's stage. The Naval Defence Act of 1889 had authorized the building of eight modern battleships, the *Royal Sovereigns*, and with it came the announcement from the First Lord of the Two-Power Standard. He declared that thenceforth it would be British policy for the Royal Navy to be 'equal to the combination of the next two strongest navies in Europe'.

Britain's reply to the *Rossiya* was HMS *Powerful* and HMS *Terrible*. They were the largest cruisers ever built up to that time. Indeed, at 14,200 tons they were almost comparable to some of the smaller battleships of the day. And, as it happened, while the *Rossiya* was preparing to keep her appointment at the Spithead Review, the brand-new HMS *Powerful* was being commissioned at Portsmouth on Tuesday, 8 June.

Captain the Hon. Hedworth Lambton, third son of the Earl of Durham, (family motto *Le Jour Viendra* – The Day Will Come), and former captain of the Royal Yacht *Osborne*, was piped aboard at 9 am to take command of the four-funnelled, 25,000 indicated horsepower, twin-screw cruiser, with her two 9.2″ guns, ship's company of 840 and capacity in her bunkers for 3,000 tons of steam coal.

Powerful had been in commission for less than three weeks when the Review was held and took no part in it. She was engaged, instead, in sea-trials. Eventually, at 8.40 am on 7 October, after taking on board 1,366 lbs of beef and 400 lbs of vegetables, she fired a 17-gun salute to the Commander-in-Chief, weighed anchor and sailed from Portsmouth for the China Station. Her first port of call was Las Palmas, in the Canary Islands, where she arrived on 12 October to take on more stores, including another 5,715 lbs of beef. She sailed on 15 October and made her way at a steady 12 knots to Simon's Bay at the Cape of Good Hope, where she took on 2,420 tons of coal. Then it was Mauritius and 9,480 lbs of beef and 800 tons of coal, Colombo, Singapore and finally to what was to be her new base, Hong Kong, on 4 January, 1898. She did the usual rounds of the China Station. From Hong Kong up to Amoy, Shanghai and Wei Hai Wei, over to Nagasaki and Yokohama, Chifu, Seudai Bay and back to Hong Kong. She rode towering waves as she sailed through monsoons in the South China Sea. She steamed peacefully between the jungle-fringed islands of the Philippines, to exercise her main armament in Manila Bay.

Not much seems to have gone seriously wrong, except when Lambton had to send young Fred Hatt, Boy Seaman, for court martial, and when Petty Officer Fitzgerald was tragically killed when he fell from the fore-top at Chifu, and when Boatswain Roberts was arrested for drunkenness and disobedience.

Nearly two years rolled by and it was time for the *Powerful* to go home. At Singapore she took on 800 tons of coal, 5,000 lbs of meat, 1,100 lbs of chocolate, 300 lbs of tea and 63 gallons of Navy rum and headed out into the calm waters of the Malacca Straits towards the blue wastes of the Indian Ocean. It was midway through the forenoon watch on 24 September, 1899.

But Jack Tar's welcome home was going to be somewhat delayed. The long-festering problem with the Boer republics of the Transvaal and the Orange Free State in South Africa was coming to a head and, instead of proceeding home by the Suez Canal, *Powerful* was going on a long detour via the Cape of Good Hope, to rendezvous there with her sister ship *Terrible*, to add their strength to the naval presence off South Africa.

Lambton put into Mauritius, only to have his ship placed in quarantine because there had been a case of smallpox on board in Singapore. Luckily, it was only for one day, and he was able to embark the 2nd Battalion King's Own Yorkshire Light Infantry – twelve officers, 437 men and three horses, who had

2

been stationed on the island, for passage to Durban. Pausing there briefly to disembark her passengers, *Powerful* lost no time in proceeding to Cape Town, arriving on Friday, 13 October, dropping anchor at 8.27 am. Superstitious members of the ship's company would have made a careful note of the date, because at 12.55 pm Able Seaman Hall, aged twenty-five and three-quarters, died of a heart attack.

The next day she joined *Terrible* at Simon's Bay, together with the light cruiser HMS *Doris* and the Simonstown guardship HMS *Monarch*. *Terrible* had been due to relieve *Powerful* on the China Station, but because of the growing crisis in South Africa had also been diverted via the Cape. Captain Percy Scott had only taken over *Terrible* from Captain C. G. Robinson on 18 September and sailed from Portsmouth the very next day. In the days before wireless, standard practice was to call at Plymouth for final orders. Arriving there on the 20th, *Terrible* took on some more stores and some relief crew intended for the destroyers *Handy* and *Hart* on the China Station. It was at Plymouth that Scott received the signal that was to trigger a dramatic turn in their lives that few on board could have envisaged. It was certainly one that none of them would ever forget:

'PROCEED VIA CAPE OF GOOD HOPE. AUGMENT SQUADRON IN SOUTH AFRICAN WATERS IF FOUND NECESSARY ON ARRIVAL THERE.'

Never one to tarry, regardless of whether an emergency existed or not, Scott sailed south the same evening. But now he was in a genuine hurry, and *The Times* reported that when she called at Las Palmas she 'took on board at that port no less than 1,850 tons of Welsh steam coal. In eight hours *Terrible* had this enormous quantity of coal in her bunkers and was on her way again to the Cape.'

Among those on board were two young midshipmen, E. G. Chichester and C. R. Sharp, both aged sixteen, who were destined to experience adventures far in excess of what they had expected when they joined the Navy only a 'dog-watch' ago. In those days life in the services for a young officer was very much a question of 'string-pulling'. Sharp's father, a chief cashier at Barclay's Bank in the City, knew a Member of Parliament, who had a quiet word with the First Lord of the Admiralty, which resulted in it being arranged for him to go to HMS *Britannia* at Dartmouth. When he passed out as a midshipman the strings were pulled again to get him sent to the China Station. Thus he came to find himself on passage in the *Terrible*, on his way to join HMS *Orlando* in Hong Kong.

For all the urgency of *Terrible*'s voyage, one important ritual was not overlooked. The traditional 'crossing the line' ceremony was executed with the usual mixture of solemnity and horse-play when they crossed the equator. The proceedings included the recitation of a long piece of doggerel, dedicated to King Neptune, composed by the Master-at-Arms, George Crowe. One verse was uncannily prophetic:

If your men should land to fight, for England, home and beauty,
Their Captain, I am sure, expects, that they will do their duty,
And emulate past naval deeds, and not return until –
Like Britain's sons, they've fought their guns, and avenged Majuba Hill.*

Terrible made St Helena by 7 October, where Sharp and Chichester managed to visit Napoleon's tomb in their couple of hours ashore, and Simon's Bay on 14 October, the same day as her sister ship arrived from the Far East. The final leg of hard steaming seems to have been fairly uneventful apart from the fact that Midshipman Sharp found that his tin trunk had been rifled and all his new white tropical uniforms stolen, making it necessary for him to fall upon the kindness of his friends in the gunroom until he could visit the naval tailors in Simonstown. That may have been his intention, but, as things turned out, it is improbable that he would have had the time to do it. But the thief was found to be a marine bandsman and, with the full force of Victorian naval discipline, the culprit was duly punished and the uniforms restored to their rightful owner.

Soon his uniforms were to involve Sharp in another problem. Their gleaming whiteness was unacceptable for the job in hand. Instead, he was soon to find himself clad in unfamiliar khaki.

* On 27 February, 1881, during the First Boer War, at Majuba Hill, at the tip of northern Natal, where it meets the Transvaal, a British Force commanded by General George Colley was routed by the Boers and Colley killed. The Boer General was Petrus Joubert, who was destined to renew his acquaintance with British Forces in 1899.

4

CHAPTER 2

SCOTT TO THE RESCUE

'Those who sup with me
Will require a Devil of a Long Spoon.'
Parody of an old Scottish proverb.

It had been plain for a couple of years or more that President Kruger was preparing the Transvaal for war. In 1897 he had signed an alliance with Transvaal's sister republic, the Orange Free State, which committed them to assist each other in the event of attack. And as a correspondent signing himself as 'Liberal Imperialist' pointed out in a letter to *The Times*, Kruger was taxing non-Boers in the Transvaal, who were not entitled to vote, in order to buy arms, a major factor behind British indignation. Kruger obtained much of this armament, including heavy artillery pieces from Germany. The Berlin *National-Zeitung* published a list of guns in possession of the Boers, which stated that they had eight 7.5 cm Krupp guns, sixteen 7.5 cm Creusot guns, eight or nine Maxim-Nordenfelt field-guns, twenty-four 3.7 cm automatic Maxim guns, eight 12 cm field howitzers (four from Krupp, four from Creusot), four 3.7 cm Krupp mountain guns, and four 15.5 cm Creusot guns. These last-named were the famous 'Long Toms', which fired a 96lb shell over a very long range. In all, with old guns, the Boers were thought to possess some eighty or ninety artillery pieces. Eventually these were to be operated mainly by French and German mercenaries.

The article avoided embarrassing British interests, in that it could well have pointed out that twenty advanced design 1 lb Maxim-Nordenfelt 'pom-pom' guns had, in fact, been bought from Britain, guns which had not yet been issued to the British Army at that stage.

It had become a matter of concern for the British field commanders that they did not have the armament to contain the long-range Mauser rifle possessed by the Boers. The Mauser fired only a small bullet, but its range, together with

5

that of the 'Long Tom', meant that the Boers were able to field a combination of some highly formidable weapons. Their advantage was to become a reality when Lieutenant-General Sir George White, VC, commander of the Ladysmith garrison, seeing his position being steadily and relentlessly threatened by the approaching enemy and realizing that the range problem lay at the heart of his predicament, cabled Rear-Admiral Sir Robert Harris, Commander-in-Chief of the Cape of Good Hope and West Africa station, on 25 October asking for naval guns with sufficient range to contain the attackers' artillery to be brought up urgently.

White had only been in South Africa less than a fortnight when Kruger's commandos crossed the border into Natal. At this stage there were 8,000 troops in Ladysmith itself and another 4,000 in the surrounding area, mainly around the town of Glencoe to protect the coal-mines. He reckoned that he had three choices for a line for the defence of northern Natal. He could make a stand on the Biggarsberg Hills, north of Ladysmith, but there was no water supply in the vicinity which ruled out that option. Or he could withdraw to the south of Ladysmith, beyond the Tugela River, which was a natural obstacle (or a natural defence, depending on one's point of view), evacuating the people as far as possible and abandoning the town altogether. But this would mean not only losing the contents of the town's arsenal and food supply, but presenting them to the enemy.

That only left the option of making Ladysmith itself the point at which he would concentrate his forces, and that was what he elected to do. It did mean, of course, that the little town of Newcastle, just inside the border, and its hinterland would be left to the Boers if they invaded, hence the quiet reception that they eventually enjoyed at the outset.

Superficially logical though White's choice may have been, he was condemned by some critics, among them Sir Arthur Conan Doyle of Sherlock Holmes fame, for three major errors which made his eventual predicament infinitely worse: (1) He failed to destroy the railway line north of Ladysmith. (2) He was lacking in judgement in 'retention of the non-combatants in Ladysmith until it was too late to get rid of their useless mouths'. (3) He ought not to have allowed the Boers to occupy Dundee so easily, which was debatable.

The Commander-in-Chief had repeatedly urged White not to let himself be besieged. Ladysmith itself was a most unsuitable spot to make a stand, being on the edge of a flat dusty plain, surrounded by boulder-strewn kopjes over which any relief force would have to fight its way. Ladysmith was, in short, a besieger's dream.

On balance, it does seem strange that White did not withdraw south of the Tugela. Over the days running up to the siege train after train had been steaming into Ladysmith laden with supplies. It would have been a simple matter, surely, to have had these left at Colenso, 15 miles down the line, and then use the empty trains to evacuate the stores in Ladysmith to safety.

Rear-Admiral Harris confirmed that he would meet White's request, but then it occurred to him that he posssessed no suitable mountings for naval guns on land, so he sent for Scott. Captain Percy Scott of the *Terrible*, in the Navy since 1866 when he was 13, and a veteran of the Ashanti and Egyptian Wars and the Congo Expedition in 1875, was a short, stocky (some said cocky) and peppery man. He was a gunnery specialist through and through. A graduate of Eastman's Naval Academy, Southsea, and the gunnery school at HMS *Excellent*, Whale Island, Portsmouth, he possessed a seemingly unlimited flair for invention and was in later life to introduce many successful innovations to Naval gunnery and general practice. When Harris asked him how soon he could give him plans for mountings for naval guns to be sent up to White in Ladysmith, Scott replied, 'Tomorrow morning, at eight o'clock.'

Writing after the War, Scott explained, 'These platform mountings were the best I could do in the ten hours given me by Admiral Harris, but, as our Army had no heavy guns at all, it was necessary to extemporize quickly a more mobile mounting which would move with the troops in the field. It was no good preparing an elaborate design. I had to investigate the resources of the Dockyard, and see what could be made quickly. In the blacksmith's shop I found some 4-inch square bar iron. This settled the design, which I drew on the door in chalk. The 4-inch bar was to be heated and a hole worked in it of sufficient diameter to receive the coned pedestal of a 4.7-inch gun mounting, the ends then being drawn down and turned for the wheels. In a minute the blacksmith was under way making it. I then went over to the plate shop and found a piece of circular five-eighth inch plate about 4 feet in diameter, with a hole in the middle of it. This was the very thing. Two pieces of angle-iron worked round the edge of it to carry a broad tyre, a brass box as a nave with a few pieces of angle-iron radiating, and there was the wheel. A wooden trail and the mounting was complete. The Dockyard worked splendidly, and in forty-eight hours we had a gun on wheels which in range and accuracy was better than any weapon which either the Boers or our Army had in the field.'

He then suggested a field mounting for the naval long 12-pounder, weighing 12 cwt, which had a much longer range than any artillery gun on either side. Using a pair of heavy wagon wheels and a baulk of timber for a trail, he organized a gun ready for land service within 24 hours.

Experts were sceptical. They declared that the 12-pounder would reduce its trail to splinters and that the 4.7″ would turn a backward somersault. Scott was adamant, and insisted on carrying out a trial, which vindicated his faith in his design. At extreme elevation the 12 pounder went 9,000 yards and the 4.7 threw a lyddite projectile 12,000 yards. Thus encouraged, Scott was given the go-ahead, and produced four more 12-pounders and two 4.7s.

A *Times* correspondent wrote, 'It is a peculiar sight to see the 4.7 fired. Many thought it would turn over, but Captain Percy Scott appears to have well calculated the stresses; there is with a full charge of cordite a slight rise of the fore-end, which practically relieves all the fastenings. Hastily put together, and crude as it looks, it really embraces all the points of a scientific mounting, and it wants a great expert to pronounce an opinion on it. The gun is mounted so high that to the uninitiated it looks as if it might turn over on firing, but it does not, and the higher angle of elevation the less strain there is on it. . . . I saw one of these guns fired with an elevation of 24 degs, and a range of 12,000 yards, and fully expected the whole thing to capsize, but it hardly moved. After the firing of several rounds I carefully examined the mounting and noticed that, crude as it may appear, a wonderful amount of practical knowledge was apparent in its construction; the strain was so beautifully distributed, every bolt and each balk bearing its proportionate share. It is in every way creditable to the Navy that when an emergency arises such a thing could be devised and made by the ship's engineering staff within 24 hours. . . . I am told, too, that he is now engaged in designing a travelling carriage for a six-inch gun, and has indeed converted *Terrible* into a factory for curiosities in gun-mountings.'

Another correspondent in Natal described Scott's design for mounting the 4.7" naval gun for service ashore: 'In this carriage lightness and mobility were the points aimed at, and Royal Artillery officers pronounce it to be far better than anything Woolwich has produced.'

In Simonstown Rear-Admiral Harris, heeding White's urgent call from Ladysmith, and anticipating that similar assistance would soon also be needed elsewhere, lost no time in ordering a naval brigade to hold itself in readiness to disembark. Including the *Terrible* and the *Powerful*, the ships off Simonstown at that point had crews totalling some 3,000 men, of whom possibly a third could be spared, together with around half-a-dozen field-guns.

Reuters cabled from Simonstown, 'The Commander-in-Chief gave a general signal last night to the Fleet, ordering the Naval Brigade to hold itself in readiness to disembark. The brigade is now busy making preparation and landing baggage. A train was kept waiting all night for the use of the Brigade. Her Majesty's cruiser *Forte* has been ordered to take in provisions preparatory to leaving.'

Both cruisers had in fact been preparing to land the Brigade. Lambton had the second part of *Powerful*'s port watch engaged on hoisting out and landing the field-guns, and the Brigade of Bluejackets and Marines carried out strenuous practice with the guns in the dock area of Simonstown on 17, 18 and 19 October. On the 20th the Brigade of seamen, marines and a party of stokers to act as stretcher-bearers, from *Doris*, *Monarch*, and *Powerful* herself, landed, led by Commander Ethelston of the *Powerful*, with one 12 pounder 8 cwt naval field-gun. The landing operation appears to have gone smoothly, with the exception of the loss overboard by accident of 'Fenders Hazel-rod 1 in No. and Cork Small 2 in No., and Hooks Boat Iron 3 in No'.

And from Cape Town came a cable to *The Times*, 'At Simonstown it has been intimated that all persons approaching Her Majesty's ships after dark are liable to be fired upon.'

CHAPTER 3

DELAGOA BAY

After discharging one man to HMS *Penelope* for prison, (this ship was subsequently used to house Boer prisoners as well) Lambton hurried *Powerful*, flat out, up to Durban, arriving there on 28 October just in time to see HMS *Magicienne* stop and seize the Dutch steamship SS *Maria* off the coast for carrying 'contraband of war'. This incident was a timely reminder of what was to prove to be a running sore for the British forces. It was also an example of astonishing lack of foresight on the part of the British Government, who had held a trump card in their hands for years, as will be seen, and had failed to play it against the Boers' ace.

On the face of it this war was destined to be an absurdly one-sided contest. On the one hand was the most powerful and richest nation on earth, with its massive resources and a huge navy able to guarantee the safe arrival, halfway round the globe, of all the men and material required to deal with the crisis, and of the many hundreds of thousands of tons of sea transport needed to carry them. On the other hand were two upstart republics, isolated, with no navy or indeed any coastline of their own, who had had the temerity to invade the territory of the former. At a cursory glance the equation simply did not balance. But there were certain other factors which needed to be brought into the reckoning. First, there was the gold.

Paul Kruger, sitting on mountains filled with gold, was the leader of a small country whose world influence was magnified many times out of proportion to its size by virtue of its scarcely tapped riches. He was able to buy just about anything he wanted by way of armaments, supplies and specialist man-power from any one of Britain's rivals. And he was able to take delivery to his land-locked republic by means of a back-door which stood permanently ajar, and immune from interference – Delagoa Bay.

Lourenço Marques (now Maputo), on Delagoa Bay, was in Portuguese

South-East Africa, (Mozambique), three hundred miles up the coast from Durban, north of the Natal border. It sat on a narrow strip of Portuguese territory, about fifty miles wide, which was all that separated the Transvaal from the Indian Ocean. A railway had been built a few years before, with German capital, linking Delagoa Bay with Pretoria, about another 250 miles inland from the Mozambique/Transvaal border, where the line crossed the Komati River at Komati Poort.

The British were fully aware that this was the only route whereby Kruger was able to obtain the means to fight them. They could easily have blockaded it if they had wished, but they faced a dilemma. Delagoa Bay was in the neutral territory of one of their oldest friends, Portugal. Understandably, the place soon became a 'hotbed of intrigue', a rendezvous for spies, secret agents and refugees of all descriptions. And all the while the steady flow of trains into the Transvaal continued.

Legally, the situation was unprecedented. On the one hand, Delagoa Bay was an international port of neutral status, on the other, it was the natural port of a belligerent power at war, namely Transvaal. And with a lamentable lack of vision, successive British Governments had failed to ratify a convention, signed by Sir Robert Morier, the British Minister in Lisbon in 1879, which gave Britain the right of access through and control over Portuguese territory between Delagoa Bay and the Transvaal. For the expenditure of a sum that Britain, at her wealthiest peak, should have considered almost as small change, there could well never have been a war at all!

As things stood, the astonishing fact was that it would have been better for Britain if Delagoa Bay had actually belonged to the Boers rather than to the neutral Portuguese! So, the question remained, what of Britain's right to enforce a blockade? Here the situation was that neutral ships were carrying cargoes to a neutral port. If it could be proved that the cargoes were 'contraband of war', i.e. useful to an enemy in the prosecution of the war, then there was a right of seizure on the high seas, but the difficulty was in the proof. Britain had always insisted on the right to search, and in fact her cruisers were doing just that outside Portuguese territorial waters off Delagoa Bay. But the searches amounted, in most cases, to little more than a sight of the bills of lading. These documents had become highly suspect, particularly as, after many a skirmish with the Boers, empty ammunition boxes were to be found scattered on the veldt marked 'Biscuits – Delagoa Bay' and the like.

The urging for a full-scale blockade grew, but in order to do this, it would have been necessary, as Britain herself had forcefully pointed out on many previous occasions elsewhere in the world, to declare war on the power whose coastline was to be blockaded. And here that power was an old friend.

11

For their part, the Portuguese also found themselves in an awkward position. They could not be charged with actually conniving to assist the Boers, but it was hard to see how they could interfere with the rights of foreign subjects and foreign commerce on what was ostensibly peaceful business.

CHAPTER 4

'GOODBYE DOLLY GRAY'

In August, 1899, the British forces in Natal were the 5th Lancers and the 18th Hussars; the 13th, 67th and 69th Batteries, Royal Field Artillery; No 10 Battery Mountain Division, Royal Artillery; 7th (Field) Company, 8th (Railway) Company, 23rd (Field) Company and a detachment of 29th (Fortress) Company, Royal Engineers; the 1st Battalion Liverpool Regiment, 1st Leicestershire, 1st King's Royal Rifle Corps, and 2nd Royal Dublin Fusiliers, and detachments of Army Service Corps, Royal Army Medical Corps, and Army Ordnance Corps. The three stations ordinarily garrisoned by British troops were Pietermaritzburg, Ladysmith and Eshowe, but it was planned to establish another at Laing's Nek. The volunteer force of Natal was 'partially paid' and consisted of about 1,500 of all ranks, all Europeans, distributed among a naval corps of ninety men, about 850 mounted riflemen, a small artillery section and some infantry. There was an armed mounted police force of about 500 men, and military training was compulsory for all boys aged 10 years or over and attending the state schools, with about 2,000 boys in the various cadet organizations.

The garrisons of Cape Colony included Nos. 14 and 23 Companies Western Division, Royal Garrison Artillery; 29th (Fortress) Company, Royal Engineers; 1st Battalion, North Lancashire Regiment, 2nd Royal Berkshire Regiment and four companies of the 2nd King's Yorkshire Light Infantry, plus detachments of the Army Service, Royal Army Medical and Ordnance Corps. There were about 1,000 Cape Mounted Rifles, and 2,000 Cape Police. With the various volunteer organizations, there were about 7,000 men with guns and eleven artillery pieces.

On many occasions before (and even more famously and drastically on two major occasions since), the British had gone to war grossly undermanned in the face of unexpected skills and fighting power, at least on land, of the enemy. This was, perhaps, a natural consequence of both naval and military chiefs being forced, almost as if by a centuries-old tradition, to wring the extra resources that their professional instincts told them were vital out of a parsimonious and myopic Whitehall penny by begrudged penny. It was no different in 1899.

As will be seen, it was not long before it became clear that this attitude had been a serious and costly misjudgment. By the end of the year the British Army had been swollen to about 250,000 men under arms. Among many others, the additional forces hastily shipped out were composed of the 1st Battalion Black Watch, 5th Dragoon Guards, 1st Aryll & Sutherland Highlanders, 1st Lancashire Fusiliers, 2nd King's Royal Rifle Corps, 1st Border Regiment, 1st Manchester Regiment, 2nd Battalion West Yorkshire Regiment, battalions of the Scots, Grenadier and Coldstream Guards, Northumberland Fusiliers, the Northamptonshire Regiment, 2nd Warwickshire Regiment, 2nd Dorset Regiment, 1st Munster Fusiliers, squadrons of Royal Horse and Life Guards, 2nd Cameronians, 1st Connaught Rangers, 1st Gordon Highlanders, 2nd Middlesex Regiment, with several more batteries of artillery and a number of Service and Medical Corps.

As the war got under way, and troopship after troopship, and train-load after train-load of fighting men, animals and equipment departed from docks and railway stations, to lurch with heaving stomachs over thousands of miles of water to add their weight to those of their colleagues already at the front, with bands playing to see them off with 'Soldiers of the Queen', 'Goodbye Dolly Gray' and other stirring songs of the moment, the flag-waving, cheering crowds gave little doubt as to the solidarity of the nation.

Notwithstanding all the euphoria at home, the Second Boer War was to teach many lessons to the British Army, but at the outbreak of hostilities about the only lesson that had been learned (or perhaps 'heeded' is more accurate) from previous conflicts was that the colour of the soldiers' uniforms needed to be changed to present a less glaring target, and so it became the first major war in which the familiar red tunic, the uniform of the famous Redcoats, did not appear. The infinitely more sensible, and now customary for most modern armies, khaki became the colour of the men's uniforms and much of their equipment. The army world became a khaki one. The Scots Greys in South Africa even painted their horses khaki!

It was the first major war that Britain had fought against a white enemy since the Crimea nearly fifty years before. It was the first war where the lesson was finally and painfully learned that the centuries-old tradition of the tight square formation, holding shape with cast-iron discipline on the field of battle, was not necessarily the irresistible force that it once was, when faced by an innovative, versatile and highly mobile enemy.

CHAPTER 5

IN THE NICK OF TIME

Powerful arrived at Durban on 28 October. Wooden carriages had been constructed by her shipwrights for the three long 12-pounders and two 4.7s loaded in Simonstown dockyard, and Lambton lost no time in getting them all hoisted out and down on to the jetty. The Naval Brigade were all ashore by 5 pm on the 29th October, and comprised: Captain Hedworth Lambton himself, Lieutenants, F. G. Egerton, A. W. Heneage, L. Halsey and M. H. Hodges, Fleet-Paymaster W. H. F. Kay, Surgeon J. G. Fowler, Engineers E. H. Ellis and C. C. Sheen, Gunner W. Sims, Midshipmen, J. R. Middleton, H. T. Hayes, R. C. Hamilton, the Hon I. L. A. Carnegie, and Alick Stokes, all from *Powerful*, with Midshipmen E. G. Chichester and sixteen-year-old C. R. Sharp from the *Terrible*, plus 267 men, being the guns' crews, small-arm companies, two engine-room artificers, forty-eight stokers as stretcher-bearers, ammunition carriers and gun-mounting parties, armourers, cooks, marine servants and a steward, a ship's corporal, a sick-berth attendant, blacksmith and carpenter.

It will be noted that Chichester and Sharp had managed to get themselves included in Lambton's mainly *Powerful* Brigade. Some more string-pulling had been done, it appears, because it so happened that Chichester's father, Captain Edward Chichester, RN, was Principal Transport Officer in South Africa at the time. It is recorded in letters that the boy hoped to get ashore with the Naval Brigade, especially as that would qualify him for a medal, and that his father had mentioned this to Captain Percy Scott. It is fair to assume that Chichester used his influence to make sure that his friend Sharp was also included.

The guns to be taken up to Ladysmith with the Brigade were two quick-firing 4.7"s, to be mounted on wooden platforms, three long 12-pounder (weight 12 cwt) quick-firing guns on the field carriages designed by Captain Scott, one 12-pounder (weight 8 cwt) naval field gun, and four Maxims, one on a tripod and three mounted on field carriages.

The amount of ammunition taken was governed purely by the limitations of what it was possible to carry, which was:

For the 4.7s, 200 rounds each of common shell, lyddite and shrapnel.

For the 12 pounders, 798 rounds of common shell, 396 rounds of shrapnel and 24 rounds of case shot.

Lee-Metford rifle ammunition, besides the 150 rounds carried by each man, 39,000 rounds.

Maxim gun ammunition, 64,000 rounds.

For revolvers, 5,400 rounds.

It seemed as if the whole of Durban had turned out to watch the loading of the men and the guns on to the waiting trains. This was something special to see. The Navy was about to go to work, the mightiest Navy in the world, with the toughest sailors, held in admiration and affection throughout Victoria's Empire. They had a look of calm and confident determination about them that tingled the spines of all who had come to watch, and to bid them farewell and good luck.

From Durban the narrow-gauge Natal Railway wound its way up, skirting hills of barren rock, lightly patched with clumps of scrub. The men, now clad in the high-buttoned khaki tunics drawn from the local military authorities, sat packed tightly in their compartments. Many a forefinger was repeatedly jammed, with a mutter, into the collar of his 'pongo's' rig that they had been forced to wear. After the loose-necked sailor's jumpers which had been everyday dress to them for years, the new attire was not only unfamiliar, it was uncomfortable.

On 11 October, 1899, the Transvaal Government had telegraphed all stations with the single word 'Oorlog' – (war). Martial law was proclaimed and next day Commandant-General Piet Joubert's Boers rode across the border into Natal near Ingogo, with supporting columns to the right and left marching through Botha's Pass, Mol's Neck and Wool's Drift. It was probably the largest body of mounted armed men that Africa had ever seen. It had rained incessantly for some days previously and they were cold and shivering, with their clothes soaked through, having slept on the mud and been unable to light fires even for cooking because of the wet. 12,000 men, composed of the Pretoria, Heidelberg, Middleburg, Krugersdorp, Standerton, Wakkerstroom and Ermelo commandos, appeared as 'an endless procession of silent misty figures, horsemen, artillery and wagons, filing past in the cold dark night along the winding road'. Poetically, it was at the precise spot where 'the black shoulder of Majuba stood up against the greyer sky.' They were preceded by the only 'regular' unit in Joubert's force, the Staats Field Artillery, with sixteen Krupp guns and two of the big 6 inch Creusot guns.

They were amazed to find themselves unopposed. For several days nothing seemed to happen as they advanced over seventy miles into Natal. To Joubert it may have seemed that the British not only had no precise idea of the numbers of Boers facing them, but also as though, like Drake on Plymouth Hoe 311 years before, they cared not.

And with exquisite timing, as if to emphasize the point, at the very moment Joubert entered Natal the new British Commander-in-Chief in South Africa, until recently Commanding Officer of the Aldershot Garrison, General the Right Hon. Sir Redvers Buller, VC, GCB, KCMG, PC, although not finishing a game of bowls, was calmly boarding the *Dunottar Castle* to the cheers of a vast crowd on the quayside in the autumn fog at Southampton, 6,000 miles and over three weeks away.

Joubert and his commandos advanced cautiously through the quiet country-side; most of the farmers and homesteaders having vacated their properties and fled southwards. On 15 October they entered the town of Newcastle, about sixty miles north of Ladysmith, unopposed by any hindrance other than the teeming rain which continued to torment them. There they rested for a couple of days, while Buller did the same at Madeira, where the *Dunottar Castle* had arrived on the 17th.

Buller was a famous and distinguished Victorian soldier, winning his VC at Hlobane in the Zulu War of 1879, when as commander of the Frontier Light Horse, he had rescued a party of his comrades in spite of hordes of attacking Zulus. In his later life, however, (although it must be remembered that he was nearly sixty years old when he set off for South Africa) he had acquired a reputation as somewhat of a bon viveur. The evidence of this could be seen in the cases of champagne and other trappings, which were unloaded on to the dockside at Cape Town when he disembarked on 31 October. By this time, however, things had begun to happen up-country and the news that awaited him was not at all good. In fact, it was disastrous.

He had had, of course, ample uninterrupted time to consider his options while cocooned on the *Dunottar Castle* as she steamed down the Atlantic Ocean. It seemed logical to take the same view as the War Office in London, i.e. that the simplest way to take the Boer capital of Pretoria was by means of a direct thrust from the Cape Colony through the Orange Free State capital, Bloemfon-tein, despite the fact that the distance from the sea was much longer than the Durban-Pretoria route, because better use could be made of the rail links northwards from the supply bases at Cape Town, Port Elizabeth and East London, which were nearer to home than Durban by several hundred sea miles.

But President Steyn of the Orange Free State, seeing the easy ride that Joubert had enjoyed in Natal, mobilized his own commandos and crossed the Orange River into Cape Colony on 1 November, hardly before Buller had had time to get his land-legs back. Instantly Buller was wrong-footed, and a vastly different light was cast on things. No longer was the easy approach to Pretoria, through Bloemfontein, an available option.

Meanwhile, elsewhere, there had been several other major setbacks for the British. At Talana Hill, a six-hundred-foot mound of red rocks and thorn bushes, on 20 October, at what became known as the Battle of Dundee, the Boers under General Lukas Meyer, thrusting towards Ladysmith, were attacked by the British in an attempt to drive them back. But the highly mobile Boers surrounded the British infantry, which ironically included Buller's old regiment, the 60th Rifles.

The disciplined British played their part perfectly, as if they were drilling in Aldershot, but they were drawn too far forward and on the edge of a eucalyptus wood at the foot of Talana the Boers cut them to pieces with a hail of Mauser bullets. The British suffered nineteen officers and 142 men killed and wounded (including their Commanding Officer, General Penn Symons, who was wounded and captured, only to die in the Boer hospital later), lost 331 prisoners and were forced to surrender, except for a mercifully detached column of 4,000 men under Brigadier-General Yule, who managed to avoid further confrontation with the enemy and endured a forced march of sixty miles back to the safety of Ladysmith through the mud and rain, reaching there on the 26th in a state of exhaustion. It was one of the most humiliating episodes of British military history, and one for which General White, who had wired Yule with orders to abandon Dundee and fall back on Ladysmith, was to be censured.

On 29 October, at Farquhar's Farm, on Nicholson's Nek, another even more serious débâcle overtook the British. With the Boers approaching ever nearer to Ladysmith, General White sent out some troops to try to halt them. These he deployed in three columns. On the right five battalions of infantry and artillery, commanded by Colonel Grimwood, were supported by Sir John French's cavalry. In the centre were four battalions of infantry, cavalry and artillery commanded by Colonel Hamilton, and on the left two battalions of infantry and artillery under Colonel Carleton.

The plan was for Carleton's column, composed of Royal Irish Fusiliers, the Gloucesters and the 10th Mountain Battery, to march through the night to a forward position at Nicholson's Nek, from whence they would pour fire onto the Boers as they fled from Grimwood and Hamilton. But things went horribly wrong. In the darkness, as Carleton's force was scrambling up a steep hill, some rocks were dislodged and tumbled noisily down the slope. This caused the pack-mules to panic and bolt into the night, taking the artillery pieces and most of the ammunition and equipment with them. Carleton had no choice but to stay where he was, hope to find the mules and guns nearby in the morning, and reorganize things in time for the action as planned. But when day broke he was horrified to find that he was not, in fact, at Nicholson's Nek but on a low hill called Tchrengula, surrounded by higher ground, and the ridges all around were occupied by Boers, 400 rock-hidden snipers, who began to rain a fusillade of withering fire down on his trapped, stranded, helpless and fully exposed men.

Meanwhile Grimwood's and Hamilton's columns had both failed in their objectives. The enemy evaded them in the darkness and they walked straight into a Boer counter-ambush near Lombard's Kop, known as the Battle of Modder Spruit, by the morning. As for French, it seems that he made a night-time tour of the veldt without any contact with either friend or foe.

For Carleton, sustaining heavy losses on Tchrengula without being able to make the slighest reply, there was nothing for it but to surrender his surviving thirty-seven officers and 917 men. All told, by the time that the other columns had straggled back into Ladysmith, General White could count 317 killed and wounded and 1,068 missing.

It had already been anticipated by White and other senior commanders that the Boers' range of fire would prove to be an insurmountable problem, hence his earlier call for naval guns, and it was already proving to have been accurate foresight. The Boers, bringing up their heavy guns on travelling bogeys from the fortifications of Johannesburg, were easily outranging and outweighing the British garrison artillery and were about to engulf Ladysmith itself.

Lambton's sailors arrived in Pietermaritzburg at 1 am, where the Governor of Natal, Sir Walter Hely-Hutchinson, turned out to meet the two trains. The wires to Ladysmith were still intact and he was able to bring Lambton up to date with the latest information from White. He expressed doubt that the Navy could reach the town before the expected battle, or before it became completely encircled. It was also feared that the Boers may have torn up the railway line farther north.

There was clearly no time for delay and the trains hurried on, fortunately finding that the track had not been destroyed, reaching Estcourt at dawn and Colenso, 20 miles from Ladysmith itself, at 8.30 am.

The line was still clear, but heavy fighting had already begun. Even above the clatter of the locomotives' pistons, they could hear the boom of big guns in the distance, echoing around the kopjes. Excitement aboard the trains grew to fever pitch as they flew up the line, running into Ladysmith at full steam.

At the station army personnel helping them to detrain the heavy guns looked at their strange new colleagues, clad in a mixture of army and navy clothing, the khaki tunics seemingly incongruous with the brown linen-covered straw sennet hats that were the Navy's usual summer rig of the period. 'Long Tom' shells screamed over the station while this task was underway, making for an uncomfortable time. But the Boers had not yet found the range and the shells landed harmlessly enough. One midshipman, probably Chichester, was heard to exclaim, 'We've been under fire, so now we'll get the medal!'

A snatch of conversation between an Able Seaman and a Petty Officer was overheard between the blasts of the exploding shells and the roar of gunfire from around the town's perimeter:

Jack, with one horny hand resting on a 12-pounder, to PO: 'Now we've got this bastard ashore, how do you propose to get it into action?'

PO to Jack, pointing at the waiting herd of oxen: 'See them fucking cows over there? Catch some of the bastards and hitch 'em on!'

Later.

Jack to oxen: 'That's got you lot fast; now you fucking cows, start fucking pulling!'

The wooden trails of the guns were lashed to wagons each hauled by sixteen oxen, and the Brigade made its way away from the station, all the time accompanied by a staccato roar of small-arms fire and of the guns of the Royal Artillery, who were throwing everything they had into an effort to silence 'Long Tom', who was maintaining his barrage of 96 lb shells, while a steady stream of ambulances came in the opposite direction, carrying the wounded from the battle.

The Brigade was ordered into immediate action. Three 12-pounders, under Lieutenant Michael Hodges, raced along Newcastle Road to the northern perimeter of the town two miles away, to Limit Hill, led by a brave young local boy on a bicycle to show them the way, the oxen rolling their eyes as they were beaten along, assisted by the sweating gun's crews on drag-ropes. Hodges, just a month past his twenty-fifth birthday, unlimbered his guns, and was just ready to open fire when orders came to withdraw.

Shells were still crashing all around and a wheel was knocked off one of the guns. Three bluejackets, Emly, Ford and Nail, were wounded and the oxen all bolted. Ordered to withdraw, all Hodges could do was to try to disable the gun before abandoning it. He tried to damage the breech with pieces of rock and heavy tools, but luckily, before this had had any real effect on the 12-pounder, enough of the oxen had been rounded up and in-spanned to the wagons. Somehow they managed to replace the wheel with a spare and ran all the guns to safety on Gordon Hill.

From below Gordon Hill Hodges was able to engage 'Long Tom' and opened up with vigour on the Boers at a range of 6,000 yards. Mr Sims, the gunner, displayed superb gunlaying and sighting. According to the report of the Spotting Officer in the observation balloon, it was only the third shell fired by the Naval Brigade that silenced 'Long Tom' for the day. Next day, however, they were disappointed to find it in action again, which meant that the damage can only have been slight.

General White congratulated Lambton on this feat of gunnery. There was no doubt that the arrival of the naval guns had surprised the Boers, who had thought themselves impregnable, given 'Long Tom's' range.

The other company, under Lieutenant Lionel Halsey, 27, another former Royal Yacht Officer, had also run a field-gun past Junction Hill and along Newcastle Road, and were ordered to retire together with Hodges to Gordon

Hill, but this gun was not a long 12-pounder and the Boers were beyond its range, so it did not go into action on that day.

Back at Ladysmith Station, all through the action the frantic work was going on to get the 4.7s unloaded, with all their mountings, gear for gun platforms, ammunition and sundry trappings. Working parties of stokers, assisted by a detachment of Royal Engineers and an 'excitable and singing mob' of native drivers, heaved and sweated all day between the trains and the waiting wagons and oxen.

The first to go out was to Cove Redoubt, one mile north-west of the town, in order to replace a 7-pounder manned by the Natal Naval Volunteers. It set off at dusk, so that its movement would be undetected by the Boers in the darkness, under Lieutenant Egerton, the Gunnery Lieutenant, with bluejacket escort, six wagons each drawn by sixteen oxen. On the way the leading wagon became stuck in a narrow rocky gully, blocking the progress of those following. All efforts to extricate it failed, despite the screaming and cursing at the animals of the African drivers, who had become fluent in the art, having worked with British soldiers for some time. A double team of oxen was sent out in the morning and, with another chorus of shouts from the drivers and snorts from the beasts, the gun was hauled up to its lofty new home.

The other two 12-pounders and the four Maxims were dragged after dark to join those with Hodges and Halsey on Gordon Hill. It was then discovered that in all the excitement nobody had seemed to think about sleeping arrangements. Being eager only to get on with the fight, they had forgotten to draw any tents from the military stores in Durban. They borrowed some rather decrepit ones from the Army, pitched them makeshift fashion, and after a supper of tinned meat, bread and coffee, the sailors slept like logs, tired and grimy.

There were known to be several Boer sympathizers in Ladysmith, so care was taken to post sentries around the guns' positions in case of any attempts at sabotage. Careful watch was kept throughout the night, the passwords being 'Powerful' and 'Terrible'. It had certainly been an eventful day and, although Sims' gunnery had scored a point against 'Long Tom' to brighten their spirits, everybody in Ladysmith was bound to be in receipt of some hot treatment in the days and weeks to come.

Nonetheless, the fact remained that the Navy, by racing to the scene in the nick of time, many miles from salt water, had managed to cover the final retreat of the rest of White's forces back into Ladysmith before it finally became encircled on 3 November, and to install guns in the town which had the ability to contain the enemy throughout the ensuing siege.

As for White, the humiliation seems to have broken his spirit as a soldier. He managed to cable the War Office, before the Boers cut the telegraph line, saying that he took full responsibility. It was his plan, and it had not worked. He then wrote to his wife a long-winded screed, steeped in misery. He was sixty-four years old, too old for soldiering. His troops had no confidence in him. He deserved to be superseded, and so on.

For all that he may have wished for the ground to open up and swallow him at that time, the immediate facts had to be faced. He was in a siege, the apportionment of blame for which had to be left for another day. With a heavy heart he set about organizing his defences.

The Intelligence Department had reported that it would not be possible for the Boers to take their heaviest guns to the highest peaks which surrounded Ladysmith. (White could, with much justification, have cited this point in defence of the criticism that was to be arraigned against him.) At the outset the eight-mile perimeter of the town's defences had therefore been set according to that belief. It soon became clear that these estimations had been sadly inaccurate when the Boers began shelling with 'Long Tom' from the summit of Pepworth Hill.

This miscalculation was yet another example of the blindfold attitude of the British top brass. They had had years in which to assess the power of the artillery that was likely to face them in the event of a conflict, but had done nothing to address this imbalance, and in truth, that was the root of the necessity for the Navy to be there at all.

White, presumably shaking himself to his senses after his initial despondency, quickly extended his perimeter of defences to a length of fourteen miles, now taking in the rocky outcrops closer to the town which were natural sites on which to position heavy guns, and brought into range much of the artillery available for the town's defence, guns which otherwise would have lain redundant behind the lines, unable to engage the enemy on his distant hilltops. Indeed, these sites had presented a potential danger in that, if ever taken by the Boers, they would have enabled them to bombard Ladysmith from point-blank range, so that by extending his lines in this way, White solved a double-edged problem.

From Caesar's Camp on its southernmost point, the new perimeter ran clockwise through Wagon Hill, Highlander's Post, Range Hill, Red Hill, Rifleman's Post, Ration Post, King's Post, Observation Hill on the northern point of the defences, to Gordon Hill, behind which lay Cove Redoubt and Junction Hill overlooking the spot on the outskirts where the railway branched to Newcastle and Harrismith, Cemetery Hill and Helpmakaar Hill. This left a three-mile gap between the last-named and Caesar's Camp, through which ran the railway line alongside the Klip River flowing south-eastwards out of town.

The extended length of the perimeter meant that it could be manned by less than 1,000 defenders per mile, so it was important for these to be well entrenched, which task was set about with all haste.

White divided the perimeter into four sections for command purposes. Colonel W. G. Knox was given the short but highly exposed arc from

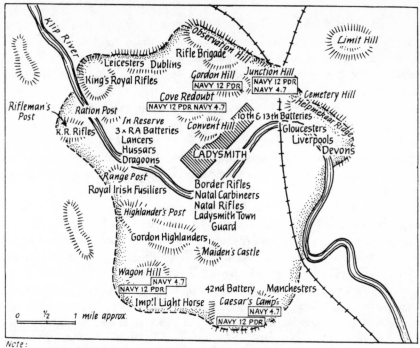

Note:
(A) The three positions of the RN 4.7 'Lady Anne' at Junction Hill, Wagon Hill and Caesar's Camp
(B) The two positions of the RN 12 PDR moved to Wagon Hill from Cove Redoubt

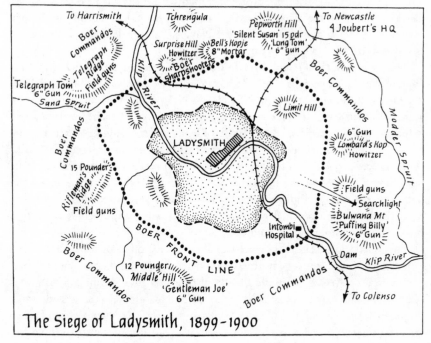

The Siege of Ladysmith, 1899-1900

23

Helpmakaar Hill back to Junction Hill, being allocated the 1st (King's) Liverpool Regiment, the 1st Devons, two companies of the 1st Gloucesters, a detachment of Royal Dublin Fusiliers and some artillery. Knox's section was reinforced by one of the Navy's 4.7s which was placed on Cemetery Hill, and the three 12-pounders on Junction Hill.

The Navy's guns were the only artillery White possessed which was able to engage the Boers' heaviest pieces, and were therefore of extreme value and had to be carefully protected. They were fixed on solid platforms and encased with substantial earthworks and sand-bagging. No Boer shell ever managed to penetrate these defences throughout the siege, despite the fact that they became obvious prime targets.

Colonel W. Royston, of the Natal Volunteers, was given the eastern section, from Helpmakaar Hill down to Caesar's Camp. This was a long, comparatively flat section and included the river plain. Royston's troops were nearly all mounted infantry, being the Natal Mounted Rifles, Natal Carbineers, the Border Mounted Rifles and the Ladysmith Town Guard.

From Caesar's Camp through Wagon Hill and northward to Flagstaff Spruit Colonel Ian Hamilton was in command, with the 1st Manchesters, two companies of the Royal Irish Fusiliers and four companies of 2nd Gordon Highlanders.

The rest of the circumference, facing north-west, was commanded by Major-General F. Howard, with infantry detachments from the 1st Leicesters, King's Royal Rifles and the Rifle Brigade. To the rear of this section was Cove Redoubt, where White placed the other Navy 4.7 alongside the 69th Battery of the Royal Artillery on King's Post.

The main artillery strength had thus been deployed to face north, which was logical. This left Dawkins' 13th Battery, Royal Artillery, on Helpmakaar Hill, together with the survivors from Nicholson's Nek of the 10th Mountain Battery under Captain Christie, plus two obsolete but useful 6.3 inch howitzers. The 42nd Battery was positioned at Caesar's Camp under Goulburn, after a heavy job of hacking a suitable path out of the rocky terrain for an approach track. The eastern-facing positions were denied any direct artillery support of their own, apart from the covering guns of the 13th and 42nd Batteries across the valley of the Klip, although Royston hit on the clever idea of constructing wooden dummy guns, which were successful in fooling the Boers into wasting a considerable amount of ammunition.

The Boers, for their part, placed a 'Long Tom' on Pepworth Hill, about three miles distant from the northern perimeter of Ladysmith, flanking the road and railway to Newcastle. It and the Naval Brigade's guns at Junction Hill were therefore within easy range of each other. On Lombard's Kop, facing Ladysmith from the east, was another 'Long Tom' with a 10.5 cm howitzer and other smaller pieces. A 6 inch Creusot and a battery of smaller guns were on Bulwana

Mountain, which looked across the valley of the Klip directly into the centre of Ladysmith, and there the Boers installed a powerful searchlight. Directly from the south, on Middle Hill and End Hill, facing Wagon Hill and Caesar's Camp, were another 6-inch Creusot and some 12-pounders.

From the west, along Telegraph Ridge down to Rifleman's Ridge behind Sand Spruit and Flagstaff Spruit, were several batteries of 9- and 12-pounders and two more 6-inch Creusots, and finally on Surprise Hill, just over a mile from the British forward position on Observation Hill, and just in front of the hump of Tchrengula where Carleton had met with disaster, was another 10.5 cm howitzer.

General Joubert had made his headquarters at Modder Spruit, above five miles north-east of Ladysmith. It was a haphazard scattering of camp-fires and horses, men and wagons, and tents of all shapes and sizes, every one of which seemed to have a row of the Boers' favourite food, biltong, strips of beef dried in the sun, suspended from its guy-ropes. He had at his disposal the very pick of the Boer forces; thought to be some 20,000 to 25,000 strong at the beginning of the siege, composed of the Pretoria, Winburg, Kroonstad, Bethlehem, Vrede, Rhenoster River, Harrismith, Ventersburg, Vryheid, Utrecht, Wakkerstroom, Lyndenburg, Krugersdorp, Heidelburg and Middlesburg commandos, supported by Irish and German brigades and companies of the Johannesburg Mounted Police, known as the Zarps.

The Senior Supply Officer of Ladysmith Garrison, Colonel Ward, with all the doors locked around him, sat down to take accurate stock of the food situation. Inside the town he counted 13,500 officers and men under arms, 5,000 white civilians, 2,500 Africans and Indians, plus horses and livestock of various descriptions. He reported to General White at the latter's headquarters in Poort Road that he calculated that the supplies of food in the town were enough to feed the humans for fifty days and the animals for thirty.

The scene was set, with the Boers to open the bowling and the British to sit tight and play as straight a defensive bat as they could until help arrived.

CHAPTER 6

'TAKE THAT KOPJE AND BE HANGED TO IT!'

Two days from Cape Town the *Dunottar Castle* passed a small steamer heading north, the *Australasian*, which had a large blackboard hanging over her side, proclaiming in large white letters 'BOERS DEFEATED – THREE BATTLES – PENN SYMONS KILLED.'

General Sir Redvers Buller noted the message through his field-glasses, doubtless with confused feelings. Did this mean that his journey was not, after all, to prove to have been necessary? Was he to arrive only to find that the war had already been won?

His fellow passengers, who included young Winston Churchill, then a war correspondent with the *Morning Post*, hurried ashore in Cape Town, anxious to find newspapers, while Buller was brought up to date with the secret war cables in hush-hush security on board. He was to learn that the *Australasian*'s message had been far from accurate.

To cap his immediate problems, he found that not only was White almost locked up in Ladysmith, but that the Boers had also besieged the towns of Kimberley and Mafeking. Ironically, each of the three major towns now under siege held a famous personage. Cecil Rhodes was in his tumbledown mansion in Kimberley, making imperious and petulant demands for relief; his friend Dr Jameson happened to be in Ladysmith, suffering from typhoid, accompanied by Cecil's brother, Colonel Frank Rhodes; and in Mafeking, far to the north near the Bechuanaland border with Cape Colony, the garrison was commanded by Colonel Robert S. Baden-Powell, future founder of the Boy Scout Movement.

That Buller needed to make an urgent reappraisal of the situation was plain. Whatever else, the plan for a straight drive through to Bloemfontein was now totally out of the question. But as his troop transports were still labouring down through the Atlantic, strung out in a line of smoke-belching, heaving chartered steamers, each crammed with hundreds of seasick soldiers, headed by the *Roslin*

Castle which was not to arrive until 9 November, there was precious little he could do but think – and wait.

On the other side, Joubert was, of course, doing some planning himself. His natural commitment to the principle of always planning a military objective so as to result in the minimum of loss of life on both sides led him to conclude that it would be best, assisted by the Free State commandos now closing in on Ladysmith from the north-west, where over 11,000 of them had been waiting on the Drakensberg passes from Oliver's Hook to Collins Pass, to bottle up the 12,000 British troops inside the town. They were, after all, the bulk of the British Army in the whole of South Africa. His advancing Boers could then wash around it, like a flow of lava around a protruding rock, and press on to the south.

He was convinced that the British would surrender and sue for peace, faced with the unpalatable fact that Ladysmith, Kimberley and Mafeking were all in a stranglehold. Held in such a grip, the towns would soon be starved into submission and the war would be over quickly and cheaply, with relatively little blood having been spilt on either side. It was a noble plan, laced with humane forethought, but on this occasion, as we know, Joubert was wrong. The British did not surrender.

Buller remained in Cape Town for three weeks while the steamers started to unload his army. Clearly now the war was going to develop on two main fronts, the east and the west, with the third front, to the south, needing little more than a holding force. Ladysmith in the east and Kimberley in the west both had to be unlocked before any broad advance could be made on Johannesburg and Pretoria.

As soon as he reached Durban, Buller examined one of Scott's 4.7-inch guns. Scott wrote:

I told him the range, and of some of the forced marches I had made the crews do for exercise. One of these marches was as follows: I wired to Commander Limpus – 'Take a 4.7 gun, WITHOUT OXEN, to Umgeni (six and a half miles), fire a round, report time of leaving and time of return.' In five minutes I got a reply, 'Have left' – and four hours later I rode out to meet them returning. They were almost back at their camp, and coming up a hill. I have never seen a finer sight. The 100 men were marching magnificently, pulling for all they were worth. It was November, that is to say, the height of summer in Natal. Everything they had on was sweated through. When they saw me they broke into double time, and Commander Limpus, watch in hand, said, 'We shall do it in four and a half hours', and they did. That was enough for General Buller and the next day he wired to send the two 4.7-inch guns and four 12-pounders to the Front as soon as possible. In our little camp, the news was received with cheers, and one

27

sailor remarked that what had done it was that 'fucking pull up from Umgeni'. I telegraphed to have a special train ready to start at five pm and to clear the line (it was a single track); at a quarter to five I was at the station, and at five o'clock, to the minute, the train, with guns, ammunition, officers, men and stores, steamed out.

During all the activity in northern Natal, it will be recalled that Lambton had already landed another Brigade, as ordered by Rear-Admiral Harris, in Simonstown, 800 miles away to the south, about a fortnight earlier, before racing *Powerful* up to Durban to catch the train for Ladysmith.

The Navy had pressed to be allowed to furnish a brigade for service on land even before the outbreak of the war, and when Harris gave the word it was done with gusto on 20 October. The personnel were: Commander A. P. Ethelston in command, HMS *Powerful,* Major J. H. Plumbe, Royal Marine Light Infantry. HMS *Doris*, Second in Command, Lieutenant F. J. Saunders, RMLI, Surgeon C. M. Beadnell, Midshipmen T. C. Armstrong and G. E. Lewin, all HMS *Powerful.*

Captain A. E. Marchant, RMLI, Lieutenant W. T. C. Jones, RMLI, Lieutenant G. W. Mc. O. Campbell, RN, Fleet-Surgeon, J. Porter, Sub-Lieutenant R. F. White, Sub-Lieutenant Newton, Assistant Paymaster B. C. Allen, Midshipmen C. A. E. Huddart, T. F. J. L. Wardle and Robertson, all HMS *Doris*.

Lieutenants F. W. Dean, RN, and Captain Guy Senior, Royal Marine Artillery, both HMS *Monarch*.

These were accompanied by fifty-three bluejackets and 290 non-commissioned officers and men of the Royal Marine Light Infantry.

Ethelston arranged to draw khaki gear from the Army Ordance Stores in Cape Town, but found that there was barely enough to go round, which resulted in a range of devious measures being taken to dye the Marines' webbing and belts, which were normally gleaming white, to match the unfamiliar drab tunics they were given to wear. Coffee, permanganate of potash, boot polish, brown paint and even ox-dung were among the substances put to a novel use.

Rear-Admiral Harris inspected the Brigade in front of his residence in the Simonstown dockyard, and they marched through the town to the station to take the train to Cape Town. All along the line thousands of people turned out to cheer, every station and embankment being thronged with waving handkerchiefs and flags. At Cape Town's Salt River Junction a staff officer boarded the train and handed Ethelston his sealed orders. The train moved off with a whistle, its destination known only to Ethelston, who said nothing for several miles.

He did make one announcement, however, which received a mighty cheer throughout the train. It had been arranged for the matelots and marines to continue to receive their daily tot of grog as usual, and this immediately put everyone into a good humour, forgetting for the moment the question of their destination.

The train steamed northwards, through the waterless and treeless Great Karroo Desert, to the junction at De Aar. Here it took the eastward branch, heading for Naauwpoort, and Ethelston sent a small pilot engine on ahead to reconnoitre for ambushes or damage to the line. The driver of the pilot engine protested loudly at being ordered to carry out this dangerous mission, until Ethelston himself offered to ride on the front buffers of the locomotive, a rash thing for an officer in command of 360 men on a special assignment to do. Nevertheless, all worked satisfactorily, except that the Commander arrived at Naauwpoort covered from head to toe in soot.

Passing through Naauwpoort, garrisoned by half a battalion of the Royal Berkshire Regiment, it was clear that the effects of war were already spreading; the town was full of refugees of all descriptions. Great stacks of supplies lay alongside the station, each covered with huge sheets of tarpaulin.

They arrived at what was to be their final destination, Stormberg Junction, on 23 October, just 50 miles from the Orange Free State. Detraining, with all their equipment, they set up camp and spent the next few days throwing up defensive earthworks and digging-in. Here, on a high dusty plateau surrounded by rocky kopjes, the South African spring weather was stiflingly hot in the daytime, but fell to a point not far off freezing at night. The variation in temperature within one twelve-hour period could be as much as 50 degrees Fahrenheit, making for a very uncomfortable time under canvas.

There had been rumours of possible Boer attacks, and many of the locals were suspected of being sympathetic to the Boers. Extreme vigilance was called for in view of the exposed position and as a precaution the men were 'stood to arms' every day at 4 am. The order came, 'No removal of boots at night.'

For the first time they were working with mules, animals famous for their stubbornness. Ethelston's men discovered that this reputation was thoroughly deserved, and much of the time they spent at Stormberg was taken up in practising the in-spanning, out-spanning, turning and manoeuvring of these fractious beasts.

Men trained and deployed for a fight are naturally keyed-up, but if they are then left to stew in inactivity for a couple of weeks they are prone to feel flat and dejected. When orders came to move, their spirits rose in anticipation of some action at last, only to be dashed again when it was announced that Buller wanted them to go down the line to Queenstown.

They reached their new camp at 7 pm on 2 November, to a cheery welcome from the inhabitants, whose nerves were stretched with the suspense of waiting for the Boers to do something. By contrast, at that exact moment, their opposite

29

numbers, commanded by the Captain of the *Powerful*, many miles away across the mountains, were about to have the door slammed shut by the Boers as they dug in at Ladysmith.

Their time in Queenstown was pleasant enough, apart from the frequent dust-storms which seemed to ruin every meal the cooks tried to prepare. It was a small town on a plain, with Bushman's Hoek and the Stormberg Mountains, over which the train had just brought them, visible to the north. In the evenings the band of the Royal Berkshires played a selection of popular airs to entertain the townsfolk. Reports of spies among the local population continued here, as at Stormberg, and Ethelston warned his men against careless talk.

Then the Boers blew up the railway line west of Queenstown, which made their position somewhat precarious, and Buller ordered them to withdraw to the coast at East London. There the equipment and stores were handed over to the Army and the gun, which they had looked after like a baby, was put in charge of the Royal Artillery.

The anti-climax of the whole episode created much disappointment, even anger, among the men. They had come here to fight, but all they had done was to go on a 1,000-mile circular tour of South Africa. And for what? Why had they not carried the fight to the Boers, instead of waiting in vain for something to happen? They could have been nicely home in Pompey by now. The rumours started. They were all going up to Natal to help relieve Ladysmith. No, it was untrue, only the Terribles were going, and the rest of them were being sent back to Simonstown to rejoin their ships.

Nearly a month had passed since their train had steamed out of Salt River Junction in Cape Town, and they had not heard a shot fired in anger, nor even seen a Boer. Their frustration was indescribable as they arrived in Simonstown on the morning of 19 November, 1899. But almost instantly, in the callous way that wars sometimes play with men's morale, their dejection was transformed into excitement by the immediate announcement that a new, and bigger, Naval Brigade was to be formed, including all the existing crews. Their train was to leave at 4 pm that very day, under Captain R. C. Prothero, of HMS *Doris*, to steam north to join Lord Methuen's column for the relief of Kimberley. Amid much cheering and back-slapping, they set about preparing to move off again.

The additional personnel of the new beefed-up Brigade were Captain Prothero himself, Lieutenant the Hon. E. S. H. Boyle, Gunner E. E. Lowe and Midshipmen W. W. Sillem, Egerton and J. F. Houston, all from HMS *Doris*, with about another 100 from the lower deck of whom half were Royal Marines, and included stokers for stretcher bearers, plus sick-bay staff and cooks. They were to take four long 12-pounders on Captain Scott's improvised mountings.

Prothero drew up his new Brigade for inspection by Rear-Admiral Harris on the lawn in front of Admiralty House in the dockyard, after which they set off for the station, marching jauntily to the music of the accompanying band and to the cheers of the usual flag-waving crowds who gathered along the road.

This time they carried straight on north to De Aar but found trouble on the line where two trains had collided, blocking traffic up or down. A replacement train was quickly shunted down from some sidings, and they were faced with the task of getting all their equipment, plus the heavy guns, unloaded and up onto the new train ahead of the blockage. Luckily there was a contingent of South African Light Horse passing and Prothero was able to enlist their help. Even then it was a four-hour job, and it was not until 2 am that they got underway again.

Methuen had left no doubt of the urgency of his need for their help in the push to relieve Kimberley and awaited them at Witteputs, with the Guards Brigade, Northumberland Fusiliers and battalions of the King's Own Yorkshire Light Infantry, Northamptons and the Loyal North Lancashires, before moving his forces up to Belmont.

It was here that Prothero's Naval Brigade found action for the first time. Indeed Belmont marked a turning point in British fortunes. After the recent disasters that had overtaken the British forces elsewhere, it was a morale-boosting event.

Methuen was faced with a long slog up the dead straight and parallel lines of the road and railway to reach Kimberley. Admittedly, it was only about 50 miles from Belmont, but there were several points of vantage for a defender standing in the way, plus the obstacle of the Modder River. The first of these to be negotiated was a line of kopjes, Table Hill, Gun Hill and Fryer's Kopje, all strewn with huge boulders, alongside the railway and road near Belmont. Intelligence reports had stated that there was a Boer laager to be found here, although the enemy chose to remain invisible to the approaching attackers.

Methuen pushed two artillery batteries and the naval brigade forward, and bivouacked his infantry, considered to be the best 'of the line' that Britain had ever put into the field, while he examined the Boer positions. Behind the three kopjes rose another higher line of peaks, with a 'nek' or saddle running through it. In this was to be found the main camp of the enemy.

After going forward to fire a few rounds into the lower slopes of the nearer kopjes to try to draw the Boers out of their positions, but receiving no response, the sailors bivouacked near a shallow spruit for replenishing their water supply, and for a few hours respite. Sleep was difficult, what with excitement of the impending battle, the cold night, the thin khaki tunics, the hard stony ground and the pot-holes that lay under the deceptively comfortable-looking long grass. Water parties went stealthily out in the blackness, only to bring back canvas buckets full of mud from the sluggish ditch. That night they dined on tinned kidneys (which nearly a hundred years later the navy caterers still use as a stand-by, and which have a most unsavoury nickname), biscuits and gritty water.

The infantry, now rested, was ordered to march off at 1.30 am, so as to be in position to attack the Boer strongpoints at dawn. Greatcoats left behind, and with full water-bottles, they went silently into the darkness, in open order, making no sound other than the swish of the scrubby grass against their puttees. But enough time had not been allowed before the first shafts of light announced the dawn and the infantry found themselves still some distance short of the Boer positions, soon to be fully exposed to a deluge of fire from the hidden Mausers. But as yet all was eerily silent. The order had been given to withhold fire and attack with the bayonet. The infantry walked on, and still both the Boers and the British artillery held their fire, the Boers remaining invisible.

As the British foot soldiers reached the bottom of the slopes of the kopje the whole mountain seemed to erupt into a thousand spurts of flame, crackling along the uneven lines of rocks. Men dropped all around, but the advance continued, albeit more thinly. This steadiness and discipline under fire seemed to unnerve the Boers and their shooting became wild and ineffective. Gradually the British fought their way upwards, in a hand-to-hand, close-quarter battle, displaying superb bayonet drill. One private was shot in the head while trying to remove his bayonet from a Boer's chest, whereupon the Boer who killed him also fell, dying instantly with a bayonet through his heart.

On the summit the infantry now paused for breath, and to allow the Naval Brigade to fire a 'softening-up' barrage at the second line of kopjes and after about an hour and a half the advance was resumed. The Boers were seen to be retiring under a white flag from their rocky ridge and the British stopped firing instantly. Then, in flagrant abuse of the white flag, some shots rang out from the Boer lines, wounding Colonel Crabbe of the Grenadiers and a reporter for the London *Morning Post*, who was following the column.

The next ridge was taken in a series of rushes, by now encouraged by the wail of bagpipes of the Scots Guards, which sound has sent chills down the spine of many an enemy and is said to be worth an extra battalion to a British regiment. The Boers fled down the far side of their stronghold, leaving sixty-four wagons and much ammunition behind. The Battle of Belmont was over.

Methuen took thirty prisoners, including a German commandant of artillery, and the Boers had an estimated eighty-three killed and twenty wounded. Outnumbering the Boers by about 9,000 to 3,500, the British losses can be said to have been costly. Fifty-three officers and men were killed, and 245 wounded.

The dead and wounded lay all around, while the ambulance corps and bearers moved among them, administering whatever relief was still of any purpose. It was said by some that the khaki clothes of some of the dead and wounded were so dyed with blood that they must have been hit several times before succumbing. Others, of a more cynical disposition, claimed that the Boers must have been using the illegal dumdum expanding bullet.

Belmont safely taken, Methuen was able to advance along the railway, with an armoured train slowly puffing alongside carrying the naval 12 pounders under Lieutenant Dean.

The Boers had had the foresight to destroy the lines as they retreated and an excellent job was done by Major Stewart of the Royal Engineers and his men, assisted by 200 coolies, in carrying out temporary repairs. Stewart carried enough girders and timbers, rails and sleepers, to repair up to twenty miles of track, but he reported that the Boers had carried out their destruction very clumsily, and he was able to keep Methuen 'rolling' with little delay.

The night of the 23rd and the morning of the 24th were spent in bivouac while Stewart carried out vital track repairs, and then Methuen marched his forces forward, seven miles over some arid veldt to Swink's Pan. Orders to arms were issued at 3 am on the 25th, ready to move up beyond the little town of Enslin, to Graspan, where the Boers were preparing to make a stand.

Prothero was told that most of his bluejackets and marines would be used as infantry when the next assault was carried out, and his mules 'lent' to the Royal Artillery to rest their exhausted horses, while the Navy's guns would follow up on the train to support them.

Here the problem of removing the Boers from some rocky kopjes presented itself in a similar style to that of Belmont two days previously, but here the strength of the defenders was thought by the scouts to be only about 400, which proved to be a gross under-estimation.

3 am came. The sailors checked and loaded their rifles. They fell into line with the 9th Brigade at 3.45 am and advanced in silence in quarter column, well spaced, parallel with the railway about a mile away on their left. In the van of the infantry, they kept up a steady pace for a couple of hours until daybreak, when contact was made with the enemy. They found the Boers well dug-in on a front of about three miles, extending eastwards from the railway. The naval brigade held the right flank of the line, together with the King's Own Yorkshire Light Infantry and the Loyal North Lancashires, while on the left were the Northumberland Fusiliers, the famous 'Fighting Fifth', and the Northamptons, with the Guards at the rear with the baggage.

If removing the Boers from their stony fortress at Belmont had been difficult, the task at Graspan was likely to be even more so. Here the approach to their kopjes was across two miles of flat, treeless, open country, without a boulder, an anthill, a ditch or any cover whatsoever. It was utterly featureless terrain. All that was on its surface was a foot-high coat of dead brown grass. And here, without any gradual sloping, the kopjes rose suddenly from the plain, with projecting rocky spurs. An aerial picture would have shown them like star-fish spread-eagled on a sandy beach. These 'legs' gave the Boers splendid positions from which to trap the British infantry in a rain of murderous cross-fire if they approached too close. It was an ideal place for the Boers' style of fighting.

At a range of 5,000 yards Dean's guns, attached to the Royal Artillery, opened up. This time the Boers did reply, and a duel began between the heavy gun emplacements of both sides. The barrage of shells thundered back and forth overhead, under which the infantry, six paces apart, started their steady march towards the kopjes.

Prothero led the advance. Behind him were Major Plumbe, RMLI, with Midshipman T. Wardle as his ADC, Captain A. E. Marchant, RMLI, Captain Guy Senior, Lieutenants W. T. C. Jones and F. J. Saunders and Colour-Sergeant Dyson heading the various marine companies, while Commander A. P. Ethelston, Lieutenant the Hon. E. S. H. Boyle, Gunner E. E. Lowe, Midshipmen C. A. E. Huddart and W. W. Sillem led the forty-five strong bluejacket company. With one company of the King's Own Yorkshire Light Infantry, the strength of the firing line on the right flank was 330.

The sun was now getting up and it was going to be a very hot day. They had already been marching for three and a half hours and nobody had yet had breakfast. Hares and partridges flew in fear across the dead grass in front of them as they approached their invisible foes.

At 7.45 am the Boer artillery ceased and immediately a torrent of Mauser fire spewed down from the rocky tops of the kopjes. The order came to advance 'at the quick' amid the oncoming storm of bullets. Six hundred yards from the nearest rocks the infantry line sank to the parched grass, trying to make themselves as small targets as possible, firing independently. It was now scorching hot and throats were parched with both thirst and excitement. They took to making short sharp rushes to close the range.

Now under 500 yards and still the cascade of defiance came from the Boer riflemen, hidden between the big boulders and making their mark with deadly marksmanship. There were many casualties.

At the very foot of the kopje some merciful shelter came to the leading lines. Here, so close were the British to the Boers that they were more or less underneath them. The defenders could not therefore train their guns on them without revealing their hiding-places and be exposed to the fire of those following.

'Fix bayonets!' somebody shouted, and the climb started, slowly and painfully, on hands and knees, up into the hard, jagged rocks. But the cost had already been tremendously high. Ethelston, Plumbe and Senior all lay dead. Prothero and Jones had been severely wounded, and Huddart, hit three times by Boer bullets, was dying. Nearly all the Petty and Non-commissioned officers of the naval brigade had also been either killed or wounded. The sailors were, for the moment, without an apparent leader, but with that special brand of discipline expected of seamen, the advance continued.

Scrambling ever upwards, over and around the huge boulders, bayonet, bullet and even rifle-butt drove the Boers backwards. The very impetus of their determined aggression gained them the crest of the kopje, headed by Lieutenant Taylor of the King's Own Yorkshire Light Infantry and Lieutenant Jones of the Royal Marines, although they were both already wounded. They were now driving the Boers down the other side. Only some scattered rearguard firing now came back at them and they soon flushed the last of the Boers from the mountain, who rushed to their horses which were tethered behind some piles of stones at the rear. They galloped away through a nearby dam, which stirred up the muddy water, thus earning some more curses from the pursuing victors.

After being reassured that the enemy were not likely to return by the sight, through field-glasses, of their baggage wagons trekking northwards into the distance, the British set about taking stock of their position. Captain Marchant of the Royal Marine Light Infantry was now the senior unwounded naval brigade officer and he assumed immediate command. Calling the roll, he found that the Navy had lost fourteen killed and seventy-nine wounded. In addition to Ethelston, Plumbe, Senior and Huddart, those killed were:

Boyle, John, Ply 8034, private, RMLI.	*Doris.*
Hurst, Henry, 188362, able-seaman.	*Monarch.*
Austin, Sidney, 187211, able-seaman.	*Monarch.*
Radford, Frederick, Ply 7470, private, RMLI.	*Monarch.*
Greagsby (?) Harry, Port. 6960, private, RMLI.	*Powerful.*
Martin, Harry, Port 6913, private, RMLI.	*Powerful.*
Metcalfe, John (?) Port 8439, private, RMLI.	*Powerful.*
Barnes, William, Port 8371, private, RMLI.	*Powerful.*
Brown, Alfred, Port 6258, private, RMLI.	*Powerful.*

The scene on the top of the kopje was one of utter carnage. A *Times* correspondent wrote, 'The hill-top was almost dripping with blood; not a boulder escaped its splash of crimson, and the innumerable splinters and chips of the ironstone blocks indicated the terrific nature of our fire. Most of the dead or wounded Boers were carried off – thirty of the more severely wounded were found in their hospital a quarter of a mile away – but here and there a dead man proved that here the Transvaal had sent its men down for the first time to meet the oncoming column.'

Fleet-Surgeon Porter, with his sick-bay orderlies and stoker stretcher-bearers, now set about their sad and grisly task of bringing in the dead for burial and tending the wounded of both sides. The plaintive cries for water from the mangled khaki bodies prostrate under the still scorching sun were to stay in the ears of the survivors for many a year afterwards.

They found Ethelston with half a dozen bullet wounds in his body, and Plumbe dead, with his faithful little terrier dog, which never left his side, even

35

to follow him into battle, guarding his corpse. Beside Plumbe lay the body of Guy Senior, his field officer.

Captain Prothero, a mountain of a man, had gone into action armed with little but his walking-stick, on which he elected to lean while his sailors lay flat in the grass to take aim at the Boers, shouting encouragement, urging them forward, and seemingly as unperturbed by the mayhem around him as if he had been taking a turn around the *Doris*'s quarterdeck. Not surprisingly, he had been hit, and fell to the ground, fortunately only wounded, but managed to rise and hobble onwards, shouting, 'Men of the Naval Brigade, advance at the double; take that kopje and be hanged to it!'

Young Midshipman Huddart of the *Doris* had displayed amazing bravery before taking the final breath of his short life. At the bottom of the hill he had been shot through the arm; halfway up through the rocks he was shot in the leg, yet, tottering forward, he still made the summit of the kopje, where he received another bullet in the stomach, which brought his end.

Even among those not wounded, such had been the ferocity and density of the Boer fire that most of them found bullets lodged in their clothes or equipment after the battle. One marine officer had his water-bottle shot away, his revolver, still in its holster, damaged beyond repair, his leather belt cut from his waist and the magazine of his rifle smashed, without sustaining as much as a scratch to his body.

The Naval Brigade was to receive many plaudits for its action at the Battle of Graspan (or Enslin), but another lesson was to be learned from it. The men had been ordered to make their clothing drab. Not a gleam of a button nor the flash of a white belt was to be seen in the bright sunshine among the ranks of the lower deck. But the officers still carried bright swords and their uniforms were spangled with shiny buttons, which turned them into conspicuous targets and which goes a long way to explain the reason for the heavy price the commissioned personnel paid in casualties on that day.

Captain Marchant of the Marines, now finding himself in command, sent the following despatch the next day to the Commander-in-Chief, H. M. Ships, Cape of Good Hope:

Royal Naval Brigade, In Camp at Esland Station,
26th November, 1899.

Sir, – I have the honour to report that the Naval Brigade was in action yesterday morning at the battle of which you have had telegraphic information.
2. The officers, petty officers, non-commissioned officers and men behaved with conspicuous gallantry, but I regret to inform you that the losses in killed and wounded were exceptionally heavy for the small number of men forming the Naval Brigade.

3. I enclose a report from Lieutenant F. Dean, who was in command of the guns during the action, as I did not see what the movements of the guns were during that stage of the action.

4. The remainder of the bluejackets who were not with the guns and all the marines formed part of the firing line, and were under the command of Captain Prothero.

They advanced with other troops and attacked a very strong position held by the Boers, who were in large force and had large guns with them. About 400 yards from the foot of an almost inaccessible hill, from which the enemy had to be driven, the line was fired on from two positions, and it was here that so heavy a loss was sustained.

I regret to inform you that at this point Commander A. P. Ethelston, Major J. H. Plumbe, R.M.L.I., and Captain Guy Senior, R.M.A., were killed whilst gallantly leading their men, and Midshipman C. A. E. Huddart was mortally wounded. Captain Prothero, both before and after he was wounded, behaved with great gallantry and coolness.

Lieutenant W. T. C. Jones, R.M.L.I., who was wounded in the hip by a bullet which has not yet been extracted, was also wounded at this stage, but undeterred charged to the top of the hill, where his wound was dressed. The conduct of this officer is deserving of the highest praise, and I strongly recommend him to your notice.

Midshipman Wardle also showed great gallantry, and remained with Major Plumbe and several dead and wounded men, and attended to them and dressed their wounds under a very heavy fire.

5. Lieutenant the Hon. E. S. H. Boyle and Lieutenant F. J. Saunders, R.M.L.I., Gunner Lowe, R.N., and Midshipman W. W. Sillem also charged to the top of the hill, gallantly leading their men all the time under a very heavy fire, and are all deserving of special mention.

6. At the top of the hill I collected as many men as possible and advanced to the furthest position, driving the enemy before us until the position was finally captured and the Boers in full retreat with their horses and wagons.

7. Lieutenant F. Dean, Lieutenant G. W. McO. Campbell, Sub-Lieutenant White, (who was in charge of the ammunition supply), and Midshipman Armstrong, who were with the guns, behaved with great gallantry in a very exposed position, which was commanded by the enemy's guns, and where they were subjected to a heavy artillery fire, which proved so accurate as to wound six men of the guns' crews.

8. Fleet Surgeon James Porter, who was with the firing line, and Surgeon Beadnell with the guns did gallant and most excellent service under trying conditions, under fire nearly the whole time.

9. It is with deep regret that I have to report the death of Midshipman

Huddart, who behaved magnificently, and still advanced after he had been twice wounded until he was finally struck down mortally wounded.

10. Midshipman Sillem was stunned halfway up the hill and remained unconscious for some time.

11. General Lord Methuen came specially to see me, and ordered the men to fall in, and complimented them on their behaviour, and expressed his regret at the heavy losses we had sustained in officers and men.

12. After the action was over, being the senior officer present, I collected the men, marched into camp, and took command of the brigade.

I have the honour to be, Sir, your obedient servant,

A. E. Marchant, Captain, R.M.L.I.
Commanding Royal Naval Brigade.

Gras Pan, 26 November, 1899
To Captain Marchant, R.M.L.I., Commanding Naval Brigade

Sir, – In compliance with your orders of this date, I have the honour to submit for the information of the Commander-in-Chief a report of my proceedings with four naval guns and four half guns' crews under my command yesterday.

2. Arrived at Gras Pan at 5.45 a.m., and observing the enemy in an apparently strong position, 5,000 yards in advance, I detrained two guns – not having enough men to handle more – and at 5.55 a.m fired one round to test range. I then waited till the Royal Artillery with six guns took up a position on my right front and opened fire on the enemy. I did the same, and subsequently advanced to ranges of 4,000 and ultimately 2,800 yards, acting from time to time on requests I received from the officer commanding Royal Artillery, who was attacking the same position – viz., two strongly fortified kopjes on either side of the railway with a well-protected gun in each.

3. About 8 a.m., I received verbal orders to retire from my position, as the Royal Artillery were about to move away to the right, and it would then be untenable for my two guns. The Royal Artillery were already moving off when I got the order, and the Boer guns, having got our range accurately, were pouring on us such an effective shrapnel fire, that I judged it impossible to carry out the order without either leaving the guns or suffering very heavy losses, both amongst our own men and the company of Royal Engineers who were helping us, if we attempted to retreat with them.

I therefore continued to fire as briskly as possible at the Boer guns, with such effect that we continuously put them out of action, first one and then the other, for as much as 15 or 20 minutes at a time. Their shells burst with utmost accuracy, and both our guns and ammunition trolly were spattered all over with shrapnel balls; but owing to my system of making all hands lie down when we saw their guns flash and remain till the shell burst and the balls flew by, we had only six men wounded when, at 9.30 a.m., the Boers finally ceased firing and abandoned their position.

4. I beg that you will submit to the Commander-in-Chief that Lieut. Campbell and Mr Armstrong, midshipman, displayed marked coolness and courage in controlling the fire of their guns and inspiriting the men, who all worked splendidly. I would recommend for favourable consideration Petty Officers 1st Class Ashley (HMS *Doris*) and Fuller (*Monarch*), who under the trying circumstances laid their guns with the greatest accuracy. I am confident that, had the Boer guns been exposed as ours were, we should have not only silenced but captured them.

5. On Friday night I found Surgeon Beadnell at Belmont Station; he had been invalided by a medical board that day and was waiting for the hospital train. Though in bad health, he gladly accepted my order to remain with the guns in view of the impending engagement, and on Saturday he rendered invaluable aid to our wounded, working close up to the guns where shrapnel balls were showering every other minute.

I am, Sir, your obedient servant,

F. W. Dean, Lieutenant, R.N.

Admiral Harris telegraphed to promote Marchant to Major and to give him command of the Brigade until a replacement arrived. This was Captain J. E. Bearcroft, HMS *Philomel*, who was to command the Brigade for the rest of its mission in South Africa.

And the now wheelchair-bound Queen Victoria sent a telegram to Harris: 'The Queen desires that you will convey to the Naval Brigade who were present at the action of Graspan, Her Majesty's congratulations on their gallant conduct, and at the same time express the Queen's regret at the losses sustained by the Brigade.'

CHAPTER 7

'NOT MUCH BRASS BAND AND GLORY'

By now, over in Natal, Ladysmith had been under siege for nearly a month. After the initial frenzied rush into action directly from the railway station, the Naval Brigade set about digging in and preparing positions for its guns. The 4.7s needed to have wooden mountings assembled from the fifteen-feet-long, 12″ × 12″ baulks of timber that had been brought up on the train with them. Sappers from the Royal Engineers dug pits for embedding the gun platforms and naval blacksmiths, using a home-made forge, which cast an eerie glow on their faces as they worked in the darkness, fixed the long steel bolts which held the gun to the mounting. They had no greatcoats and it rained all night, but the hard work built up a healthy sweat and by the morning all was nearly ready for them to haul the Junction Hill gun on to its mounting, helped by their new neighbours, the Liverpool Regiment.

But right at the very outset tragedy overtook Lambton's Naval Brigade. On Thursday, 2 November, only a matter of hours into the siege, the sailors and marines were still busy building up a parapet of sandbags around their precious 4.7 on Junction Hill. The 'Long Tom' on Pepworth Hill, 6,500 yards away, had already loosed a couple of rounds at their position, with uncomfortable accuracy and they had replied in an effort to silence them.

At about 9 am a flash and a burst of white smoke appeared on Pepworth Hill, which told them that they had about 25 seconds to take cover before the shell arrived. This one brushed the top of their half-built sandbag parapet, just missing the gun, but it caught the Gunnery Lieutenant Egerton, smashing into his legs. Surgeon Fowler was on the spot and did all he could for Egerton, but his injuries were severe and he was losing blood rapidly. The bluejackets lifted him tenderly and placed him in the shelter of a nearby dhoolie until he could be taken to hospital in an ambulance wagon. On the way he tried to be cheerful, smoking a cigarette and joking that he supposed that this would mean he would not be playing cricket for a while. But the loss of blood and the shock were too great and he died that night.

HMS *Powerful*'s log records that three ratings reported wounded after the action, namely 149587 Leading Seaman W. Ford, 159638 Able Seaman John Emly and 172445 Ordinary Seaman John Nail.

Gun crews and stokers worked busily through the night to finish the job of 'digging in' their guns. Parapets were strengthened with sandbags four deep, and earth and rocks, the latter prised from the stubborn terrain with much difficulty, piled outside. Traverses were excavated, six feet deep and shuttered up 'shipshape' with wooden boards, from the guns to the ammunition magazines which had been dug out of convenient nearby hillocks.

Twenty-five odd rounds were fired daily by the 4.7s during the early part of the siege, but this soon had to be restricted owing to shortage of ammunition as the days and weeks wore on, until eventually long periods elapsed when they were absolutely quiet. Chief Engineer C. C. Sheen of the *Powerful* wrote: 'Sharp comes the order, "Fire"; down comes the horny hand on the lanyard; click goes the striker; the gun flies back and forwards again with a deafening crack, a little acrid yellow haze comes floating in through the embrasure and one of those precious 200 khaki-coloured lyddite shells is speeding on its way to the Boer gun nearly four miles away. The breech is swung open, the empty cordite cylinder pulled out, the man crouching with the shell in his arms jumps to the gun and shoves it well home through the smoking breech, another jams in a fresh charge; with a bang the breech is closed, the gun is ready again and there is still plenty of time to see what the first shell is going to do. Everyone cranes forward eagerly; over on the Boer ridge, close to Long Tom, comes a splash on the brown slopes, a great yellow-grey cloud shoots up, and the shell has done its work.'

It was a well orchestrated display. They had all performed it a thousand times before in the Gunnery School or in practice at sea. Even now that it was the real thing, they could have done it in their sleep, a gun's crew of six bluejackets laying, loading and firing their 4.7, while a party of four stokers hurries silently along the deep trench back and forth from the ammunition magazine to fetch the 40lb shells, one by one, up to the gun.

The Boers, at first at any rate, seemed to be treating the whole thing as a more or less part-time hobby, taking pot shots with the Mausers at any careless picket soldier who lifted his head, and now and again languidly firing a couple of shells at the British gun emplacements, as if they were trying to win a prize at a fairground stall.

G. W. Steevens, of the *Daily Mail*, who was to die of enteric fever in January, observed, 'It must be said that the Boers make war like gentlemen of leisure, restricting their hours of work with trade-unionist punctuality. Sunday is always a holiday; so is the day after any particularly busy shooting. They seldom begin before breakfast, knock off regularly for meals – the luncheon interval is 11.30 to 12.00 for riflemen, and 12.00 to 12.30 for gunners. They hardly ever fire after teatime, and never when it is raining. To do them justice, they did not at first try to do wanton damage in the town. They fired almost exclusively on the batteries, the camps, the balloon, and moving bodies of troops. In a day or two the troops were far too snugly protected behind schantzes and reverse slopes and grown far too cunning to expose themselves to much less. The inhabitants were mostly underground, so that there was nothing really to suffer except casual passengers, beasts and empty buildings.'

But it had to be admitted that Joubert's tactics did have an effect on morale as the weeks dragged on. The never-ending need for vigilance, combined with the boredom, the heat, the rain and the uncomfortable life in dug-out shelters in the ground, all put a tremendous strain on the defending troops.

Nevinson, the *Daily Chronicle* correspondent, wrote, 'The smudgy khaki uniforms soaked through and through, stained black and green and dingy red with wet and earth and grass; the draggled greatcoats, heavy with rain and thick with mud; the heavy, sopping boots; the blackened, battered helmets; the blackened, battered faces below them, unwashed and unshaved since the siege began, the eyes heavy and bloodshot, with sun and rain and want of sleep; the peculiar smell – there is not much brass band and glory about us now.'

Already people were beginning to crave for the little luxuries denied to them by the siege. One young officer, who had been heard to express continual impatience with the slowness of the relief column, confessed to Nevinson that it was not so much a letter from his sweetheart that he craved, but a supply of Quaker Oats!

A little while after arriving in Ladysmith, when the initial fury of the siege had abated and everybody was able to catch their breath, Lambton was pleasantly surprised to be presented with some unexpected, but very welcome, reinforements in the shape of Lieutenant E. C. Tyndale-Biscoe, R. N. (retired), and Lieutenant E. Stabb of the Royal Naval Reserve. These officers had found themselves in Ladysmith at the outbreak of hostilities and did not hesitate to place themselves under his command. Both of them were to succumb, eventually, to the enteric fever which swept through the besieged community, in Stabb's case, fatally.

On 16 November another casualty occurred when Able Seaman Masters vaulted over the parapet of his gun and sat on his own bayonet. Luckily, he was not seriously hurt, even though it seems that it went in right up to the hilt. The Medical Officer's report stated, 'Bayonet passed through port cheek of backside'.

Lieutenant Lionel Halsey entrusted an African runner with some letters to his mother,

Cove Redoubt,
Ladysmith,
Friday, November 10th.

My dearest Mother,

Little did I ever think or ever dream of writing to you from a town that is
and has been for 10 days in a state of siege. I have been unable to write a
word before, as we have been hard at it day and night, erecting and firing
guns – but to make a long story short I am now up here, which is a hill
about 500 feet above the Town, and have got a 4.7 inch gun and ten men
to take charge of, and a most interesting job it is. We have been fighting
every day since we came up except last Saturday and Sunday when there
was an armistice on to move the Hospital and sick outside the Town,
preparatory to the Boers shelling it. Now the shelling is more or less over,
at least they have been firing away from about 20 guns for a week, and
have done a surprisingly small amount of damage and the loss of life is also
very small, though I regret to say we have lost such a good dear chap,
Egerton by name – he was our Gunnery Lieutenant; he had charge of the
other 4.7 we brought up, and while they were firing a Boer shell came in
and struck him, shattering one leg and smashing up the other. He was so
plucky about it, and just remarked as they were putting him on the
stretcher, 'I'm afraid this will do for my cricket'. He lit a cigarette while
being carried down – poor chap, he recovered consciousness after the
operation of amputating both legs, but the shock was too great and he
died 12 hours after he was wounded.

We have had 4 other men of ours wounded, one very severely and 3
slightly. We arrived up here in the nick of time without a doubt and as far
as we could we saved the situation with our guns. A general engagement
was going on when we steamed in on the train, and our 12-pounder guns
were there, and then taken straight out to the front and did very well, so,
as you may imagine, the Navy is very popular here and nothing is good
enough for us.

The Naval Brigade consists of Captain Lambton in command, Heneage,
Hodges and I are the Lieutenants, Fowler our surgeon, Kay, Fleet
Paymaster doing transport, 2 Engineers, 2 mids and 260 men, 2 - 4.7
guns, 4 - 12-pounder guns and 4 Maxims.

We have had a real rough time and a hard time into the bargain, being
up day and night very often, and even now, it is Friday, and I have not
had my clothes or my boots off since Sunday, but I am as fit as a fiddle,
couldn't be better, and a fine ginger beard coming on. Our position here
is undoubtedly a very poor one, but with luck we ought to be able to hold

out till relief comes, which will, I trust, be in a week or so. Our men are most cheery and get on A 1. with the soldiers.

We have 8,000 troops here now, which sounds a lot, but it is a big valley to hold and we are absolutely surrounded by the Boers in every direction, and they are getting guns up every day, and therefore every day it gets hotter for us and we had a grand fight yesterday; I have got two Boer guns to try and knock out and I absolutely silenced them both yesterday, though I fear I have not hurt the guns at all, and now I am waiting in my Redoubt for them to open fire on me, so you see we live in a world of intense excitement.

We are all hungry for news of the outside world; it is not a nice sensation at all being bottled up like this and the sooner we get out the better I think we shall all be pleased. Weather, taking it all round, has been good, though we have had one or two filthy days, wind and wet, which is very unpleasant, as there is no shelter. I managed to get hold of a bit of canvas on Sunday, and I have now rigged up a sort of tent for myself, as I can hardly ever get into camp, and of course I always have to be up here at night. I have met such a lot of fellows I haven't seen for years – half the cavalry officers seem to have been at Eton or elsewhere with some of the family, and there are two Regiments here who were in the West Indies when I was out there. They all come up and see one, and bring food and stuff for our men, as of course we are employed all day, and they are simply cooped up and can do nothing.

If we all get out of this all right, it will be a splendid day for the Navy, as Heaven only knows what would have happened if our guns had not arrived in the nick of time, and we only just got through, as the Boers cut the Railway and telegraph on the Wednesday. We had got two more guns and a lot of ammunition on the way up from *Powerful*, but it did not get farther than Maritzburg, so we are rather short, at least we have to be very sparing with it, though if we are relieved in a week it will be all right.

It is now 8 a.m. and we are having a quiet forenoon, as they haven't opened fire yet, but I shall have to in a short time as they are throwing up an earthwork on a hill about 5,000 yards away, and directly I can see the gun arriving I shall put a shrapnel or two into them if the authorities will let me. This is such a change from our usual daily routine on board, and I never before realized what real excitement was.

I sent or rather asked Fred Morgan to send a cable to Cecily for me on 31st, so I hope she got it. I told him Barnett, Waterend would be enough address. I thought of her being married while I was under a hot shell fire at the time, and I know she would have been so unhappy if she had known it. I had so hoped to have been at the wedding, however, 'God disposes.' We are in a most humiliating position here, surrounded by a lot of Boers, but there's no help for it, and they have just opened England's eyes a bit, or at least I hope they have. What we shall do when the Relief Column comes goodness only knows. It would be very nice to go all the way up to Pretoria with them, but I rather doubt them taking us, as our guns are not very mobile, in which case we shall probably stay here.

Dr Jameson, Col. Rhodes, Willoughby and others of Jameson's Raid are all here in this place, and will have a short existence if the Boers get hold of them. Colonel Rhodes is a real ripper, he employs his time looking after the wounded and sick, and kindness is no word for all he does. The other day I was talking to him up here in my Redoubt, and he noticed, I suppose, that my face and lips were frightfully sore, because this morning he sent me a tube of Lanoline, which is most acceptable.

The Skipper has been up here and we have been selecting another place to mount one of our 12-pounders which is at present down below here, they are as certain as they can be that there will be a big attack in force tomorrow, and we are making all preparations for every emergency. I do hope we repulse them all right, as I don't think they will try again. If only they would come out into the open we could hobble them, but one never sees a Boer hardly; however, to get in here they must come out for a short way, and of course our cavalry will be all ready. They were sniping into our camp all day yesterday but did not harm at all, I'm glad to say. Our camp has been shelled almost daily with the most wonderful luck for us, only one man having been wounded – a shell went into his tent, where he and 9 others were and not one of the others was touched, the man who was hit was wounded rather badly in the shoulder. I haven't heard today how he is.

If I get a chance I will add to this, you must pass it round if ever you get it, as I cannot write any more letters possibly. Even this is done line by line, as I am continually jumping up.

Your ever affectionate son,
Lionel.

Monday, 13th: – Here we are, still bottled up and still expecting an attack in force.... I think we must have given the Boers a good drubbing this morning as they are very piano this afternoon.... I just missed Arthur at Durban, where I believe the *Philomel* is now, as she was due there two or three days after we came up here; for all I know he may be landed with guns at Maritzburg. I do hope I shall see him....

Tuesday 14th, 8.30 a.m.
The Relief Column ought to be leaving Durban today and I expect will have a tough fight to get in.... I do bless that rug you gave me years ago,

with the air-cushion in the corner – it is luxury, much envied by others. . . .
Heaps and heaps of love to you all. I should so like to catch a glimpse of
you instead of listening to shell whizzing by.
Your affectionate son,
Lionel.

The Boers have not attempted to storm or take by stealth any of the
positions around the town from which effective Mauser fire could be
poured in. Their defeat on 9th November, when they were driven back
with a loss of 700 to 800, seems to have convinced them that it would be
folly to depart from their traditional tactics.

On 9 November the Boers had made a half-hearted attempt to attack the town.
There was no hand-to-hand encounter, but there was a fierce exchange of rifle
and short-range artillery fire. As the battle was dying and the Boers retreating
back to their laager beyond the kopjes, the naval brigade guns fired a 21-gun
salute in honour of the Prince of Wales, whose birthday it was. The troops gave
three cheers for the popular Prince and sang the National Anthem to the
accompaniment of the last few enemy shells shrieking through the air. Then
they sent a pigeon to Durban with birthday greetings for cabling to His Royal
Highness, and it gave a boost to everybody's spirits when it was known that the
bird had arrived safely and the Prince acknowledged the message with thanks.

The Naval Brigade camp was an odd hotch-potch of white tents, sheets of
tarpaulin, old sails and pieces of battered corrugated iron. At first it was sited
on the summit of Gordon Hill, but this was in full view and range of the Boer
howitzer on Surprise Hill. The folly of this choice of position was proved one
day when the Boers managed to land a shell almost on top of the cook's galley.
The cook was frying onions at the time and it burst just in front of him. The
air was full of flying shrapnel, pieces of rock and other debris. Luckily he was
unhurt, but stood there amazed, holding a frying-pan full of mud and stones.

It was thought wiser to move the camp to a more sheltered position after
that, and on 19 November the Naval Brigade shifted its trappings round the
shoulder of the hill, out of sight of the Boer gunners. Their new home was
partly in the garden of a cottage occupied by a refugee family from Johannesburg
who had had the misfortune not to get on the last train out of Ladysmith. It
was a pretty spot, with its fruit trees and cactus, and gum trees full of weaver
birds. The officers pitched their tents between the trees and borrowed tables
and chairs from a local chapel. Such an idyllic place seemed rather incongruous,
what with the thunder of the guns and the shells passing overhead.

Lionel Halsey, however, in command of the 4.7 Princess Victoria and a 12-
pounder up on Cove Redoubt, found himself leading a lonely and uncomfortable existence. Perched some 500 feet above the town, he had a line of sight to

all angles of the compass, but on the other hand he was a prominent target for the Boers. He needed, therefore, to be constantly alert and, as he was some way away from the main naval camp, he lived up there, eating and sleeping by his guns, which were 700 yards apart, which meant plenty of walking for him.

Once a routine was established, his crews turned in every night at 10.30 pm and manned the guns again at 3.30 am. Halsey was happy to be in a comparatively healthy spot, away from the worst of the dangers of enteric, but the tiny piece of canvas that he rigged up to serve as a shelter only managed to keep the very worst of the rain from soaking him.

It was a favourite spot for snakes, centipedes, scorpions and tarantulas, besides an abundance of white ants, and the bluejackets needed to be on the alert for all of these unpleasant pests as well as keeping an eye on the Boers. Bedding needed to be shaken out every night before turning in, but even then the thought of such unwelcome visitors hardly encouraged pleasant dreams. One sailor disturbed a snake in his blankets. He was lucky not to be bitten, but did receive a spit of poison in his eye which gave him several painful hours.

The big 4.7s needed to be mounted on sturdy platforms. Indeed, the first time Halsey fired the one on Cove Redoubt she jumped, and had to be re-mounted, which caused frantic work all through the night to dig an eight-feet-deep pit in which to sink the four huge baulks of timber on which the ordinary ship's mountings were bolted, all to be covered in with earth and stones well rammed down.

Fleet-Paymaster W. H. F. Kay, of the *Powerful*, played father figure to the younger officers. He had been in many a tight corner throughout his years in the Navy; on the Nile, in the Burma and Abyssinian campaigns, he had perfected the art of making oneself comfortable with whatever resources were to hand, even if they had to be 'borrowed' or obtained by the force of 'prayer'. His organizational skills did much to improve the life-style of his colleagues as the siege settled into a boring routine. He acquired books, packs of cards and a football as if by magic, but his crowning success, earning him much gratitude, was the purchase of all the remaining beer in Ladysmith for £30.

From 1 November to 5 December 3,264 Boer shells were recorded as falling in Ladysmith, killing thirty-one civilians and wounding 145. Ladysmith Town Hall, which was being used as a hospital, was badly damaged, despite the Red Cross flag flying over it. One shell wrecked Mr Carter's house. Another fell dangerously close to the jail, in which the Boer prisoners were being held. A third struck the Standard Bank, and others destroyed the convent, and also the porch of the English Church. Colonel Rhodes, brother of Cecil, had a narrow escape when a shell fell close to him.

Young Midshipman Sharp managed to purloin one of the stone balls that fell from the Town Hall clock tower following its rude assault from 'Long Tom'. It is indicative of the lad's youthful determination that he even managed to carry the unwieldy object home, where it sits to this day on a special plinth in a lovely Cornish garden, with a plaque beneath it proclaiming its historical significance. It is believed, on the basis of information received from a reliable South African informant, that the civic authorities in Ladysmith would appreciate its return.

CHAPTER 8

UP THE LINE

At last, on 12 November, the *Roslin Castle* docked in Durban, made fast to the jetty and put her gangways down to let the first of Buller's army come ashore. Many more were soon to follow. There were the *Lismore Castle* and *Yorkshire* on the 14th, the *Gascon* on the 15th, the *Hawarden Castle* on the 16th – and so it was to continue for a long time to come. As soon as their feet had touched dry land they were packed into railway-trucks for the trains to hurry them up the line to the front at Estcourt.

After landing Lambton and the Ladysmith Naval Brigade at Durban, HMS *Powerful* had returned to Simonstown. This left Captain Percy Scott, in HMS *Terrible*, to make the final arrangements for the assembly of a larger Brigade to be landed at Durban, mainly from his ship to assist with the relief of the siege and to push the Boers out of Natal altogether.

Terrible ploughed her way up to Durban in a force eight gale, arriving there on 7 November. Immediately she docked, at 8.30 pm, her Naval Brigade contingent began to move ashore. The Naval Brigade was to be commanded by Captain E. J. Jones of HMS *Forte*, and his full complement of officers, when finally assembled, was:

From HMS *Terrible*.
Commander A. H. Limpus
Lieutenants F. C. A. Ogilvy, S. R. S. Richards, J. S. Wilde, G. P. England,
Sub-Lieutenant S. Newcome,
Surgeons E. C. Lomas and C. C. McMillan,
Engineers J. F. Arthur and A. E. J. Murray,
Assistant Engineer F. J. Roskruge,
Gunners, J. Wright, E. J. Cole, and E. Williams.
Midshipmen P. F. Willoughby, R. T. Down, R. B. C. Hutchinson,
   A. C. Ackland, A. E. Sherrin, H. E. W. C. White, G. M. Skinner,

G. L. Hodson, W. W. Hallwright, H. S. W. Boldero, and
J. A. G. Troup.

From HMS *Forte*
Lieutenants F. W. Melvill and G. P. E. Hunt,
Staff Surgeon F. J. Lilly,
Acting Lieutenant J. M. Steel,
Gunner E. Holland.

From HMS *Tartar*,
Lieutenants J. E. Drummond and H. W. James,
Staff Surgeon J. Hughes.

From HMS *Philomel*,
Lieutenants A. Halsey, C. R. N. Burne, A. Deas and F. A. Clutterbuck,
Midshipman W. R. Ledgard,
Clerk W. T. Hollins,

Natal Naval Volunteers,
Lieutenant Anderson, in command,
Lieutenants Chiazzari and Barrett.

Thirty guns were landed within two days of the ships docking, comprising of
4.7s and 12-pounders to be fitted on Scott's special mountings and carriages,
plus many machine guns.

Scott himself was to remain in Durban, with two companies of bluejackets
and one of Royal Marines, to ensure the defence of the port. At that point in
the war the area around Durban was felt to be vulnerable and, of course, it was
vital that the port should not be cut off as a supply link. The High
Commissioner appointed Scott to the post of Military Governor and Commandant of Durban, thus placing the town under martial law.

Gun positions were quickly set up, guarding the main roads and railway into
the port, and the Naval Brigade divided into three sections, under Commander
Limpus, Lieutenant Richards and Lieutenant Wilde respectively. There was
already in the town an armoured train, manned by a crew from HMS *Tartar*,
which was later to figure in a famous episode. (Nine years after the War General
Botha told Scott that, but for these naval guns, he would have flown the
Vierkleur over Durban Town Hall, an assertion to which Scott agreed, as the
British had no army in Natal outside Ladysmith, and the Boers were south of
the Tugela and in control of the railway. With Durban itself in Boer hands,
and therefore with their supply lines cut, British fortunes would indeed have
been at a low ebb.)

The Umlass Waterworks, about fifteen miles from town, was an important
position to defend, and a 12-pounder gun position was established on a rocky

outcrop overlooking it, under Captain Mullins, Royal Marines, and Sub-Lieutenant Newcome. To get water it was necessary for the guns' crews to force a path through thick undergrowth to reach the Umlass River. In doing this, one of the bluejackets had an alarming experience. He trod on a giant python, nineteen feet long. Luckily it was not hungry and tried to slide away, but Sergeant Peck shot it through the head and the skin was kept as a memento.

Durban was swarming with refugees, criminals and spies, both loyal to the Empire and otherwise. In the interests of security, therefore, one of the first things that Scott did was to impose a curfew from 11 pm to 5 am, with all public bars closing at 9 pm. An unlucky experience befell the Commandant himself. When asked to produce proof of identity on one of the first nights of his own curfew, he could not do so and was promptly arrested and detained in a cell at the police station overnight. The arresting constable apologized profusely in the morning, but Scott was pleased to congratulate the red-faced officer for his good work.

Now well known as an innovator, Scott was constantly bombarded with ideas from all kinds of people who were convinced that they had invented formidable secret weapons with which to bring the Boers rapidly to their knees. One elderly lady suggested a huge net, attached to six powerful rockets, which could be fired into the air over the Boer positions. This would ensnare the enemy in their droves and all our troops would have to do would be to pull the net back to their own lines on the rope thoughtfully provided by the inventor. Another fanciful idea was put forward by an eccentric gentleman in the form of a shell filled with a special chemical. This would be fired at the Boers and, when it burst among them, would emit a dense black fog which would induce inertia and disorientation among the enemy, thus enabling our troops to walk in and quietly capture them all. He had not yet invented the special chemical and was unsure by what means the British themselves would be rendered immune from the effects of it.

Scott was to stay at his post of Military Governor for the entire time that the *Terrible* remained on station and several commentators have lamented the fact that he was never to witness first-hand the superb contribution that his various inventions made towards the eventual winning of the war, being denied the privilege of watching them in action.

No time was lost in the deployment of advance parties to defend some key positions. Lieutenant James was despatched with some Tartars and two 12-pounders to defend Frere, the most northerly point on the railway line to Ladysmith still in British hands. Lieutenant Arthur Halsey of *Philomel* had a special interest in the expedition. He was the elder brother of Lieutenant Lionel Halsey, who was then commanding the 4.7 on Cove Redoubt in Ladysmith. The elder Halsey was sent, with some Philomels and two more 12-pounders, to defend Pietermaritzburg. Lionel, as yet, could have no knowledge that his

51

brother had gone ashore with the Naval Brigade, but he told his diary, hopefully, that 'he may be with General Clery's column at Estcourt for all I know.'

Lieutenant Steel, with some Fortes, was assigned to defend the railway at Mooi River, and some more Tartars with a 7-pounder were installed on an armoured train which was to make periodic exploratory forays north into Boer territory. This train was to become famous. Winston Churchill, war correspondent for the *Morning Post*, it will be remembered, had landed at Cape Town from the *Dunottar Castle* at the same time as General Buller. Anticipating that more immediate news was likely to emanate from the Natal front and anxious to produce some interesting copy for his editor so as to justify his £250 per month salary, plus expenses, he had taken urgent passage in a coaster for Durban, accompanied by J. B. Atkins of the *Manchester Guardian*, and thence by rail up to Estcourt. The young Churchill was already extremely well-connected, and it was not much of a surprise to him to find two old friends already there, namely Leo Amery of *The Times* and a Captain Haldane. Haldane, (later to become General Sir Aylmer) was nursing a slight wound in Estcourt, while waiting for the big push up to Ladysmith, but nevertheless had been assigned to take his troops the next day on the armoured train to reconnoitre north, as there had been sightings of Botha's patrols close to the line. He invited the reporters to join him.

Having inspected the train and declaring it to be 'in short, a death trap', Atkins and Amery declined the invitation, but Churchill could not resist and at 4.30 am on Wednesday, 15 November, he clambered over the seven-foot-high steel walls of the contraption. It steamed off, packed with Haldane's soldiers and a 'wretched little muzzle-loading 7-pounder gun from HMS *Tartar*, mounted on a truck and manned by bluejackets'. All went smoothly as far as Chieveley and they had just started the return journey when they were ambushed with some ferocity by Louis Botha's men. The engine driver piled on all steam and the train hurtled down the steep gradient towards Frere, flinging its startled occupants from side to side against the walls of their steel box. This fell neatly into Botha's plans, because he had placed large rocks on the track farther down the line, which derailed the leading truck, hurling its passengers into the air and causing many severe injuries. The engine and carriage, plus the truck with *Tartar*'s 7-pounder, stayed on the rails. The sailors managed to get off three shots before a Boer shell struck the old muzzle-loader, knocked the truck sideways and bowled over two of the gun crew.

Most of the party were taken prisoner, including Churchill himself, with only one of the sailors making it back to Estcourt. Churchill's story of his capture, and subsequent escape from Pretoria, half-starved, and hiding for fourteen hours in a wood, watched by a vulture 'who manifested an extravagant interest in my condition, and made hideous and ominous gurglings from time to time' has provided enough material for many a book.

CHAPTER 9

A HAT TRICK OF VICTORIES

Lieutenant-Colonel Kekewich, affable, rotund, bald and forty-five years old, was in command of Kimberley garrison. He had been sent there by Sir Alfred Milner, High Commissioner for South Africa, in August, 1899, in the light of the developing crisis, to report on the town's defences, and had found them to be more or less non-existent. Grudgingly, he was allocated a few companies of his own North Lancashires and half a dozen obsolete light field guns. Then the war broke out, the Free State commandos crossed the border into Cape Colony three miles to the east of the town, and Kimberley was besieged.

Physically, Kimberley was a most unattractive spot. It sat on a flat, arid, treeless, windy plain, nudging the perimeter of the Kalahari Desert. It suffered from an inhospitable climate, with enormous variations in temperature and incessantly strong winds. The only attractive feature was what lay underneath it – diamonds. Many men had become rich in Kimberley, but none richer than Cecil Rhodes. He and his De Beers Company owned Kimberley, more or less. Rhodes detested Kekewich, and made a pest of himself by constantly gibing at the professional soldier's handling of the situation and making perfectly absurd suggestions of his own.

At last, on 21 November, a coded telegram arrived at the very moment that Lord Methuen was rattling over the Orange River bridge, fifty miles to the south, to start his advance up the long straight railway towards Belmont and Graspan. It told Kekewich that relief was on the way. It should be with him in five days. He was to watch for searchlight messages in the sky. Here was another of Captain Percy Scott's inventions. He had taken searchlights from the *Doris* and the *Terrible* and mounted them on railway trucks, with a flasher attachment based on the principle of a Venetian blind (it was the pre-cursor of the Aldis Lamp) for morse communication with both Ladysmith and Kimberley. Shining on to the clouds, it had proved extremely successful in tests over distances as much as forty miles.

After Graspan, the Naval Brigade, still awaiting the arrival of their new commander, Captain Bearcroft, moved forward by train, the line having been repaired by Major Stewart and his Royal Engineers, to bivouac at Klokfontein, where they arrived on 27 November. They transmitted their call sign by Scott's searchlight, its giant beam slanting high into the night sky towards the besieged Kimberley. 'M.D.' 'M.D.' 'M.D.' At last they were close enough to receive a repy from the Kimberley searchlight, perched on top of the Wesselton Mine. 'K.B.' 'K.B.' 'K.B.' Contact had been made with the outside world.

At 4.30 am on the 28th the Naval Brigade moved forward about a mile and a half to a range of 4,800 yards from the Modder River, where they had been told they would breakfast. Methuen had reconnoitred the terrain ahead personally the previous afternoon. He had ridden right up to the river and inspected the iron bridge across it. All seemed plain sailing. He had been briefed by his scouts that the Boers intended making their stand at Spytfontein, which was some miles up the line past the bridge.

But the Boers had, yet again, deceived a British commander, and, it would appear, his scouts, by their ingenious tactics. On his visit to the bridge Methuen had been, unbeknown to him, a mere 300 yards from a five-mile-long line of 9,000 cunningly camouflaged Boers, who had not uttered a sound to betray their presence. Comprised of Free Staters under De la Rey facing the British left, and Transvaalers under Cronje on the right, they had entrenched themselves along both banks of the Modder under heaps of brushwood and shrubbery, so cunningly deployed that 'even the best field glass could not detect their outline'. They had concealed a pom-pom, two field guns and some Maxims on the north bank, and more long-range guns on higher ground a couple of miles back. And in the night they had destroyed both the iron railway bridge over the Modder and the line itself a couple of miles south of it, which made it impossible for the armoured train to be of any use to the British in the fight that followed.

But Methuen had been led to expect only token resistance from a handful of Boers at the river. Cheerfully, therefore, his forces, now reinforced by the 1st Argyll & Sutherland Highlanders, marched in the early morning sunshine towards the tree-lined banks of the Modder and Methuen ordered his cook to prepare his breakfast.

At 5.40, the Boers having held their fire until the range was less than 800 yards, the British were met by a murderous torrent of what was described as probably the most concentrated rifle fire of the whole war. Along the Boer line an annihilating crackle of shots came from the Mausers and the leading ranks of British fell to the ground, almost to a man, either killed or wounded. Above all the rifle fire could be heard the steady drumbeat of the Boer's Maxim, which quickly wiped out the Scots Guards own Maxim detachment.

Quite unprepared for an attack of such ferocity, and unable to advance further, or indeed to retreat without being pursued by a hail of bullets, the British infantry did the only thing possible. They threw themselves down and tried to mount a counter-attack. Three Boer shells landed among the wagons of the Naval Brigade in the early course of the action, but mercifully none burst. Although the Navy's 12-pounders did manage to silence the enemy's Maxims for a while, the Boer's long-range rifle and pom-pom fire was still pinning the infantry down with venomous accuracy.

As the sun rose higher, the day became scorching hot, reaching 110 degrees Fahrenheit, and the British army learned another painful if relatively unimportant lesson. The kilt is not an ideal article of clothing in which to send infantry armed with modern long-range rifles to fight in a hot climate. The Argylls, prostrate on the ground, suffered badly from sunburn on the backs of their bare legs. Indeed, such was the closeness of the attention the Boers were paying to their targets that each time a lick of breeze ruffled the kilts so the wearers could expect the thud of another hail of Mauser bullets.

The day wore on and Metheun moved four of the Naval Brigade 12-pounders forward to throw the Boers off the range, but it was a bad position from which to shoot and they were pulled back again under heavy fire. In the late afternoon the 62nd Field Battery arrived, after a long forced march, to beef up Methuen's artillery strength. They were dead beat, but went into action immediately, sending several well-laid shells into De la Rey's Free Staters. This extra firepower did enable some of the British infantry to struggle across the waist-deep Modder towards evening, when the Free Staters crumbled and fell back. They had been fighting for over twelve hours. Men were exhausted, plagued by the colonies of ants among which they had lain, and desperately thirsty. They were as relieved to reach the waters of the Modder River as if they had been given a week's leave.

Night fell and the infantry were recalled. Methuen, temporarily hors de combat, handed over command to General Pole-Carew. British losses were counted as twenty-four officers and 460 men. In the morning they found that the Boers, with their customary unpredictability, had gone. The only occupants of the Boer trenches were five brave but dead Highlanders. The lanterns and torches of the ambulance parties of both sides cast ghostly flickers in the pitch darkness as they picked their way among the rushes and over the sandy foreshore towards the groans of the wounded, and to pick up their dead. It was 29 November 1899.

Despite Methuen's hat trick of victories of Belmont, Graspan and Modder River, the British were still far behind 'on points' as November drew to a close. After seven weeks of fighting, Ladysmith, Kimberley and Mafeking were still held as if in the coils, as one humorist punned it, of a Boer-constrictor. The Boers had bloodied the nose of the embarrassed British lion at Dundee, Elandslaagte, Nicholson's Nek, Lombard's Kop and Willow Grange, and even where they had been beaten back with a swipe of the mighty paw in the west, they had taken a terrible toll by way of numbers killed, wounded and captured.

And from the British viewpoint, December was to turn out even worse. Over the run-up to Christmas, the British Army was destined to experience what was almost certainly the most humiliating week, up to that time, in all its long history. They called it Black Week.

CHAPTER 10

BLACK WEEK

It will be remembered that the first Naval Brigade had landed, under the doomed Ethelston, at Cape Town on 20 October and had taken the train up to Stormberg via De Aar. They had languished there for ten days before being pulled back to Simonstown after another fortnight's sojourn at Queenstown, not having seen a single Boer. This journey had taken them on a wide sweep of the countryside containing the vital junctions of Naauwpoort and Stormberg, both of which General Buller now elected to abandon and to fall back on De Aar and Queenstown. He was to receive much criticism for this, but, in his defence, he probably realized the difficulties he would face in fighting the Boers in hilly country, as had been the experience north of Ladysmith. And in strengthening his forces around De Aar, he protected a vital point on his advance to Kimberley and Mafeking, and also threatened Bloemfontein.

On 18 November Lieutenant-General Sir William Forbes Gatacre, KCB, DSO was appointed to command the 3rd Division on the Southern Front. Gatacre, 56 years old and in the Army for thirty-seven years, was a dashing and energetic officer. Some even described him as a little too daring. The troops called him 'Back-acher'. Anxious to lose no time, he set up his base in Queenstown, from whence, on 21 November, he pushed forward a small force, composed of the Irish Rifles, the Berkshires and some Cape Mounted Volunteers, with six small mountain guns and some Maxims, to reconnoitre Bushman's Hoek, the pass through which the railway wound down northwards to Stormberg. At this time the Boers had been playing a waiting game, their usual tactics. On the 27th they pounced, seizing Burghersdorp and Stormberg Junction, thus cutting Gatacre off from De Aar.

Gatacre waited in vain for reinforcements, but Buller had few troops available, and by 1 December only a couple of battalions of infantry had arrived, with no artillery or cavalry. Eventually, a couple of exhausted field batteries turned up, the 74th and the 77th, but they were of little use. They had come straight from the ship, without any training of their horses, which turned out to have been pulling omnibuses in England only a few weeks previously, and many of them objected strongly to artillery work, 'with much kicking and rearing, combined with an obstinate determination to remain absolutely stationary'.

Locally Gatacre was under mounting pressure from the British loyalist farmers to push forward in order to prevent further looting of their properties and livestock by the Boer incursionists. Therefore on 9 December he entrained 2,500 men of the Northumberland Fusiliers, the Royal Irish Rifles, the Royal Scots, a few Cape Mounted Police and twelve 15-pounder guns up to Molteno, intending then to carry out a night march on Stormberg. His plans went hopelessly awry. A vital telegram was not transmitted. Chains of command broke down. Whole columns of men got lost in the dark. His scouts were incompetent. The result was that an exhausted British force, having marched for many miles through the night, (some even fell asleep while in action), were ambushed and heavily defeated in the morning at Stormberg, losing 600 prisoners and eighty-nine killed to a Boer commando of 800 men. That was the start of Black Week.

Pole-Carew's troops approached the Modder River with extreme caution on the morning of 29 November. It was eerily quiet after the previous day's fight. A peaceful ripple of the leaves of the bullet-scarred willows and poplars and the swaying of the broken stands of rushes lining the river banks was the only movement they could see; there were certainly no Boers anywhere in sight. A cock crew in the village a little way off. The British feared a trap. But it was true. The Boers had left the Modder and fallen back on Magersfontein.

Modder River Station was a pleasant place in normal circumstances, consisting mainly of hotels of motley construction, set in a woodland scene, with its two rivers, the Modder and the Riet, its ironbridge and its railway station. But the British found it much damaged. Scarcely a building or a tree stood that did not bear scars of yesterday's battle. There were 150 dead horses in the street, there were dead Boers in the river itself, and scattered everywhere were thousands of spent cartridge cases. The baked-mud wall of the adobe-built houses were peppered with holes where the British shrapnel balls had spattered them. The great banks of prickly pear had been cut to pieces. Normally impenetrable, their needle-sharp defences had been no match for a rain of Lee-Metford rifle bullets. Crippled branches hung drunkenly from the trees all around.

In peaceful times it was where the well-to-do of Kimberley came to picnic or enjoy a little boating on the Modder. It was a veritable oasis, escape to which from The Great Hole and its heaps of spoil provided pleasurable relaxation. This summer, however, there was to be none of that. This summer the picnickers would spend under house arrest in Kimberley. This summer the pleasure resort had become a war zone.

Here Captain J. E. Bearcroft joined the Naval Brigade to take command, together with several other reinforcements from the ships, who were: –

Commander S. V. Y. de Horsey,	HMS *Monarch*.
Major A. G. B. Urmston, to command Marines,	HMS *Powerful*.
Lieutenant-Commander W. J. Colquhoun,	Royal Victorian Navy (Aus).
Lieutenants E. J. K. Newman, W. S. Poe,	
G. I. Raikes,	HMS *Monarch*.
Captain R. H. Morgan. R. M. L. I.	HMS *Monarch*.
Lieutenant L. O. Wilson, R. M. L. I.	HMS *Monarch*.
Sub-Lieutenant M. G. Newton,	HMS *Doris*.
Surgeon E. P. Mourilyan,	HMS *Doris*.
Gunner Ball,	HMS *Doris*.
Midshipmen Robertson, J. W. Rainier,	
F. Saunders,	HMS *Doris*.

Pole-Carew needed to pause for breath, await supplies and reorganize his manpower resources after the fierce encounter they had just fought. Not the least of his chores was the task of repairing the Modder River railway bridge before he could continue his push towards Kimberley. The indefatigable Major Stewart and his Royal Engineers set about constructing a temporary bridge and approaches. The labour involved was enormous and the bridge was in danger of being washed away by the first rains, but Stewart was confident that he had designed it in such a way as to facilitate rapid repair if need be. The Boers had demolished the original bridge with repeated charges of dynamite, probably looted from Kimberley. Its ruins stood there, the southern end hanging like a necklace and the northern end standing bolt upright, twelve feet in the air.

Scouts had confirmed that the Boers were indeed digging themselves in on the Magersfontein kopjes, six miles back, just before Kimberley. Pole-Carew decided that heavier long-range artillery would be essential if he were to force them from this stronghold and telegraphed Rear-Admiral Harris in Cape Town requesting one of the naval 4.7s which were in readiness there.

With the practised skill that sailors possess in making themselves at home wherever they happen to be, the Naval Brigade set up its Officers' Mess in the spacious billiards room of one of the hotels and settled down to await the 4.7 and further orders.

All was not going smoothly for the Boer Generals. Firstly, Cronje's Transvaalers had opened fire at much longer range than the 400 yards they had agreed on when starting the battle, which took away much of the power of the punch that had been intended to put the British to flight. Secondly, De la Rey's son, Aadrian, had been killed late in the day. And thirdly, the already suspect morale of the Free Staters, after Belmont and Graspan, had finally broken.

Then they found themselves in disagreement about whether to follow Cronje's plan and fall back on Spytfontein, or De la Rey's, who favoured Magersfontein. Top-level telegrams flew between Presidents Kruger and Steyn, who were both disturbed, and quite understandably so, by the sudden cracks that had appeared in the relationship between the commanders. Steyn hurried over from Bloemfontein, bearing a message from Kruger calling for unison. In the end De la Rey's scheme was adopted. Stand at Magersfontein, and there was still Spytfontein as a reserve line of defence if things went badly.

They set about digging a twelve-mile-long defence line at the base of the Magersfontein kopje, using commandeered African labour to hack out the stony red earth. In front of this they placed a screen of acacia branches to camouflage their position, and in front of that a knee-high horizontal barbed-wire entanglement, several yards across, which would be invisible to the attacking infantry until they were nearly upon it.

A short six miles down the line, at the Modder, Methuen was now sufficiently recovered from his wound to enable him to resume command. He set up his HQ at the Crown and Anchor Hotel and began to plan his next move.

On 4 December the Kimberley searchlight signalled that they had enough food for another forty days, but Methuen wanted to get the job done. He had already wasted over a week waiting for his wound to heal and for reinforcements. The Royal Engineers had cobbled together a temporary bridge over the Modder by 8 December, so, as soon as the extra troops, equipment and guns, including the Navy's 4.7 from Simonstown, arrived on the 10th, the latter was brought up to shell Magersfontein. The Naval Brigade christened their new gun 'Old Joey' (after Joseph Chamberlain) and brought it into action with vigour. The Boers sat tight and made no reply.

Next day, the 11th, at three o'clock on a Sunday afternoon, Methuen gave the order to advance. The plan was for the Highlanders of the Black Watch, Seaforths and Argylls to attack with bayonets at first light next morning under a fierce artillery barrage, and hope to repeat the exercise they had carried out at Belmont by taking the fight into the kopjes themselves. They moved off in the pre-dawn gloom, in the middle of a tempestuous storm, in close order.

As it happened Methuen's hope was a vain one. Not only did he fail to pull off a victory Belmont style, but the Boers repeated their Modder River trick against him. This time Cronje's men's nerves held. They waited for the leading line of Highlanders to come within 400 yards of their trenches before the now familiar sizzle of Mauser fire suddenly erupted from between the acacia branches of their camouflage screen. And of course 'Old Joey' and the rest of the artillery had been shelling the deserted kopje behind the Boer trenches. There was scarcely a soul on it, except for a few scattered burghers with the old-fashioned Martini-Henry rifles, which fired black powder, thus giving puffs of smoke to draw the British fire, while the majority of the Boers, and there were now 6,000 of them, were at the foot of the kopje in their trench, armed with the smokeless Mausers.

Surprised on the march as they were, the losses sustained by the Highland Brigade were heavy. Once more, as at Modder River, the infantry soon found themselves pinned down by murderous and accurate rifle fire from the entrenched Boers. And once more it was the artillery who came to their rescue. The Naval Brigade moved to within a mile of the Boer line, a highly dangerous manoeuvre, being well within the reach of the Mauser rifles. That morning the Boer artillery chose to remain silent. By firing lyddite shell the sailors managed to enable the infantry to hold their positions, although the ordeal of being pinned down for a nine-hour stretch, again without water, was exhausting for them and morale-sapping in itself.

Although a few Black Watch and Seaforths had actually reached the eastern face of the kopje, by early afternoon they had quickly been either rounded up or killed. The rest of the infantry on the right flank were ordered to fall back a few hundred yards so as to regroup prior to making an orderly withdrawal back to their supplies of water. But the Highlanders' morale had disappeared. It had been too much even for their famous fighting spirit. The trickle of men to the rear, as ordered, developed into a stampede. They had been well and truly defeated. Even the skirl of the pipes was insufficient to raise their fighting spirit. The Boers continued to shoot them down as they ran, and so ended one of the most shameful days ever to befall a Highland Brigade. Most of them died with bullets in their backs.

Out of 3,500 Highlanders fifty-seven officers and 700 men were killed or wounded, including their Commanding Officer, Major-General Wauchope, who was killed. The ambulance parties found his body next day, only a couple of hundred yards from the Boer trench. All told the British had lost sixty-eight officers and 1011 men.

At the Crown and Anchor Hotel Methuen lived in hope, all through the long night that followed the battle, that he would find in the morning that the Boers had again retreated, as they had at Modder River. But he hoped in vain. They were still there, secure in their trench.

Reuter's cabled next day, 12 December, from Modder River: 'Twelve ambulances started early this morning under a flag of truce to collect the wounded and to bury the dead. General Wauchope's body was found near a trench. He had been shot through the chest and in the thigh. A few wounded were found near the trenches. Several wounded Boers were taken to the hospital on the side of the hill. The ground in the vicinity of the enemy's trenches were strewn with dead.'

The Times special correspondent had wired from Modder River, at 7 p.m. on 10 December, i.e. on the evening before the battle:

We have been shelling the Magersfontein kopjes at the eastern end of the Spytfontein range. Beginning at 4.15, the naval 4.7″ gun made excellent practice at 7,000 yards, shelling the Boer western position. A howitzer battery, with half of another battery, followed from the right. Lyddite and common shells were used by both. The effects of the lyddite were extraordinary, the projectiles throwing up clouds of ironstone dust extending two or three hundred yards, and visible for ten miles. Many Boers were cut off from retreat on Douglas by the artillery fire and retired into the kopjes, which are apparently one mile in depth.

The range terminates on the east with an abrupt saddle-rock some 150 feet high. The Boer entrenchments run round the whole front position some two miles long, due east and west. The western ends of the trenches follow the contour of the kopjes, and afford a retreat. The formation of the central plateau of the range indicates that there is a plain on the northern side of the kopjes, stretching to Kimberley and affording an opportunity for the cavalry when the enemy are dislodged.

The effect of the firing of lyddite by the naval gun is distinctly felt where we write. The enemy are returning the fire from three or four points, but ineffectually. Much rain fell at midday.

That Methuen should have been aware of such intelligence is scarcely credible. That he should not have adopted a more adroit battle plan in the light of it is even more so. As it was, he had sponsored the second chapter of Black Week.

Up the line in Kimberley the roar of the guns at Magersfontein had been clearly heard all day on 11 December. The besieged inhabitants prepared to receive their rescuers with all due festivity. But no rescuers came. The only communication they received from the outside world was from the Boers, who flashed them late on the very afternoon of the battle, 'We have smashed up your fine column.'

At Modder River Station the Naval Brigade was detailed to guard the new bridge and the immense pile of stores and baggage on the south bank while the exhausted army rested. It was a precarious moment. Several times parties of Boers had been seen moving around in the distant kopjes, and if they were to attack and destroy the valuable material and animals being guarded by the sailors and marines it would not only have delayed any further British advances towards Kimberley for a very long time, but would have probably compelled them to fall all the way back to Orange River to consolidate. On one occasion Bearcroft's men were called to action stations when a cloud of dust signalled the approach of a sizeable force, but it turned out to be nothing more than a swarm of locusts.

Meantime Methuen brooded in his Crown and Anchor Hotel Headquarters, his dreams of glory shattered. 'I must bear my fate like a man,' he wrote, 'and hold my tongue.'

Redvers Buller arrived in Pietermaritzburg on 25 November and over the next ten days devoted all his attention to the organization of his Ladysmith Relief Force. Before leaving the Cape he had sent Lord Methuen off to relieve Kimberley with his 9th Brigade, supported by General French and his cavalry, and artillery strengthened by the Naval guns. General Gatacre had been sent to the north-eastern part of Cape Colony to counter the Boer activities north of Queenstown.

That left Ladysmith to be unlocked, and the fact that Buller had moved his base up to Natal indicates that he was confident that Methuen and Gatacre would be able to carry out their briefs without undue difficulty, while he, the Commander-in-Chief, attended to what was, as he saw it, the central problem to the whole war, the relief of Ladysmith – relieve Ladysmith, move on to Pretoria, blocking the Delagoa Bay railway at the same time, and meet up with Methuen's forces there, who would have already taken Bloemfontein on their way up. That was the plan. The Boers would no longer be in a position to maintain the siege of Mafeking or to continue with their tiresome antics in the south. They would be forced to sue for peace.

Major-Generals Lyttelton, Hart, Barton, Hildyard and Clery had already been sent up to Natal, with Clery taking command of the forward position base at Frere, a mere twenty-five miles down the railway line from Ladysmith.

By early December, by rushing train-load after train-load of soldiers up to Frere, straight from their transports as soon as they docked in South Africa, Buller had amassed an army of about 21,000. Now he was ready to move. He carried out careful reconnaissance of the country ahead, armed with a large telescope. It was an endless panorama of kopjes, through which the road and railway threaded, and in a hollow in the centre of it, straddling the railway, was the village of Colenso, a single-street settlement of simple tin-roofed houses where both road and railway crossed the Tugela over two bridges. Colenso did not look like the sort of place to be taken easily. Through the glass he could see the strongly fortified kopjes of Red Hill and Grobler's Kloof to the left, beyond the river, which was hidden at this point in its deep bed by dense brushwood. Commanding the two bridges was the low hill of Fort Wylie, and to the extreme right were the heights of Hlangwane and Monte Cristo, and the 4,000 feet high Mount Inhlawe, on the steep blue slopes of which the Boers had dug excellent defensive lines.

Buller decided on a feint. He ordered Major-General Barton to take his four battalions of English, Welsh, Scottish and Irish Fusiliers to a position immediately in front of the Boers' defences at Colenso to distract them. Captain Jones,

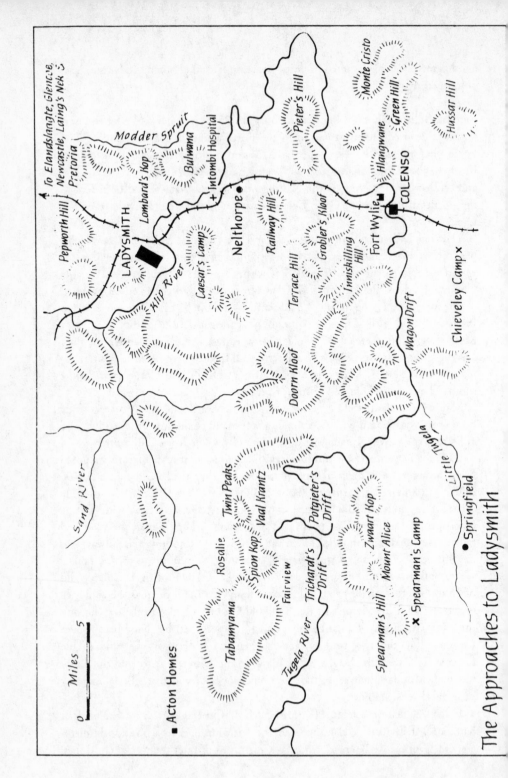

The Approaches to Ladysmith

of HMS *Forte*, followed close on Barton's heels with the Naval Brigade from *Terrible* and *Tartar*, and set up positions at a range of 7,200 yards from the Boer emplacements on the nearest kopjes.

Then, late in the evening of 12 December, one day after Magersfontein and two days after Stormberg, Buller set out with the bulk of the remainder of his forces on a night march, sweeping wide to the west towards Potgeiter's Drift. But something made him change his mind before the troops had marched very far. It was to prove a crucial moment in his life. Perhaps his instincts all told him that he would be foolhardy to move so far from the line of communication that the railway provided. Almost certainly (he practically confirms this in his signal to the War Office) the news of the disasters at Magersfontein and Stormberg had dealt his confidence such a shattering blow that he just was not thinking clearly. It is obvious that he was in no fit frame of mind, as a commanding General, to fight and win a battle. He signalled both the War Office in London and General White in Ladysmith that he had changed his mind and would be coming through Colenso after all. Only hours before, he had been firmly of the opinion that such an approach was impossible.

The wording of his signals was in such defeatist terms that Buller was never, for the rest of his life, to be allowed to forget them. He was never to live down the ignominious stain of Colenso, despite his subsequent victories. To the War Office he sent: 'This operation [i.e. his original plan to sweep to the left] involved the complete abandonment of my communications, and in the event of success, the risk that I might share the fate of Sir George White and be cut off from Natal. I had considered that with the enemy dispirited by the failure of their plans in the west, the risk was justifiable, but I cannot think I ought now to take such a risk. From my point of view, it will be better to lose Ladysmith altogether than to throw open Natal to the enemy.' By now, mid-December, the word 'Ladysmith' was ingrained on every British heart at home, and Buller could not have chosen more unsuitable words with which to express himself.

His forces now consisted of sixteen infantry battalions and five artillery batteries, plus Jones's sailors and a mounted detachment commanded by the newly arrived Lord Dundonald. In the modern European armies of the time, the ratio of artillery to infantry was around five guns to every thousand men. Buller had only thirty guns, but 21,000 men, which, on paper at least, indicated a woeful lack of artillery with which to try and carry out an offensive operation in difficult mountainous country. It is true that he was reinforced by the two 4.7s and fourteen 12-pounders of the Naval Brigade, but these were very cumbersome in such a terrain as this, being drawn by huge lines of plodding oxen through countless drifts and dongas, and all the while vulnerable to attack from a highly mobile enemy.

Captain Jones's naval guns hammered shells into the Boer-held kopjes all day on 13 December without any reply whatsoever. In fact, apart from a scurried few movements to be seen on the hillsides when a British shell fell uncomfortably close, there was no indication that the Boers were present at all.

By the 14th Hildyard, Lyttelton, Hart and Dundonald had all swung their brigades to the right, following Buller's change of mind, and encamped north of Chieveley, well in sight of Colenso. Jones brought his guns up closer and heavily shelled both Fort Wylie and another fortified kopje far behind it at 10,000 yards. Again the Boers were silent. The impression was that they did not intend to hold the line of the Tugela and were falling back to strengthen their defence of Ladysmith itself.

That evening Buller, in conference with his Major-Generals, resolved to force his way over the Tugela the next day. He delegated each of his brigades a crossing-point on a front straddling the two bridges. Part of the Naval Brigade was to take up position on top of a slope facing Colenso, about two miles away, with the two 4.7s and four of the 12-pounders. This was to comprise the central battery, under Commander Limpus, and would take up position about 800 yards west of the railway, some 3,000 yards back from the river. The guns were assigned as follows. No 1 4.7 Lieutenant England and Chief Petty Officer Bate; No 2 4.7 Lieutenant Hunt and Chief Petty Officer Stephens; 2 × 12-pounders Lieutenant Richards, Petty Officer Jeffrey and Sergeant Roper; 2 × 12-pounders Lieutenant Wilde and Petty Officers H. Mitchell and Metcalfe. The Natal Naval Volunteer detachment, under Lieutenants Anderton and Chiazarri, were allocated to support the 4.7s. Mr Cole, gunner, and Chief Gunnery Instructor Baldwin were attached to the battery for general duties.

Another six 12-pounders, with Lieutenant Ogilvy as the senior naval officer, were to be attached to the command of the Colonel Long of the Royal Artillery on the right of the railway. This battery comprised the *Tartar's* two 12-pounders under Lieutenant James with Petty Officers Epsley and Bird; 2 × 12-pounders under Lieutenant Deas with Petty Officers Symons and Ward; and 2 × 12-pounders under Mr Wright, gunner, and Petty Officers Venness and Taylor. The remaining two 12-pounders, commanded by Lieutenant Burne with Petty Officers Mullis and R. Mitchell, would stay in the rear, on Gun Hill, to guard the flanks.

In the morning, long before the sun came up to herald an intensely hot day, the infantry had piled their greatcoats on wagons to be taken to the rear, packed 170 rounds per man into their ammunition pouches and started to move forward in skirmishing order, cheerfully anticipating, as they had been told, that the Boers would not defend their lines with much stubbornness as they were on the point of falling back.

The Naval Brigade, too, had been called at 2 am for breakfast and were on the march before 4 o'clock, rolling easily down the gentle slope, over the dewy grass of the veldt. All was quiet except for the rumbling of the wheels, the snorts of the oxen and the occasional shout of a Kaffir driver.

At 4.45, at a range of 4,000 yards, the sailors' 12-pounders opened up with a tremendous crash, pouring a deluge of common shell and shrapnel on to Fort Wylie. As before, the Boers' guns were silent. Jones brought his 4.7s into play at 5.20, keeping up a steady bombardment for an hour, while Colonel Long moved his batteries, with Ogilvy's 12-pounders in their rear, up on the other side of the railway, to within close range of Fort Wylie.

Now the sun was up enough to cause the damp grass to steam, making observation of distant movements difficult, even through glasses. But still the invisible Boers made no reply to the British onslaught, which seemingly confirmed that they were indeed retiring and did not intend to fight that day.

The infantry had almost reached the river when the Boers came into action at last. Firing from a triple row of trenches and rifle pits, they hurled a cascade of Mauser bullets, backed up by a steady beat of pom-pom fire from scattered positions in the kopjes. From farther back behind the Boer rifles, heavier guns began to join in the fight. They were using smokeless powder, which made it impossible for the British gunners to spot their hidden positions so as to reply.

Colonel Long had been convinced that the enemy had retired, following reports from his scouts, one of whom had actually walked on the road bridge without hearing a shot or seeing a Boer. Despite the pleadings of some of his junior officers, who sensed a Boer trick (and, incidentally, in contravention of Buller's explicit instructions), he moved his batteries very close to the Tugela and only 1,200 yards from Fort Wylie.

It was Long's Royal Artillery gunners, having rolled into a suicidally close position to the Tugela, far in advance of the British infantry, who bore the brunt of the Boers' opening storm of fire. With practice-drill discipline they unlimbered, coolly picked up the range and began to shell Fort Wylie. Lieutenant Ogilvy's 12-pounders, being heavier and slower to manoeuvre, were last in position. Two of them had just crossed the last donga when the Boers opened up. The sudden barrage killed many of their oxen and, in the midst of the chaos, the rest stampeded and the native drivers all ran away.

With great difficulty Ogilvy's sailors got their guns unlimbered and began to pour shells on to the enemy emplacements in an attempt to ease the pressure on Long's guns just ahead. Now, under the full attention of the naval guns firing lyddite, Fort Wylie was enveloped in clouds of smoke and red dust, rising vertically into the sky. A Boer gun had just been brought into action from a position on the Fort and Petty Officers Venness and Taylor, both renowned for their deadly aim with a ship's gun, turned the fury of the battle into a sporting occasion by calmly challenging each other to see who would be first to knock the Boer out of action. A mighty cheer went up from all around when Taylor won the contest and they saw the big gun topple over.

But the 'Long Toms' had begun firing from a range of 7,000 yards, and after half an hour the Royal Artillery batteries, hopelessly outranged, were completely knocked out. Stranded, with only a few oxen and with the 'Long Tom' shells falling all around them, the Naval Brigade's 12-pounder crews heaved and strained on the guns' drag-ropes to haul them back to a safer position in a donga. Pulling the heavily laden ammunition wagons back to safety was a highly perilous manoeuvre. With no oxen and only one team of artillery horses available, it had to be done by hand. Every available muscle was applied to the job, and even General Buller, who was close at hand, dismounted with his attendant staff to put their shoulders to the wagon wheels. Help came to hand when somebody produced another team of eight horses to extricate a wagon from a donga. Amid a storm of Mauser bullets, a young Ordinary Seaman, Frank Hayles, leapt on to one of the leading horses, but within seconds it was shot dead. Cutting the corpse free of the traces, he jumped on another, and that too was hit. Still in the donga, he stopped the wagon to pick up several rifles that had been jerked off the back as it lurched along, whereupon Buller shouted, 'Push on, Jack, or you'll lose the wagon and the whole lot for the sake of a few rifles!'

Ogilvy had been forced to leave behind the spare ammunition wagon, but a local farmer-driver, a Mr Pringle, owned the wagon and with astonishing coolness managed to inspan a few oxen and single-handedly bring back the ammunition safely.

The 4.7 gunners, far back, sweated all the morning in the terrific heat. Here again was a contest between the guns' captains, C. P. O.s Bate and Stephens, whose efforts were later described by Buller as admirable. Although they displayed some very accurate gunnery in silencing the 'Long Toms' on Fort Wylie with lyddite shells, there were an estimated fifteen of the latter, in scattered positions, and the British guns were simply outnumbered. They were, at this point, the subject of a new-fangled invention. During the course of the action, a biograph (movie camera) was set up alongside their great guns, looking like a tea-chest stuck on top of a tennis umpire's perch, to film the battle.

Up ahead the infantry were undergoing severe punishment. *The Times* correspondent wrote:

At 6.30 am the Dublin Fusiliers with the Connaught Rangers advanced across the open ground under fire, and as they came into the curve of the river, the Boers opened up an enfilading as well as a front fire on them. The ground was very dry and every bullet could be seen striking up a spurt of dust. The fire was terrific. Besides the musketry fire, the enemy shelled them with three guns, one directly ahead at short range ... the 63rd and 64th batteries on the left seemed to be unable to silence their fire, and the naval battery, which was the only one capable of doing it, was concentrat-

68

ing its fire on Fort Wylie. The Dublins and the Connaughts advanced magnificently against the almost overwhelming fire; men falling at every step . . . and yet there was nothing to tell where the enemy was concealed. Not a single head was visible, nothing but a long line of smoke and an incessant crackling roar. . . . At last our men reached the river, but where there should have been a ford there was 7 feet of water. [the Boers had dammed it downstream.] the few who tried to cross it, overcome by the weight of rifle and ammunition, were drowned.

The naval guns continued to give the inevitable British retreat covering fire, as the wagons rolled back carrying thirsty and angry troops. Eventually General Buller ordered them to retire as well, and they were back on Shooter's Hill by late afternoon.

Lieutenant Richards' Royal Marines gun crew had fired 317 rounds from their 12-pounder during the day. They had completely disabled one cunningly hidden Boer gun, which had been firing smokeless powder. Richards managed to spot its location through his telescope and Sergeant Roper hit it, square-on, with his second shot. The next look through the glass revealed a gun-muzzle pointing drunkenly skywards.

There were few casualties among the naval personnel. Able Seamen Newstead, Webster and White were wounded, and another bluejacket received what was termed as a 'scratch'. In White's case, while he was lying dangerously wounded by a shell-splinter in the back, his 'oppo', Able Seaman Campling, had stayed behind to guard him, after the guns had retired, until the ambulance picked him up. Campling had then advanced, on his own, to join the infantry in the firing line and was officially recorded as 'missing' until he later returned to receive an appropriate rebuke. Lieutenant Ogilvy himself had had a narrow escape. He had been standing, looking through his field glasses at his fall of shot when no less than three Maxim shells had passed between his legs without touching him.

It was the infantry who had been slaughtered at the Tugela. The Dublins, the Connaughts, the Devons and the Royal West Surreys had paid a fearful price.

The surgeons, including the Naval Brigade's, worked until late in the night attending to the wounded as they were brought in by the stretcher-bearers. All through the evening the ambulance wagons had been swaying and tottering back across the stony veldt, bearing men with terrible wounds the sight of which turned the stomachs of even the hardened surgeons. Burnt black by the sun, with clothing stiff with dried gore, some died on the journey back. Others thrashed around on their stretchers in delirious agony, awaiting merciful chloroform, while the less seriously wounded dipped big army mugs into buckets of Bovril and drank deeply, grateful to be alive.

Then it started to rain and tarpaulins were hurriedly thrown over the stretchers. But all the while the surgeons bent over the helpless forms, stitching and amputating, until the wet grass became littered with mangled pieces of arms and legs, creating a grisly scene of horror lit by flickering lanterns.

Buller had lost seventy-one officers and 1,025 men killed and wounded, including Colonel Long, mortally wounded with Mauser bullets through the liver, and the Boers had captured three guns and nine ammunition wagons.

From Chieveley Camp, the next day, Lieutenant Ogilvy sent his report to Captain Jones:

Sir, – I have the honour to submit the following account of the part taken by the 12-pr guns forming the battery under my command during the action in front of Colenso. Acting on orders received from Captain Jones R.N., I reported myself to Colonel Long, C.R.A., who directed me to attach myself to him until the guns were placed in a suitable position. I therefore directed Lieut. James of *Tartar*, to lead the battery behind the Royal Artillery field-guns, and told him that we were to form up on the left of the Royal Artillery guns when they came into action. About 6 a.m., the guns being in column of route march with Naval guns in the rear, I was riding beside Colonel Long about 450 yards from Colenso Station, when he directed Colonel Hunt to bring his guns into action just in front of a deep donga running across our front at right angles to the railway. He then told me to come into action on the left, and proceeded to arrange our different zones of fire, while the Royal Artillery guns were getting into position. In front of us was a line of trees up to which our skirmishers had advanced, also a few artillery outposts. Just as I was about to address my guns where to go, and as the Royal Artillery were unlimbering, the outposts turned sharply and a murderous fire, both rifle and shell, was opened on the guns and ammunition column. I immediately galloped back to my guns and found that the fire had caught them just as the two centre guns were going through a drift across another donga parallel to the before-mentioned one, but about 400 yards in the rear. When I arrived I found that all the native drivers with the exception of those for Lieut. James' gun teams had bolted. These guns had just crossed the drift, so I directed him to take up a position on the left and opened fire on Fort Wylie, from which the majority of the shell-fire appeared to come. About this time, my horse was shot through the shoulder by a rifle bullet. The two rear guns under Lieut. Deas, of HMS *Philomel*, not having crossed the drift, I directed him to take the ground to the left and also open fire on Fort Wylie. The two centre guns under Mr Wright, gunner, of HMS *Terrible*, were unfortunately jammed with their ammunition wagons in the drift, the wheels of the wagons being locked and the oxen turned round in their yokes. I managed by the aid of some artillery horses to extricate these guns from the drift and to bring them into action on each side of the drift to the rear of the donga, one of the horses being shot whilst doing this. I could not manage to move the ammunition wagons as the rifle and shell-fire was too severe at the time, a one-and-a-half-pounder Maxim-Nordenfelt being particularly attentive, and sending three shells into the drift at every discharge. Repeated messages for more men came back from the Royal Artillery batteries, and these were sent to the front by a Royal Artillery sergeant in charge of the ammunition column. After about half-an-hour's firing, as I should judge, the Royal Artillery guns were silenced, nearly all the men being apparently killed or wounded. Soon after this, the fire from Fort Wylie slackened considerably. The Commander-in-Chief now rode up and directed me to move our guns and ammunitions as soon as I could. The guns were got away each by a team of artillery horses, who galloped up the hill to the rear. The wagons were far more difficult owing to their weight, the large circle they required to turn in, and to the fact that they had to be got out of the drift and turned round by the guns' crews before the horses could be put on. About this time a most brilliant feat was performed by two teams of artillery, who galloped to the front, against a murderous fire, limbered up and rescued two guns; a similar attempt by one other team, at least, resulted in the entire team, as far as I could see, being destroyed. The advance of the infantry on an open plain, with little or no cover against a most heavy rifle fire from intrenched positions, was also a magnificent sight. The conduct of our men without exception was particularly fine, the day being a very hot one and the work hard. The way Nos 1 and 2 guns' crews of the *Terrible* got their wagons out of the drift under heavy fire from shell and rifle was quite up to the standard expected of all seamen. I cannot conclude without mentioning the way Lieut. James of the *Tartar* selected the best position and opened fire with great effect. Lieut. Deas, of the *Philomel*, unfortunately had a gun capsize as they were moving off to the left to come into action, but managed to mount it quickly and brought both guns into action. After the first few minutes these two officers took entire charge of their respective guns and brought them safely out of action; Lieut. James coming again into action on the left under the direction of Captain Jones. Mr Wright, gunner, worked his guns well, and was of great assistance in withdrawing them. Surgeon Macmillan, R.N., Lieut. Palmer R.A.M.C., were conspicuous in their attendance to the wounded. Our loss was very small, three wounded, one of them very slightly, and I attribute this to (1st) the Fort Wylie guns and rifle fire being directed principally on the R.A. guns, which were some 300 yards nearer than we were; (2nd) to the enemy directing most of their fire on our ox teams and wagons, they being so much more conspicuous than the guns. 28 oxen were killed, wounded or lost.

I might mention that Mr Boldero and Mr Hodson, midshipmen, and Mr Hollins, clerk, were attending on me noting ranges and carrying messages between the guns during the four hours we were working at the drift.

I have the honour to be, Sir,

Your obedient servant,

F. C. A. Ogilvy,

Lieut. Commanding six 12-pr guns, attached to 2nd Division.

To Captain E. P. Jones, Commanding Naval Brigade.

Black Week was complete.

CHAPTER 11

CHRISTMAS WITH JACK

Buller had spent fourteen hours in the saddle under the broiling sun, and the pain of the slight wound he received cannot have added to his composure. He was furious with Long for the crass and disobedient behaviour which caused both men and guns to be lost.

He sent to White, by heliograph, 'I tried Colenso yesterday but failed; the enemy is too strong for my force, except with siege operations, and these will take one full month to prepare. Can you last so long? If not, how many days can you give me in which to take up defensive positions? After which I suggest you firing away as much ammunition as you can and making the best terms you can. . . . Also add to end of message: Whatever happens, recollect to burn your cipher, and decipher and code books, and any deciphered messages.'

And to the War Office, 'My failure today raises a serious question. I do not think I am now strong enough to relieve White. . . . My view is that I ought to let Ladysmith go, and occupy good positions for the defence of south Natal and let time help us.'

For the British Government, this was an intolerable attitude for a British General to adopt. Yet again he had advocated the abandonment of Ladysmith. Without more ado, he was sacked.

Three times in five days, at Stormberg, Magersfontein and Colenso, had a British general hurled his troops at the fortified trenches and kopjes of the Boers head-on like runaway trains at buffers at the end of the line, and with a similar result. There had been far more damage caused to the train than to the station. What was more, the station masters' offices at Kimberley and Ladysmith had not felt the least shudder from the impact. The stupendous bravery displayed by the Guards at Belmont, the Navy and Marines at Graspan and the Dublins at Colenso had all counted for nought.

Buller's pessimistic heliographs to General White had not been the only communications to Ladysmith after the Battle of Colenso. Arthur Halsey

73

managed to get permission to let his besieged brother know of his presence with the relief column, and soon the mirrors were flashing a somewhat more optimistic message: 'All well at home. C. to be married in London: hope to see you soon.' To which Lionel replied, with stiff upper-lipped economy of verbage: 'All well – wire home.'

'Bobs' was having his breakfast in Dublin when the morning papers arrived, bearing brief cabled news of Buller's reverse at Colenso. He hurried from the table to scribble a long telegram to the Secretary of State for War, Lord Lansdowne. Now was his chance to press home the oblique claims for Buller's job which he had been making for a long time. He had been bombarding the War Office with suggestions for the better prosecution of the war ever since it began and was convinced, having read Buller's telegrams, that the latter had lost his nerve long before Colenso. In fact, he had said so in a letter to Lansdowne on 8 December, a good week beforehand, and followed it up with a secret private visit two days later.

Field-Marshal Lord Roberts of Kandahar and Waterford, VC, KP, GCB, GCSI, GCIE, or just 'Bobs' aged sixty-seven and a lithe five feet two, was one of Victorian Britain's heroes. He had come home from India in 1893 after forty-one years overseas, mainly on the sub-continent, where he had won his VC in the Indian Mutiny of 1857. But it was his march on Kandahar, Afghanistan, in the summer of 1880 for which he was most famous. The British Consul in Kabul had been murdered the previous year and Roberts was appointed to lead the small army which was sent in to avenge the crime. With the startling rapidity that was to become his trademark, he invaded Afghanistan, entering Kabul within days. After pausing there, he suddenly cut loose, and, living off the land, his column of 10,000 troops made the 320 miles to Kandahar, in sweltering heat, in twenty-three days.

There cannot have been many Generals who held the affection of their troops as strongly as 'Bobs'; maybe not even Wellington. Julian Ralph, of the *Daily Mail*, wrote, 'His army will do anything for him; march longer, starve harder, go without tents, blankets, and rum more days and weeks, and die in greater numbers for him than any other man alive.' Of his portrait, it was said to possess 'that perfectly balanced combination of justice and mercy, vigour and refinement, inflexibility and consummate tact, which have made Lord Roberts equally loved and feared.'

Unbeknown to Roberts, as his latest cable was on its way to Lansdowne, the Defence Committee had already decided to appoint him in Buller's place, and their telegram to him was on its way to Ireland, where he was Commander of the Forces. One other thing was unknown to Roberts. His only son, Freddie, had died at Colenso, with five Boer bullets in his body, while making an heroic attempt to recover some guns, which was to earn him a posthumous VC.

On receipt of Lansdowne's cypher, Roberts immediately left for London.

Accounts differ as to the actual sequence of events as regards his knowledge of the loss of his son. Some record that Lansdowne broke the news to him in London, but from the *Times* account of his departure from Dublin it would appear that he already knew about it:

> Lord and Lady Roberts and their two daughters left Dublin last night for London. They travelled to Kingstown in the same train as Mr and Mrs Chamberlain. Lord Roberts, who left the Royal Hospital at a quarter-past 7 o'clock, received a very cordial send off from the hospital and all the pensioners turned out to witness his departure. Lord Roberts' party, who were in deep mourning, had entered a private saloon carriage before the arrival of Mr Chamberlain. Sir David Harrel, Under-Secretary, Major-General Gosset, Mr John Atkinson, Attorney-General, and Lord Justice Fitzgibbon were on the platform. Only some 60 other persons were present. As the train moved out of the station there was a tremendous outburst of cheering, in which the railway porters and other officials took an enthusiastic part.

The appointment of Roberts and the firing of Buller presented a ticklish problem for Lansdowne. He anticipated all kinds of obstruction, especially from the eighty-year-old Queen. It was decided that she would not be told until it was *fait accompli*, and to soften the blow by leaving Buller to retain the command in Natal under Roberts as supremo. To Lansdowne's relief, all appears to have gone according to plan. Victoria was acquiescent. Salisbury raised no objections, but made the proviso that Lord Kitchener, then in Egypt, should be appointed as Roberts' Chief of Staff. Furthermore, the War Secretary's concern that whatever the Defence Committee decided should receive the approval of the people was satisfied. He was sure they would like this. And they did.

From then on events moved fast. The Cabinet sent Buller a telegram to the effect that his suggestion to abandon Ladysmith was regarded as 'a national disaster of the greatest magnitude' and Roberts arrived at the War Office to confirm acceptance of his appointment. It was thought that Buller would resign rather than endure the humiliation of his relegation. But this was not to be. On the contrary, it was rumoured that it was Buller himself who had suggested Roberts as his replacement. In truth, after the black gloom following Colenso had passed, he was probably grateful that the weight had been lifted from his shoulders.

On Saturday, 23 December, a bare week after the news of Colenso had reached London, and amid the usual thunder of applause at Waterloo Station, Roberts departed to Southampton, where he joined the same *Dunottar Castle* which had taken the unfortunate Buller to the Cape. Kitchener was already at sea in the cruiser HMS *Isis*, steaming flat out at eighteen knots, on his way from

Alexandria to Malta, where he was to transfer to HMS *Dido*, for Gibraltar, to rendezvous with the *Dunottar Castle* when it arrived there.

And then it was Christmas. Christmas seemed to have crept up on a nation preoccupied with less festive matters. The two months of fighting had hardly shifted the Boers back an inch, especially where it mattered. And all at a fearfully high cost in blood. The famous upper lip had needed to become stiffer and stiffer. The morale of the country was understandably deflated, but the spirit was not broken. Christmas would, perhaps, be a more sombre occasion than usual, but like all Christmases, it was a time for reflection and taking stock. Behind the stiff upper lips scanning the headlines and casualty lists each morning hid rows of gritted teeth. Such was the anxiety of the nation that *The Times* actually brought out an issue on Christmas Day.

As the *Dunottar Castle* lurched her way towards Cape St Vincent that Christmas Day on her way to pick up Kitchener at Gibraltar, the three Naval Brigades with the British forces in South Africa were all trying their best to make it into a holiday. Bearcroft's men were still on guard over the huge baggage and ammunition piles that were being amassed at Modder River in the west. In Natal, on the Sunday morning after Colenso, during a convenient eclipse of the moon, the central battery under Commander Limpus were moved back from Shooter's Hill to Gun Hill, where, having positioned the guns, they were encamped until the middle of January. Ogilvy's 12-pounders were sent down the line to rest with the bulk of Buller's army at Frere. And Lambton's crews were still ensnared in Ladysmith.

With her customary thoughtfulness for her troops, the Queen decided to send each man at the front a personal Christmas gift. Lansdowne received a letter from Sir Fleetwood Edwards at Windsor Castle, on 19 November:

Dear Lord Lansdowne,

The Queen commands me to inform you of her anxiety to make some little personal present as soon as possible to each of her soldiers serving in South Africa. Her Majesty has decided upon sending chocolate, which she is given to understand will be appropriate and acceptable.

It will be packed for each man in a tin that has been specially designed for the occasion. The Queen hopes that you may be able to arrange for its conveyance and distribution.

Believe me, yours very truly,

Fleetwood J. Edwards.

The Queen's order for the chocolate was equally divided, with careful diplomacy, between the firms of Cadbury, Fry and Rowntree. The chocolate, which was in 'cake' form so as to be suitable either for drinking or eating as a sweet, was supplied in tin boxes each containing half a pound, or enough to make about a dozen good mugs-full. The tins were oblong, printed with decorative designs in blue and silver on a background of red, in the centre of which was a portrait of Victoria. One hundred thousand of these were required, and there were many manufacturing and logistical difficulties which had to be overcome before the order could be completed, mainly owing to the shortage of time. The contract for the manufacture of the tins was also divided between three firms, one being Hudson, Scott & Sons Ltd of Carlisle, who made 33,000 of them.

Elsewhere at home the men were not forgotten either. Lady White, wife of the besieged General in Ladysmith, launched an appeal on behalf of all those incarcerated in the town, which quickly raised £3,000 and 600 parcels. In reply, three doughty ladies from West London, Margaret and Dora Scott Turner and Alma Mary Howell, hastened to publicize a similar appeal on behalf of the 2,500 trapped in Kimberley and the 800 in Mafeking.

The Naval Brigades had special attention from various quarters. The Mayor and Corporation of Portsmouth sent £100 to Admiral Harris for the welfare of his men, and the famous Aggie Weston, whose Sailors' Rests have since been a home-from-home for many generations of Royal Navy matelots, made the following appeal in the columns of *The Times*:

Sir,

The gallantry of our sailors as well as of our soldiers is in the mind of the whole country. Jack, with his naval guns, came to the rescue at Ladysmith and turned the tide; the battle of Graspan, or Enslin, which has just been fought on the road to Kimberley, has been called the 'sailors' battle', so heavily did the brave bluejackets and marines of the naval brigade, both officers and men, suffer. But, as might be expected from Jack's dauntless gallantry, the battle was a victory.

I am honoured by the Navy with the title of 'Mother', and I am anxious to cheer the hearts of the brave boys at Christmas and the New Year. There are between 600 and 1,000 men at the front, and I want to send each a Christmas pudding, a ration of tobacco, and a pipe, and possibly socks, to replace those worn out in climbing kopjes. I have consulted the bluejackets at the home ports as to these gifts, and they suggested and voted vigorously for puddings, 'baccy and socks. I shall be sending out immediately, and I shall be very glad to receive help from all friends of the Navy who may be disposed to aid me.

All gifts, marked 'Christmas and New Year's Cheer for Jack at the Front', will be duly acknowledged. Cheques to be drawn to Agnes R. Weston or paid into 'Royal Sailors' Rest Account, National Provincial Bank, Landport, Portsmouth'. All cheques and postal orders to have & Co. written across them. Will my kind helpers address to me, 'Miss

Weston, Royal Sailors' Rest, Portsmouth' and send at once, as Christmas and New Year are at hand? Jack's rations when fighting are often short, and his privations great, and it cheers his heart to know that his friends in England never forget him.

Yours very truly,

Agnes R. Weston,

Royal Sailors' Rest, Portsmouth.

It was now high summer in South Africa and in such an arid area, only a stone's throw from the tropics, life became uncomfortable for those living under canvas. At Modder River the erstwhile picturesque setting had become a dusty desert. The camp had grown into a big depot as more and more supplies poured in, preparing for Methuen's push up to Kimberley. Horses, mules, oxen, wagon-wheels and marching feet had churned up the ground when it was muddy, and now, as their numbers grew, they ground it into a fine dust which found its way into food, eyes, ears, blankets, clothing and even managed to get inside pocket-watches. All this despite the men taking refuge in their tents, with the flaps and doors lashed down tight.

The cool morning breezes turned, as the sun rose, into hot swirling gusts which drove the dust into whirlwinds, spiralling high into the blazing blue sky, which caused the animals to stampede, flattening tents and smashing equipment. Water became scarce, creating terrible thirst. The Modder was, by now, reduced to a trickle, and its muddy water needed to be boiled before drinking. All the same, enteric (typhoid and paratyphoid) fever, which was to deplete the British forces by greater numbers than Boer bullets in the course of the war, was beginning to take its toll of the bluejackets. One of Bearcroft's midshipmen, Robertson, was one of the first to succumb to it.

A flurry of cables emerged from the front, via *Times* correspondents and Reuter's, over Christmas, as if to say 'don't forget us':

Modder River, Dec. 23, 6 pm. The unparalleled absence of rain is becoming serious, though it injures the Boers far more than it does us. . . . Experiments made with wireless telegraphy have shown that the excessive dryness of the air and the soil here, and the slight impediments in the latter, cause obstructions in the earth current. The difficulty has been partially overcome by attaching the wire to the railway or to a wire fence, thus increasing the area of contact, or by using zinc troughs filled with wet earth. The fall of rain, which is now overdue, will facilitate the working. The Boer plant confiscated was made by Siemens and Halske, not by Signor Marconi.

And a cheerfully re-assuring message from Reuter's:

The Boers every day throw a few shells into our lines, firing from extreme range. The shells fall within the line of outposts at about 700 yards from our encampment. They seldom burst, however, and do no damage. Our naval gunners believe that the Boer gun must be raised to its highest possible elevation and fired as a venture. A small party of Boers have been observed in the neighbourhood of our extreme right, but they retired on the approach of our cavalry.

Our position is now one of extreme security, and splendidly adapted either for defensive or offensive operations. A long rolling plain extends on all sides, bounded on the north by the Magersfontein Range, too distant, however, to affect our position. The water of the Modder has been analysed and pronounced to be of exceptional quality (!). Our troops are extremely healthy, and have recovered entirely from the fatigues of the last fight.

Reuter's: 'Modder River, Dec. 24. The force encamped here wishes to send Christmas greetings to all friends and relatives at home.'

And from Orange River: 'Dec 25. The news of the appointment of Lord Roberts and Lord Kitchener has been received with jubilation by the troops here. The men have a marvellous confidence in Lord Roberts, from whose presence every advantage is anticipated, from success in the field to a first-rate commissariat.'

Boxing Day seems to have been quiet, but on 27 December, dateline 5.10 pm. Modder River, came:

Last night the Boers began a heavy fusillade which lasted 20 minutes. They seemed to imagine that we were designing a night attack. Their fire disclosed two miles of trenches, fully manned, and two guns. Today the Boers heavily shelled our left, wishing to silence our naval gun. Their practice was excellent, many shells falling within 20 yards. We replied from the right with a few well-placed shells. Rain fell heavily today. The weather is breaking up.

December 28, 11.30 a.m. At half-past eight last night there was a repetition of the Boer scare of the previous day, a continuous fire being opened along the whole of their trenches and kopjes. . . . Guns, Maxims and rifles were all employed for 20 minutes and thousands of rounds were fired aimlessly into the dark. We replied with only two rounds of our 4.7. This nervousness of the Boers is a wholly new feature and causes much amusement in our camp.

From information found on the battlefield, it is certain that Cronje employs half his force in watching by day and half by night. It seems probable that the consequent weariness will be found intolerable, and combined with the absence of water and the outbreak of typhoid reported by a doctor, will render their position impossible.

And from Reuter's at Modder River the same day:

The Boers disclosed three of their guns yesterday afternoon. A naval gun which up till then had been silent immediately fired a lyddite shell at them. The shot burst close to the embrasure of the enemy's guns, upon which the Boers at once ceased work. Lord Methuen ordered three naval guns to be laid while daylight lasted and about 11 o'clock last night they began to fire at intervals of a few minutes. The Boers replied with a heavy rifle fire from the Magersfontein ridges. Our outposts did not fire a single shot in reply. Suddenly firing ceased, but was renewed half an hour later as vigorously as before. Early this morning the Boers opened with two guns but they were quickly silenced.

Over at Frere Captain Jones' Brigade were doing more or less the same as their colleagues in the west – awaiting reinforcements. Just to keep the Boers on their toes, they were firing spasmodic 4.7 lyddite shells into the enemy emplacements at all kind of irregular times. Quite often, even in the depths of the middle watch (midnight – 4 am) the silence would be broken by the sudden crash of a big naval gun, and a few seconds later a pyrotechnic display would sprout on the slopes of a kopje four miles away.

Then General Buller decided that the road bridge at Colenso was being too useful to the Boers and must be destroyed. The sturdy stone-piered bridge, with its iron superstructure, was addressed by the 4.7 of Lieutenant Hunt and Chief Petty Officer Stephens. They threw thirty shells at the bridge and, although they hit it several times, it remained intact. Thus developed yet another sporting contest, when up stepped Lieutenant England, with the other 4.7 and CPO William Bate, whose lethal aim could land a naval shell on a sixpence at four miles. Bate hit the bridge. So did England. Bate took his second shot and the spans of the bridge toppled like a row of dominoes.

One of the 4.7s was showing signs of wear and Jones wired down to Scott at Durban for a replacement. When the new gun arrived, it has to be taken from the railway to Gun Hill for mounting, a distance of half a mile. This task provided an excellent opportunity for a display of superb co-ordination of human muscle power. There were no tripods or sheer-legs available, and the two-ton gun had to be man handled entirely from the rail-truck.

CPO Baldwin was in charge of a party working 2,000 fathoms of six-inch rope into a mantle covering for the armoured train engine to protect it from shell blast. The finished product gave the engine an appearance uncannily similar to a giant Afghan hound, and it was christened 'Hairy Mary'.

All in all the sailors were enjoying a welcome division from shipboard life. Here there were no decks to holystone; no brightwork to polish; no hammocks to scrub, and games of football to be enjoyed in the cool of the evening. Even the food made a pleasant change from the monotony of the fare at sea, especially at Christmas. Many hampers arrived from Durban, both from civilian friends and from their mates still aboard *Terrible* and the other ships. Books and magazines, pipes and socks, all flooded in.

And a thoughtful gentleman in Peckham Rye, London, one Andrew A. W. Drew (in fact he was the uncle of Commander de Horsey, HMS *Monarch*, who was about to celebrate Christmas 1899 with the Naval Brigade at Modder River), sent 3,500 sheets of writing paper, plus stamped envelopes and indelible pencils, saying that he hoped that an equal number of anxious mothers, sweethearts and wives would receive letters, free of charge, from their Jack or Joe at the front, which they could not otherwise get.

On Christmas Day, at 102F in the shade, and in full sight of each other, it seems that Briton and Boer observed a time of truce, if only for a few hours. This was especially fitting in a country whose name means Christmas. After Church Services in the morning, there were organized sports in the afternoon and a smoking-concert in the evening. The Naval Brigade played a prominent part in the jollities. Bennet Burleigh, war correspondent of the *Daily Telegraph*, describes their antics perfectly in his *The Natal Campaign*:

Christmas and Boxing Days, as I have indicated, were ushered in by the drums and fifes merrily making the rounds. There are those who prefer the gentler home waits, but there is that peculiarity with the fife and drum, those irritant early wakers from sleep, that their martial pulsations catch the heart and set the blood aglow thumping through the veins to their rhythmic beating. 'Jack's the lad for work, and Jack's the lad for play,' and our bluejackets were the boys who provided the lighter vein of amusement. Christmastide in South Africa, and Natal in particular, has been frizzling hot. Here the sun was over the yardarm. A band of jolly Jack Tars made the round of the camp, capering and singing, preceded by a sailor on horseback bearing a Union Jack and followed by nearly half-a-score of messmates making ridiculously rough weather on muleback. The sailors seated on a gun-carriage were two. Of their number, one represented John Bull, the other, a marine, personated Oom Paul – whom the tars and soldiers generally prefer to call 'Ole Kroojer'. Kruger had his hat, pipe, and umbrella, and real good fun the sailors made of the business, John Bull giving 'Kroojer' no end of nasty knocks, and occasionally sitting upon his chest, whilst Pat and Sandy further fairly bedevilled the wretched one. The tars and soldiers sang bravely during the marchings, and at the sports 'Rule Britannia' set to new words, and all the popular catchy airs of the day, were laid under tribute to enable the men to describe with gusto what they had in store for Kruger.

After their Christmas dinner, which included 10,000 plum puddings generously sent out from England by Messrs J. Lyons, the Tommies queued in long lines to have a look through the big naval telescopes that the sailors used for gunnery spotting. From here it was even possible to see the crew of the Boer Long Tom, 'Puffing Billy', working on Bulwana Hill twelve miles away. Sometimes the mountain would be hidden for several seconds within the green-grey cloud of a bursting lyddite shell as one of Lambton's 4.7s trapped in Ladysmith hurled a defiant shot on to Bulwana. But not today. Today was peaceful. The Boers spent it singing hymns.

It had rained heavily in Ladysmith, which was a mixed blessing. Forage for the animals had been running short, and the change in the weather heralded a welcome sprouting of grass within the perimeter of the defences. But for the time being, with so many feet and hooves confined inside such a small area, the ground became churned into a sea of slippery mud, creating much discomfort, especially for those inhabitants who took shelter in the holes they had dug into the steep banks of the Tugela.

The wet spell and the high temperature (it reached 104°F on some days) meant that the danger from enteric fever was greatly enhanced. General White now had well over 800 men on the sick list, mainly due to enteric and dysentery. Midshipman Sharp had just reported sick with the latter and he recorded in his log that Able Seaman Archer had died on the 13th from his head wounds.

On 22 December a Boer spy was caught and sent down for incarceration in the prison at Estcourt. It was none other than the Reverend Harmes, director of the Hanoverian Mission in Ladysmith, who had been frequently visiting the Boer laager to report on the movements of the British positions within the town. The British had been forced constantly to shift the positions of vital guns and stores because the Boers had been seen to find the ranges quite quickly. It was now clear that this had been largely due to Harmes' information. He tried to claim the protection of the German flag, but General White would hear nothing of that and off to gaol went the parson, together with his accomplice, a German farmer named Stucke.

As was their habit, large numbers of African drivers and runners decided to change their allegiance, seemingly on impulse, just before Christmas. One hundred and twenty of them flocked into Ladysmith, saying they were tired of working for the Boers. Their information was that the British rifle and common shellfire was having practically no effect at all on the Boers, but the lyddite shells were wreaking havoc in their trenches. They said the trenches were so full of dead they had to be filled in, making a mass grave. The Boer laager was full of women wailing. All this was, of course, treated with utmost caution as to its reliability.

The Boers stepped up their bombardment on Dingaan's Day, 16 December, starting with a twenty-one gun salute at dawn. This was the Transvaal Republic's day of patriotism, celebrating the twin occasions of their victory over the Zulus in 1838 and of the raising of the Boer flag at Heidelberg in 1880. On the 18th the Boers scored their highest total of killed in one day so far, when twenty-one men and a dozen horses died. General White's headquarters suffered a direct hit on the 21st, forcing the General to move to a new base on Convent Hill. The next day the Gloucestershire Regiment lost five men, killed by a single shell while they were eating their breakfast, and Midshipman Chichester was taken out to Intombi Hospital Camp with enteric fever.

Then there was silence. Starting on Christmas Eve, no shells came at all, as the sternly religious Boers called a temporary halt to hostilities for two days. At least, that was what it had been assumed that they would do. But to everyone's surprise, on Christmas morning two big bangs were heard. Later two shells were found embedded in the soft ground. Each had the message written on its casing 'Compliments of the Season', and was stuffed, not with high explosive, but with Christmas Pudding!

The Christmas festivities within Ladysmith itself were, perforce, demanding of the greatest originality and initiative on the part of the organizers. Scarcity of luxury goods had forced prices to levels unaffordable by the majority. Whisky was £5 a bottle, if indeed it could be found at all. Potatoes were 3d each, chickens £1 and eggs a shilling each. Nevertheless, White authorized the release of a certain amount of the reserve food stores, so that a passable Christmas dinner was had by all.

The wardroom steward at Naval Brigade headquarters, with the customary guile of his calling, managed to produce two turkeys, a suckling pig (there would have been two, but a Boer pom-pom shell killed the other early in December), some champagne and stout, and enough ingredients to make a giant Christmas duff for his fourteen officers. And Arthur Halsey managed to get permission from General Buller to send a heliograph to his besieged brother that all was well at home.

After Church Service, the round of social visits for pre-lunch drinks continued until it was time to eat, and then, having consumed their heaviest meal for nearly two months, everyone joined in the fun-making, with Lambton and his Jolly Jacks, by all accounts, being the life and soul of the party.

A giant 'Christmas Tree', made up of several different types of tree, was draped with a vast number of toys and knicknacks for the children of the town. These had been rescued, long ago forgotten, from the dark recesses of many a cupboard. Over 200 excited children assembled in the 'hospital' for the party.

Regimental Sergeant-Major Bill Perrin of the Imperial Light Horse was Santa Claus, assisted, among others, by Colonel Frank Rhodes, whose brother Cecil was still grumbling in Kimberley.

There were sports, with a tug o' war competition and gymkhana. The Natal Carbineers had made oil-drums and paraffin tins into a comic steel band, accompanied by tin whistles. The Gordon Highlanders played their bagpipes and there was a singsong, followed by dancing until the early hours.

Boxing Day saw an unpleasant return to reality, however, when the bombardment began again, catching a group of officers of the Devons at breakfast, killing several of them.

New Year's Eve, 1899, was one of those times that would remain clear in the memory for years to come. Everybody would remember exactly what they were doing and who was there when midnight struck to herald the advent of 1900. Lieutenant Burne of the *Philomel*, at Chieveley, noted in his diary that he turned out with Whyte, one of his Midshipmen, at midnight and struck sixteen bells on an old 4.7 brass case. Then they had a bowl of fine punch with slices of pineapple in it, which they shared with the duty watch, and everybody wished each other Happy New Year. Then he records that, as a gesture of goodwill, they sent the Boers some 4.7 liver pills.

The dutiful Lionel Halsey wrote again to his parents; this time to his father, with New Year greetings:

Princess Victoria Battery,
Ladysmith
2nd January 1900.

My dear Father,
   Things are of course for us just as monotonous as ever, and we are in precisely the same position as we were two months ago, though I regret to say that many of our men have gone over to the great majority, chiefly from Enteric.... The only thing is to be cheerful, always, whatever happens.... After all, we are all right here and have food for a long time yet, though the cavalry have gone to pot (horses I mean) and are useless, there being no hay left at all.... We had a very good Xmas Day under the circumstances.... Dickson and King, A. D. C.'s to Generals White and Hunter, came up to my parapet with a bottle of whiskey to drink the New Year in; we had such a great night, and drank all sorts of toasts ...
   Snakes are getting very bad, and one has to be very careful ... I had two messages from Arthur yesterday, one rather unintelligible, viz., 'C. married on 21st November also P. Copper two days later, best wishes for 1900', and another one which I was so glad of 'All well at home' – I can only suppose he means Podge.

84

1. Captain Percy Scott of HMS *Terrible*.

2. Flag Captain Reginald Prothero of HMS *Doris*.

3. *(Left)* Lionel Halsey. Taken after the Battle of Jutland in 1916, when he was a Commodore in HMS *Iron Duke* and Captain of the Fleet.
4. *(Below left)* Commander A.P. Ethelston of HMS *Powerful*. He was killed at Graspan, 25 November, 1899.
5. *(Below)* Captain the Hon Hedworth Lambton of HMS *Powerful*.

6. Biograph camera filming the Battle of Colenso, 15 December, 1899. A naval
   4.7" can be seen in the background.

7. Naval 12-pounder field guns firing on to Spion Kop from Mount Alice.

8. Boers loading a "Long Tom".

9. Armstrong gun and Boer crew outside Ladysmith.

'I'm not going to write any more as I am down to my last sheet of paper and have to borrow, which is very hard to do nowadays. Our clothes are all worn out, and we are a funny looking crowd altogether.

Best love to Mother and all, and the best of good wishes for 1900 from

Your ever affectionate son,

Lionel Halsey.

It had been ghostly quiet in the kopjes around Ladysmith, but the eeriness of the night was broken about midnight on 5/6 January by the sound of Boer hymn-singing, presumably on account of it being Epiphany. Most of the senior British officers guessed that this was a ruse to cover the fact that most of their tormentors had moved off to the south to counter Buller's build-up of reinforcements. So they ignored it.

General White had issued orders for some of the Naval Brigade guns to be re-located, the Boers having found the ranges to an uncomfortable degree of accuracy. The two 4.7s had been christened 'Lady Anne' and 'Princess Victoria' by the men, and the former, together with two of the 12-pounders, was to be moved to the south-western perimeter at Wagon Point, which was a high promontory on the extreme edge of Wagon Hill.

Moving the big 4.7 naval gun was quite a daunting operation, involving three ox wagons, thirteen bluejackets, twenty-five sappers and an escort of a company of Gordon Highlanders. By a quarter to three in the morning they had hauled two of the wagons to the top of the Point, with all the tools and the wooden gun platform. The other wagon, containing 'Lady Anne', was waiting at the bottom. They were in the process of lowering the platform into the stone-built emplacement when bullets started to pitter-patter on the boulders around them, to the accompaniment of whining ricochets. The sappers' lanterns had provided a perfect target for the Boers, who now switched on a powerful searchlight from among the kopjes. In the confusion that followed some men scrambled down into the stone sangar, a small fortress of rocks built for picket duty, others crouched in the gun emplacement itself, whilst some, being unable to find their rifles, panicked and tried to run away until halted by a Royal Engineers Lieutenant with a drawn revolver.

Their assailants were a hundred Free Staters, who now poured over the ridge. Gunner Sims, later promoted to Lieutenant for his bravery, showed great presence of mind by yelling at his men to steady them, in the same voice that he used at gun-drill on the foc'sle of the *Powerful*, ordering them to number off: One! Two! Three! Four!

The rifles cracked back and forth for two hours through the night. The rock-strewn slope threw off patchy shadows in the unremitting pale-yellow glare from the searchlight. Both sides crouched behind any available boulder, not knowing whether they were firing at friend or foe.

A couple of miles away to the east, at Caesar's Camp, Colonel Ian Hamilton's men were also under attack from a force of Transvaalers. Hamilton had been somewhat lax in not burning off the scrub which covered the approaches to his section of the perimeter, and the Boers, skilled stalkers, had taken full advantage of this cover. No real trench-work had been done and the little stone 'forts' which formed the only line of defence were set back on the inner side of the ridge, which was very soon taken by the attackers. From this position the Boers were able to wreak havoc on the defending picket line, the Manchesters, who fell in large numbers.

Awoken in his headquarters by the recently installed field-telephone connected to each section, General White learned that his complete perimeter was under storm. Knox's 'A' section and Howard's 'B' section at Observation Hill were coping with their attacks, but real danger existed on the southern edge at Wagon Hill and Caesar's Camp. White quickly ordered out reinforcements of Imperial Light Horse and more Gordon Highlanders. As they left town, a wayward Mauser bullet killed the Gordons' commander, Colonel Dick-Cunyngham.

The battle raged on, often hand to hand, and soon it was dawn. More and more troops poured out of Ladysmith, trying to force their way up the slopes of Wagon Hill. But the Boers were now the defenders, having taken the crest, and were able to repel every wave of attack with unerring rifle fire. At one point some Boers were spotted working their way towards the 4.7 gun pit. If 'Lady Anne' were to be damaged beyond repair, the British would have lost a vital tool. Hamilton's men raced to save the gun with seconds to spare, diving over the sandbagged stone parapets headfirst. As they turned to direct their fire onto the enemy, they saw how close it had been, because the ends of their rifle barrels were almost touching the waistcoated chests of their targets as both sides mowed each other down.

At Caesar's Camp, the Boers of the Heidelberg commando had broken through the Manchesters' line. Only a determined bayonet charge by the Gordons, accompanied by Midshipman Carnegie and his G Company, scattered them, and the Scots were able to reoccupy the picket-line rifle pits. Carnegie, weak though he was, fought with commendable bravery, ordering his men to advance with fixed bayonets and getting to close quarters with the attackers, shooting four of them dead himself before being hit in the neck and arm and carried to the rear. Then Major Abdy, with his 53rd Battery, Royal Artillery, galloped out towards Intombi with six field guns, calmly unlimbered and rained shrapnel shells on the eastern slopes of Caesar's Camp which effectively silenced the remainder of the Heidelbergers. But as the sun rose the Boers opened up with 'Long Tom' from the top of Bulwana, straddling Abdy's guns with 94 lb shells.

It is said that Joubert himself was watching the battle from the top of the mountain, and that it was his wife, who often displayed more ruthless determination than her spouse, who ordered the 'Long Tom' to direct its fire on Abdy. Be that as it may, it was not long before the Navy's other 4.7, Halsey's 'Princess Victoria', was brought into action from Cove Redoubt over four miles away, and was able to silence 'Long Tom' with a few of its dwindling supply of lyddite shells.

The day, and the battle, wore on. White heliographed Buller in Chieveley, asking him for a supporting action against the rear of the Boers to relieve the pressure on the defenders of the town, but it seems that little was done. It is not even clear whether Buller ever received the entire message, because, as it was being transmitted, a thundery hailstorm blew up and the signallers in Chieveley watched as the flashes from the mirrors faded into the grey blur. The torrential rain and jagged thumbnail-sized hailstones came down so heavily that visibility was reduced to a few paces and fighting became impossible.

It was now late afternoon and General White could see that it was vital that the Boers should be driven back from the crests of the ridges before dark. He threw all his reserves, three companies of the Devons under Colonel Park, into play. About 5 pm Park gave the order, 'Fix Bayonets', and the Devons set off under a slowly clearing sky to take Wagon Hill.

But the Boers had fallen back behind a fresh line of rocks, and opened fire before Park's men could use their bayonets, killing three of them and wounding several more. The resolute Devons pursued the enemy down the slopes until they were close to the banks of the flooded donga. Here the Boers made a desperate stand, some of them actually being drowned, but the main body managed to hold their ground. And so the fighting continued well after dusk, nearly eighteen hours after it had started, until an armistice was called for collecting the wounded on both sides.

In the morning it was seen what terrible carnage had been wrought. Abdy's shrapnel had mutilated some of the Boer corpses on the slopes of Caesar's Camp so badly that they had to be buried in the spot. On top of the hill were fifty-two dead Boers.

The exact number of Boer losses is uncertain, but some estimates put it as high as 700. On the British side there were seventeen officers and 158 men killed, and 221 wounded. Among the severely wounded was 172753 Able Seaman Albert Ward, HMS *Powerful*.

Five VCs were won that day, by Lieutenant Masterson of the Devons, Privates Pitts and Scott of the Manchesters and posthumously by Lieutenant Digby Jones of the Royal Engineers and Trooper Albrecht of the Imperial Light Horse.

The luckless General White now took to his bed, smitten with the dreaded fever.

CHAPTER 12

SLAUGHTER AT SPION KOP

The chartered steamers had continued landing their seasick khaki-clad cargoes at Cape Town and Durban all through December, to be squeezed into the trains waiting at the quayside and then rolled up the line to Methuen at Modder River, and on the Natal front to Chieveley, where Lieutenant-General Sir Charles Warren was assembling his 5th Division.

Buller had now had three weeks since the débâcle of Colenso in which to cogitate and brood. True, he had spent a far from happy Christmas. True, he had been fired and his successor was about to arrive from England to supersede him. But he was to retain command in Natal and his build-up of reinforcements had been proceeding well, notwithstanding that he did not enjoy a very cordial relationship with Warren. Much of his self-confidence had returned, creating a more positive frame of mind. He resolved that another attempt to break through to Ladysmith was now feasible. It was clear that a push straight through Colenso was no longer an option, so he decided to revert to his original plan, discarded disastrously at the last minute, of swinging to the west and crossing the Tugela at Potgieter's Drift. Rather than leave his lines of supply exposed, he chose to move his base across to Springfield, a sixteen-mile trek away.

By 10 January, 1900, all was set to move. Twenty-five thousand men and 650 wagons streamed out of Chieveley like a giant khaki python creeping over the veldt, so long that its head was almost at its destination before its tail had left the point of departure.

The *Manchester Guardian* correspondent, Churchill's friend Atkins, gave a wonderful description of the scene:

> It seemed endless, this rope made of all the strands that hold an army together – infantry, guns, gunners, ammunition, horsemen, wagons with forage, rations and tents, wagons hung all over like a gypsy van with chattering utensils, kaffirs plying whips like fishing-rods, bakers, cooks,

farriers, telegraphists, typewriters, paymasters and paymasters' clerks, telegraph wires and poles, sappers, chaplains, doctors, ambulance wagons, bearers, 'body-snatchers', signallers with flags and heliographs, sailors and naval guns, headquarters staff, cobblers, balloons, aeronauts, limelight flashlights, traction engines with heavy lists to port or starboard, pontoons, etc, etc.

A hundred years before, Napoleon had commented that no army carried as much baggage and impedimentia on the march as the British, and it was no less true here. Even without the drawbacks presented by the awful weather conditions, Buller's army would have still been like a gigantic lumbering khaki caterpillar, crawling its way over the bumps and ridges of a cabbage-leaf. And faced with such light travellers as the ever-watching Boers, its very slowness gave the enemy every opportunity to anticipate the likely point at which the next 'play' would need to be made, ample time in which to throw up well-dug trenchworks and to plan their defence tactics accordingly. Any elements of surprise that were available to be exploited, therefore, were usually at the disposal of the Boers, and denied to the British.

Before leaving Chieveley the army carpenters had constructed some dummy wooden guns to leave behind on Gun Hill to conceal the sailors' departure, but the Boers heliographed Buller, 'Ha! Ha! Ha!, you will not fool us so easily!'

The unrelenting rain and thousands of feet, hooves and wheels had turned the kopje-dotted landscape into a muddy nightmare, the champion churners being the heavy guns and wagons of the Royal Artillery and the still heavier ones of the Royal Navy. They struggled and squelched their way through the clinging, sucking mire, often with the wagons sunk axle-deep. And still the rain came down. Several horses and mules died trying to haul sunken wagons and guns from the quagmire, having strayed from the road, such as it was. On countless occasions the oxen simply stood stock still with their sides heaving, unable to go any further without rest, up to their bellies in the mud, so that they appeared to have no legs and the wagons looked like sledges.

Buller had imported a couple of steam traction engines as an innovation for transporting heavy equipment in such terrain, but their very weight became a disadvantage in such dreadful conditions and they floundered helplessly on roads that had become little more than canals of mud.

George Crowe, Master-at-Arms of the *Terrible* wrote, 'One good old navy drag-rope and a hundred horny-handed sailors would – and often did – take a heavy ammunition wagon or a 4.7 inch gun where no traction engine under full steam with an open throttle-valve or a prize team of oxen could approach within a respectable distance. Besides, men can be easily controlled, but engines and oxen – both extremely useful in their proper spheres – either stop dead when they should be moving, or bolt away when they are required to stop, and both consume a quantity of water that would suffice for a hundred thirsty tars. Moral: – drag-ropes, and good long ones.'

Four of the Naval Brigade's 12-pounders were left behind at Chieveley, under Lieutenant Burne, together with the railtruck-mounted 4.7, while the remainder moved up to Potgieter's Drift with the main army. On the march up from Chieveley the Navy was more fortunate than most of the soldiers, in that they had wagons under which to try to snatch some sleep, sheltered from the worst of the downpour. They halted about 7 pm at Pretorius Drift, ate a makeshift supper and crawled under their wagons.

All night long Warren's Fifth Division tramped and slithered past the stationary wagons, with the jingling harness, rumbling wheels, curses of the drivers and whinnying of the horses all combining to make any proper sleep impossible for the sailors, and in the morning they faced the difficult prospect of crossing Pretorius Drift, which was in full flood after the heavy rain.

The track through the Drift was just a narrow cutting through its steep banks, only four paces or so wide and full of stinking black mud. The wheels and oxen hooves sank in deep, and on the way through the water the wagons tilted at alarming angles, threatening to capsize. It was hard work indeed, taking fifty oxen and 200 sailors, marines and soldiers to pull each gun up the steep northern bank. They toiled all morning getting across, and, once safely over, paused for a well-earned dinner of bully beef and biscuits.

They marched on all the rest of the day to Springfield, during which it never stopped raining, and bivouacked there. Next day they crossed the Little Tugela by the bridge, which the Boers had failed to destroy and for which they were very grateful. Then over the narrow Lindeque Spruit without mishap, arriving at Potgieter's Drift on 11 January.

Burne arrived from Chieveley with his four 12-pounders to join up with the main Naval Brigade on the evening of 16 January. Having been ordered to do so with all haste, he and his men were dead beat as they stood in their black greatcoats, plastered with mud and still dripping with rain, clutching steaming mugs of Maconochie's soup before crawling under the wagons to sleep.

General Buller ordered Captain Jones to position his guns on Spearman's Hill, which was a big kopje with a dome like St Paul's, towering over the Tugela by the Drift. The two 4.7s were set up on Mount Alice, a pimple on the hump of Spearman's Hill, one thousand feet above the Tugela, with the 12-pounders on the lower slopes, about a mile nearer the Boers' lines.

The top of Mount Alice is clearly visible from Ladysmith and direct heliograph communication was now possible. It was a pleasant spot, with plenty of lush grass for the animals, bracingly clear air and lovely trees of mimosa and cactus giving shade for the off-duty watches. The slopes led down to another drift, across which was the road to Ladysmith, which could be seen winding its way around the kopjes into the distance. Behind these stood the central feature

90

of what has been described as the most beautiful panorama in all South Africa, the ominous hump of Lookout Hill, or, as the Boers called it, Spion Kop.

Spion Kop, a craggy, steep-sided natural fortress, commanding the centre of a double row of kopjes which formed the Boers' defensive line, also served as a watchtower which provided them with the means to anticipate every move of the slow-moving British forces. It loomed over the wagon-road to the north that Buller must use if he were to make any progress towards Ladysmith.

Through the big navy telescope the Boers could be seen engaged in the preparation of entrenchments and gun emplacements covering every weak point at which Buller's infantry might try to get close. Large numbers of reinforcements were also plainly seen in the laagers further to the rear.

If Buller's attempt to relieve Ladysmith by this route was to succeed, Spion Kop would have to be taken, which was not going to be easy. In the event it was to result in what must be one of the bloodiest battles in all history, when measured in terms of lives lost per square yard of battlefield.

The general battle plan was for the British artillery to pepper the Boers defence works and pin them down under such heavy fire as to allow General Sir Charles Warren's infantry to sweep round behind the western flank of the enemy and destroy their positions.

The Boers had continued frantically to dig trenches and throw up earthworks at Brakfontein and high on Spion Kop for about a week. The Navy guns and Lyttelton's 5-inch howitzers had been bombarding them with regularity in an attempt to soften up their resistance, but had received hardly a reply. It was a familiar pattern.

Around 9 am on 17 January Warren started to move his troops into position. All day long they rattled across the pontoon bridge over the Tugela, coming under long-range rifle fire from the trenches in front of the distant kopjes. On the opposite flank Lyttelton's guns began an intense bombardment of Brakfontein and some infantry were pushed forward to divert attention from Warren's advance, but the Boers were not to be fooled, or drawn. Sitting tight in their trenches, they replied with a few 'sporting' shots from their Mausers. The British feint to the right had not produced the desired effect.

For reasons that are not entirely clear, other than that he considered his originally planned route to outflank the Boers via Acton Homes to be too long, Warren now revised his thinking. He decided to take a much more direct path, heading for Fairview and Rosalie. This involved a head-on confrontation with the Boers and was a much more difficult trip in terms of the terrain to be traversed. By the 20th Warren had made little progress along his new route and his ponderous pace was causing acute frustration to the watching Buller, who, taking the view that the nettle had to be grasped if the situation was not to degenerate into a stalemate caused by Warren's dithering, ordered the naval guns to be brought across the Tugela on the 21st.

Now on the north bank, they moved forward to a range of about 4,200 yards from Boer trenches and Ogilvy deployed them in a convex curve, with James's *Tartar* guns on the extreme right and Burne's in the centre. To their front was Lyttelton's Brigade, with its Royal Artillery field guns and howitzers mounted on a cluster of small kopjes.

George Crowe said that from this angle Spion Kop reminded him of the Rock of Gibraltar, both in shape and size, which provides a good picture in the mind of the magnitude of the task that faced any attacking forces. From here the 4.7s could fire clean over the summit of Spion Kop at the Boers' lines in the rear, but firing at invisible targets means that the fall of shot cannot be reported to the gunner without the luxury of forward spotters, therefore much ammunition is wasted; so the futile practice was discontinued. Nevertheless, shortly after midday, hearing reports that a large body of horsemen was approaching from the direction of Ladysmith escorting many covered wagons, the contents of which were unknown, Lieutenant England of the *Terrible* tried a speculative shot with a 4.7 lyddite shell at a range in the order of 18,000 yards. A few minutes later several riderless horses were seen trotting between the kopjes, and, according to scouts, the wagons appeared to have dispersed, so it can be safely assumed that England had scored a lucky hit.

Warren now seems to have become temporarily revitalized. He persuaded Buller, against his superior's better judgement it must be said, that the best method to secure the Kop would be by means of a night attack by infantry. Accordingly, at dusk on the 23rd half of the Lancashire Brigade under General Woodgate, plus 200 of Thorneycroft's Mounted Infantry and a few Royal Engineers set off towards the south-western spur of the mountain. There were about 1,600 in the column, plus mules to carry water bags, spare ammunition and stretchers. In the stretchers they carried about twenty shovels and twenty mattocks to dig the trenches which would enable them to hold their ground while they awaited reinforcements – twenty picks and twenty mattocks to dig trenches for 1,600 soldiers!

With Lieutenant-Colonel Alec Thorneycroft, a twenty-stone lion-hearted giant, in the van, they started to climb cautiously upwards around the huge boulders on the lower slopes. No talking and no smoking was the order. Nearing the top, they were surprised by the sudden appearance of a big cream-coloured spaniel, an incongruous apparition, which trotted out of the gloom towards Thorneycroft, wagging its tail and jumping up at him with a friendly greeting. Only one excited bark would be enough to reveal their presence and ruin the entire expedition. It could also cost many British lives. 'For God's sake, we'll have to kill it,' somebody whispered, and a rifle pullthrough was produced with which to garotte it. But the killing of it may have produced a yelp or a gurgle, and in the end the British love of animals prevailed. The pullthrough was converted into a lead and the spaniel was led down the hill by a boy bugler, still wagging its tail, happy to go with its new master and oblivious to the close call it had had with death.

By 4 am Thorneycroft's men were almost at the crest. There was a thick mist and it was a dark night. So far they had not been seen. But in the murk the advance party stumbled on a startled Boer picket, which loosed off a fusillade of bullets. As the rifle flashes flickered, barely visible through the fog, they threw themselves down, holding their breaths while they waited for the telltale rattle which told them that the Boers were reloading their Mausers, at which point they made a concerted bayonet charge, accompanied by much cheering, yelling and screaming, which drove the defenders from the plateau. It seemed to have been all too easy.

The Royal Enginers then got to work, digging a three-hundred-yard trench on what appeared to be the forward brink of the plateau. It was hard work, because there was only a thin crust of soil above the solid rock of Kop, and they only had a little more time before dawn would burn off the fog which was now their protector.

An imperative factor in the success of the operation was for heavy guns to be brought up to the summit with all haste, so as to command the range of kopjes and protect the general advance. Woodgate set the Engineers to cutting a track up the hill. But the Artillery commanders were dubious about the ability of their 15-pounder mountain guns to make such a precipitous climb. There was only one thing for it, Woodgate decided. He would have to call in the Navy. The bluejackets had already demonstrated that they were willing and able to go anywhere at any time. He sent a message down to Warren and Buller to say that he was securely entrenched but needed naval guns urgently.

At about 7 am, when the fog lifted enough for the top of Spion Kop to be visible through his telescope, Buller was able to assess the true picture. It was not pleasant. The battle had not been won at all. In fact, it was only just about to start.

The Boer picket that had been put to flight by Thorneycroft's bayonets had reported to Botha's headquarters, about a mile to the rear. Comfortably settled down for the night in their lonely eyrie, with their boots off, they had been taken completely by surprise. Stumbling in terror down the grassy slope at the rear of the Kop, away from the steel of the British bayonets, they had fled as fast as they could. Botha listened stoically to the news that the British were at the top of Spion Kop, and announced, quite simply, that they would have to take it back. His own heavy guns could be trained on the plateau held by the British. In fact, they could be brought to bear from two emplacements on the low hills of Tabanyama, at a bare 4,000 yard range, and trap the invaders in a deadly crossfire. Closer still, on Spion Kop itself, there were several excellent positions from which riflemen could fire, point blank, at the British. The vital factor, from Botha's viewpoint, was speed. He had to act before Buller could consolidate a force with heavy guns on the summit.

He called up all the reinforcements that could be spared from those holding Warren in check, about a thousand men in all. Coffee cups were thrown down, hats jammed on heads, feet thrust into unlaced boots, ammunition stuffed into bandoliers, horses rapidly mounted and off they galloped towards Spion Kop, some arriving in less than a quarter of an hour after Botha had issued his orders, and began to scramble up the grassy slopes.

The British had made a fearful mistake. What had seemed, in the thick fog, to be the forward edge of the plateau was in fact nothing more than a sharp dip between two peaks. It was here that they had sweated and toiled to dig a mere scratch in the rocky ground. It could not be described as a trench. It was not even deep enough to protect a prostrate man satisfactorily from rifle fire. And it was in a vulnerable, rather than a commanding, position, because the Boers were able to enfilade it from a prominence known as Aloe Knoll.

As the first of the burghers neared the crest of the slope, a line of helmeted heads popped up from behind the rocks and a blaze of Lee-Metford bullets rained down on them, killing many. But the helmets were only those of the British forward picket, guarding the frenziedly digging sappers trying to construct a new trench, and soon, as more and more Boers arrived, they were able to drive the British back. More British troops, waiting behind the crest in the rear, were ordered forward and the battle ebbed and flowed as the morning wore on.

Boer riflemen had taken up positions directly overlooking the plateau on which the British were trapped, and their 'Long Toms' and deadly Maxim-Nordenfelts had opened up from the distant kopjes. Bullets from the Mausers and Lee-Metfords swept back and forth across those three acres of butchery like showers of sleet. Warren's batteries and the Naval Brigade's 4.7s and 12-pounders joined in, all plastering the battleground with shots that produced great cartwheeling shards of splintered rock. Murderous fountains of shrapnel flew in every direction.

The carnage was awful to behold. It was a scene from hell. Headless bodies and bits of limb, clad in tattered shreds of uniform, littered the ground all around and filled the trenches in piles, some providing a merciful barriacade in death to shelter those who still lived to fight.

The intrepid Atkins wrote to the *Manchester Guardian* of:

That acre of massacre, that complete shambles, at the top of a rich green gully with cool granite walls (a way fit to lead to heaven) which reached up the western flank of the mountain. To me it seemed that our men were all in a small square patch; there were brown men and browner trenches, the whole like an over-ripe barley-field . . . I saw three shells strike a certain trench within a minute; each time struck it full in the face, and the brown dust rose and drifted away with the white smoke. The trench was toothed against the sky like a saw – made, I supposed, of sharp rocks built into a rampart. Another shell struck it, and then – heavens! – the trench rose up and moved forward. The trench was men, the teeth against the sky were men. They ran forward bending their bodies into a curve – they looked like a cornfield with a heavy wind sweeping over it from behind.

About 8.30 am Signalman Large of the *Terrible*, on attachment to the army signallers, received from General Woodgate, half by heliograph, until a shell smashed the apparatus, and the remainder by flags, 'Am exposed to terrible crossfire, especially near first field dressing-station; can barely hold my own; water badly needed. Help us. Woodgate.'

Woodgate was, in fact, already mortally wounded by a shell splinter which struck him above the right eye, and within a few minutes the flags waved again and Large received, 'Reinforce at once or all is lost. General dead.'

By late morning the British situation had become critical. On Woodgate's death, the command fell to Colonel Crofton.

Warren's next actions were to infuriate the already impatient Buller. There were 10,000 troops at his disposal on the left bank with which he could have aided Crofton. Instead he heliographed Lyttelton to send up two battalions and some mounted infantry. Buller had intended to use these men in a thrust to the right, thus turning the British advance into a two-pronged attack. But now Warren had wrecked the plan.

As for Crofton, he seems to have vanished from the scene as soon as he had tramsitted his plea for support. Some reports suggest that he had 'lost his head'. Buller wired to Warren at 11.40, 'Unless you put some good hard fighting man in command on the top you will lose the hill. I suggest Thorneycroft.'

Warren agreed, and ten minutes later the heliographists on the summit received the order that Thorneycroft had superseded Crofton in command. The runner who bore the message to Thorneycroft fell dead across the big man's body with a bullet in his head and it was only later that another officer shouted to him above the din to tell him that he was a General.

Soon afterwards a pocket of Lancashire Fusiliers became cornered, and somebody waved a handkerchief in surrender. Thorneycroft had an angry, red-faced appearance even when he was calm. Now his complexion grew puce with fury. Hobbling forward on his stick, despite an injured ankle, he shouted that he was in command now, that he did not allow surrenders and that the Boers should go to hell.

More and more men were thrown into the deafening maelstrom as the afternoon wore on. The Dorsets, the Imperial Light Infantry, the King's Royal

Rifles and the Scottish Rifles all tramped up the hill to join the battle, covered by Ogilvy's 12-pounders, who fired over the heads of the leading line. A Boer sniper's nest, spied through a telescope, was hit spot-on by the 4.7 of Lieutenant Hunt of HMS *Forte* just as a company of British infantry was about to climb straight into its trap.

Apart from these incidents, all the long-range naval guns were, in truth, wasted at Spion Kop. They were kept parked in the vicinity of Potgieter's and thus unable to render any real assistance other than conduct an ineffective bombardment of the summit of the Kop. Lieutenant Burne of the *Philomel* expressed in his diary the frustration he felt at his lack of involvement, writing that it was 'a surprise and a blow to learn that his guns were taken to the rear' and being 'dragged up Criticism Kop by eighty Durhams, who were now his escorts'.

As the sun went down the thunder of the shelling died away, to be replaced by the ghastly moans, screams and delirious cursing of the wounded as they cried for help and water. But still the battle raged on, with spits of rifle fire penetrating the eerie blackness.

The twelve hours of nerve-shattering violence had taken its toll on both sides, not only in terms of blood, but in the sheer ability to take much more of it without cracking up completely. The Boers, composed almost entirely of irregulars, were dependent on the willingness of their men to fight to a greater extent than the British. At any hint of a setback or even a barn-door stalemate, they were prone to simply drift away from the battlefield with a metaphoric shrug of the shoulders and reappear to fight again the next day somewhere else. Now, suddenly disheartened after the gruelling day's fighting which had seemingly been fruitless, they gradually melted away into the twilight. Soon, only a handful of Boers were left at the summit of the Kop.

Botha was appalled when news reached him in the middle of the night. He tried to exhort the remaining burghers to stay, but his pleas fell on deaf ears. Then his messenger returned from General Schalk Burger's main camp, whence he had been despatched with an appeal to stand firm, to tell him that he had found nobody there. All the men, horses, tents and heavy guns had vanished. The Boers had fallen back towards Ladysmith.

Master-at-Arms George Crowe later poured scorn on the British commanders. As he wrote: 'Several assertions have been made that guns could not possibly have reached the summit unless a track was previously prepared for them. But to those who still adhere to that opinion, the writer respectfully points out that when naval field guns *cannot be wheeled* to where they may be required, they are either parbuckled, dragged, hoisted, or even carried there. Where men can walk, a field gun can be made to follow by one or other of the common methods just mentioned.'

In the end Warren did dispatch a party of 1400 sappers, under Lieutenant-

Colonel Sim, to dig emplacement pits, twenty-three feet wide, for two 4.7s, plus smaller ones for some mountain guns, and to prepare some better trenchworks for the infantry. And Lieutenant James of HMS *Tartar* set off into the blackness of the night with his 12-pounders and a mountain battery of Royal Artillery to haul their guns up the narrow twisting path, pausing every couple of minutes both for breath and to allow stretcher-bearers to pass on the way down or water-carriers to pass on the way up.

But Thorneycroft had had enough. Twelve solid hours of fighting was more than he could take. Like the Boers, he had decided that it was better to retire to fight another day. 'Better six good battalions safely down the hill,' he mumbled, 'than a bloody mop-up in the morning.' He started to lead the remnants of his men down the hill, and near the bottom met Sim and his sappers on their way up. Sim handed him a note from Warren imploring him to hold the Kop at all costs, but it was too late. Thorneycroft and his men were dead-beat and continued on their way down. Farther down still, they met the sweating sailors with their 12-pounders, who learned that the summit had been evacuated. Everyone was sick at heart as James withdrew his guns and they tramped back to Potgieter's.

The crowning irony of the Battle of Spion Kop was that both sides wrongly assumed that they had lost it and retired. The difference was that the Boers came back. Soon after dawn next morning, as Buller's ox-drawn wagons, thirty-five heavy guns, mules and ambulances rumbled back across the pontoon over the Tugela at Trichardt's Drift, Botha was on the summit of the Kop, gazing down at them. Behind him, burial parties from both sides were carrying out their grisly work. On the British side, they were trying to deepen that suicidally shallow trench enough for it to serve as a mass grave.

The Boers lost 335 in the fighting, and the British 243, plus over a thousand wounded. All this had taken place on an area about the size of a football pitch. The 2nd Lancashire Fusiliers had suffered the most. They had gone into action 800 strong, but only 553 of them answered the roll call next day.

And it had all happened at a spot which, on another day, was described as 'an earthly paradise; a country of arable soil and splendid pasture, where brown-clad doves emit plaintive love songs, of twittering tom-tits and green-plumaged sunbirds, of huge grey-coated secretary birds and gaudy butterflies that would gladden the heart of the entomologist.'

As for Buller, the black mood of bitter despair that had taken him after Colenso did not reappear after Spion Kop. He addressed his exhausted army, thanking them with all his heart for their bravery and sacrifices, adding that he was convinced that they had shown him the way to Ladysmith. Now, more than ever, he was confident that he possessed the key to the door.

CHAPTER 13

GRANT'S GUNS GO ASHORE

As Buller's frustrated and downcast army was arriving at Potgieter's Drift, the *Dunottar Castle* was tying up at Cape Town, a day early in fact, to land Roberts and Kitchener. Roberts had never been of the opinion that it was Ladysmith which represented the key to the winning of the war. Indeed, he had made his views on the subject well known at home before even being appointed as Commander-in-Chief. Little Bobs was a confirmed Western Route to Pretoria man.

Many at home agreed with this line of thought. Although Ladysmith had become the focus of world attention, and Cove Redoubt, Bulwana and Junction Hill all, by now, household names, it was argued that the supposed paramount importance attaching to its relief was false, emanating purely from the heart, and had no basis when addressed by cool military thinking.

'Bobs' and K, now ashore in Cape Town after their lengthy cruise, set about organizing the big build-up for the push towards Kimberley and Bloemfontein. One of the first items on the agenda was the ordering of two more 4.7 guns. News of this sent a ripple of excitement around the ships anchored there.

There had never been any shortage of volunteers to join the various Naval Brigades ashore. Indeed, being guardships on station for the past two months had resulted in considerable boredom for many of the crews. As a method of letting off steam they had taken to making frequent 'practice runs' with gun-carriages and all their paraphernalia, sweating up Red Hill to the cheers of the local people. When the news of the two new guns became known, therefore, and the consequent need for more bluejackets to go ashore with them, there was a general clamour to be included.

In the end Commander W. L. Grant of HMS *Doris* was appointed to lead the new detachment, with Midshipmen G. H. Lang and J. Menzies, also of the *Doris*, Lieutenant J. A. Fergusson of the little HMS *Barossa*, and Surgeon T. T. Jeans and the appropriately named Gunner J. Cannon, both of HMS

Monarch. They were to take fifty-nine ratings and marines, mainly from *Doris* and *Barossa*.

The choice of devoting his immediate attention to Methuen's area of operation was not only in keeping with Roberts' conviction that the War was to be won on the western front, but also one of extreme tact in leaving Buller to run things in Natal with the minimum of interference from the new Commander-in-Chief. Clearly, any dealings between Roberts and Buller would require delicate handling if the main task in hand, i.e., defeating the Boers, were not to suffer.

At Modder River, however, Methuen's forces had seen little action since the disastrous massacre at Magersfontein over a month previously, apart from routine reconnaissances and Bearcroft's naval guns periodically reminding the Boers of their presence by lobbing a couple of shells on to their lines, to which the other side would reply with a blaze of Maxim fire.

CHAPTER 14

STALEMATE AT VAAL KRANTZ

South of the Tugela Buller rested his army for over a week after Spion Kop. The Boers, for their part, retired behind the kopjes. Not a shot was fired as both sides, demoralized after the savage butchery they had inflicted on each other, quietly licked their wounds.

Experience told Buller that the full fighting will of his army would take a while to return. Therefore he was content to pause, but it was no comfort to reflect that the eyes of the Empire, indeed the whole wide world, were gazing upon them. Every man in Buller's army knew that, right down to the youngest drummer boy. The khaki bull had now charged the gate twice and the gate had not broken.

However, this was no time for him to sit idly in his tent. There was much thinking to be done, the upshot of which was his conclusion that Vaal Krantz must be taken in his next major move. Vaal Krantz was a series of ridges between Spion Kop to the west and Doorn Kloof to the east. The successful capture of Vaal Krantz, followed by a flanking attack on Brakfontein, would pull the Boers away from their strongly held positions around Spion Kop, and stretch their defensive line, hopefully enough to enable Buller to make a breakthrough to Ladysmith.

All day on Sunday, 4 February, and well into the night, it was clear to the sharp-eyed Boers that something big was afoot as long lines of wagons, guns, troops and animals formed up to plod and rumble their way in various directions towards newly allocated positions.

The Number One 4.7, under Lieutenant England, was to be placed on Signal Hill, and Number Two, commanded by Lieutenant Hunt was to remain on Mount Alice. This would give them lines of fire enabling them to sweep the entire left flank of the operation. Lieutenant Burne's 12-pounders, plus the two 5-inch guns, were to be emplaced on the lower slopes of Zwaart Kop, with Ogilvy and James on the absolute summit behind them.

In a clever ploy, Lieutenant Ogilvy's battery, together with Lieutenant James's *Tartar* guns and the Mountain Battery plus two guns of the Royal Field Artillery, had set out on the previous Friday evening, under cover of darkness, to make their way secretively to the top of Zwaart Kop, which would give them a strong commanding position. Such a move was, perhaps, evidence that the British were at last realizing that in order to defeat the Boers they would need to display more guile.

So many of the manoeuvres of the Naval Brigade had taken place accompanied by a violent thunderstorm that it almost seemed to be an automatic feature. This was to be no exception. As they set off down Mount Alice, at about 9 pm, with their new escort of about 100 Scots Fusiliers, the heavens erupted, the rain streamed down, and very soon the now familiar mudbath was created. They skidded and slithered their way, often sideways, down the steep track to Potgieter's, then turned eastwards. By midnight they had reached the neck, or col, connecting Signal Hill to Zwaart Kop.

If daybreak came before they were all over the ridge, they would be in full sight of the Boer lookouts and the whole enterprise would be ruined. The plan was to rest behind the ridge, safely hidden, during the following day, and then strike out again for the summit when darkness fell again. It was a race against the sun.

Each of the guns and the ten wagons was hauled separately over the neck, using a treble team of forty-eight oxen and every available man on the drag-ropes. Twice No. 4 gun tumbled over sideways on the rough terrain, but, at a cost of much sweat and quiet cursing, all had disappeared from view by dawn.

The following night, although somewhat refreshed by a day of inactivity, they faced a stern task – Zwaart Kop itself. Indeed, it had been argued in several quarters that it would be an impossibility to take heavy naval guns up there at all. There were no roads or tracks up the steep brown cragginess of Zwaart Kop, although the Royal Engineers had blasted away some of the worst rocky obstructions, so that a rough path, if it could be called that, could be traced.

The ascent fell into three phases. First, there was a rough scree-covered slope of about 20 degrees angle of ascent, which was cleared by the same means as on the previous night, with forty-eight oxen and the men on drag-ropes. Then came a steeper prominence, or shoulder, which required the added assistance of the Scots Fusilier escort on the drag-ropes, while the sailors pushed and manhandled the spokes of the wheels. Finally came the worst section. The last 100 yards were strewn with huge jutting boulders, and here the angle of ascent was in the order of 45 degrees, on which it is nigh impossible to stand, let alone do heavy work.

Having carried out a thorough reconnaissance, in anticipation of the problem, Ogilvy had requisitioned a long wire hawser from the Balloon Section. This was centred and the bight fastened round the trail of the gun. Then the ends of the hawser were passed through leading blocks which were hitched on two stout and convenient trees at the top of the rise, and long hemp drag-ropes bent on to them. Then the heaving began, each rope being manned by fifty men, and the guns warped up the precipice. The soldiers, unaccustomed to much hauling on ropes, unlike the sailors, suffered severely from bleeding and blistered hands. After a couple of 'stand-easies' to catch their breath, and despite a couple of capsizings, all was safely on the top of Zwaart Kop before the morning mist had cleared.

The plateau of Zwaart Kop was an open meadow, save along the northern edge which was thickly lined with trees, thus providing ideal camouflage cover. Those trees obstructing lines of fire were sawn nearly through and then steadied by guy-ropes, so that they could be pulled down quickly as soon as the guns were required to come into action.

At 7 am on Monday, 5 February, the Royal Artillery Batteries and Naval 4.7s on Mount Alice and Signal Hill opened up in a feigned attack on Brakfontein on the British forward left, while to the right, waiting under Zwaart Kop ready to mount the real attack on Vaal Krantz, were Hart's, Hildyard's and Lyttelton's Brigades, under General Clery, plus the 1st Cavalry Brigade and a battery of Royal Horse Artillery.

Then, covered by a heavy bombardment, with the thunder of the guns echoing up the valley, the infantry closed to within a mile of the Boer trenches. Here the Boers made their first reply by way of concealed pom-pom and heavy Mauser rifle fire, and their 'Long Toms', firing from the slopes to the north of Spion Kop, quickly found the range, splashing 94 lb shells on to the British lines and batteries with extreme accuracy.

Throughout the morning the artillery duel raged. The British howitzers now came into action, hurling 50 lb lyddite shells at the Boer trenches, causing tremendous carnage with their powerful explosions.

The British infantry had been firmly pinned down, but Ogilvy's guns had managed to cover the Royal Engineers as they threw a pontoon across the Tugela, just east of Zwaart Kop, and Lyttelton's Brigade were able to cross over by midday.

But as they moved forward across the open ground, three guns, which had been raking Ogilvy's battery on the summit of Zwaart Kop from a concealed position on Doorn Kloof, switched their attention to the British foot soldiers. Fortunately, few casualties were incurred and many of the Boer shells failed to explode on impact with the soft ground. Lieutenant England's 4.7 and Ogilvy's 12-pounder battery, from 10,000 and 6,000 yards respectively, gave a fierce retort to these guns in an effort to silence them, whilst Hunt's 4.7 and the Royal Artillery guns divided their firing between Spion Kop, Brakfontein and the Vaal Krantz ridges.

In the afternoon Lyttelton's men made a fearsome bayonet charge on the

Boers' positions and took the first low ridges of Krantz Kop. For this they were rewarded with the combined fury of the whole of the Boer artillery. There was little cover, but they were lucky that the light was failing and they spent the first hours of darkness in throwing up earthworks and generally securing the ground which they had won.

Failing light can have a reward for gunners, albeit for only a short time before nightfall and just after dawn. The bright light of a South African summer's day on the veldt can present a problem with mirage. This tends to disappear in late afternoon and early mornings, and the 4.7 Lieutenants took every advantage of this. Every telescope was trained on the Spion Kop crests and intense eyes endeavoured to spot the semi-concealed Boer guns there. The range was known and the barrage begun. Firing ceased from the Boers' guns and a prisoner later confirmed that the 4.7s had inflicted serious damage on them.

Lieutenant Burne, with no less a personage than Sir Charles Warren camped right alongside his 12-pounders, had been shelling the left flank incessantly all day. When nightfall came and the firing ceased, he found just sufficient energy to record that he had expended no less than 250 rounds during the action before crawling to his bivouac to sleep.

During the night the Boers played the same trick as the British had done by secretly moving a 'Long Tom' to the top of Doorn Kloof and stationing numerous machine-gun posts and pom-poms among the kopjes. In the morning Lyttelton's force, marooned on the ridge that they had captured, and with no support forthcoming, found themselves facing a blaze of fire from across a wide arc and could do nothing much except to keep their heads well and truly down.

At about 7 am England's 4.7 dropped a shell plumb on the magazine of one of the 'Long Toms', which created a terrific explosion and a huge column of smoke. The big gun was silenced for a very long time, but the British infantry continued to be pinned down and harassed by the fire from the invisible smaller guns, which had started to use shrapnel shells.

About 8 am Buller asked Lieutenant Burne personally whether he could silence two Boer guns who were proving to be a particular nuisance, namely a 'Long Tom' and a 3-inch, at 6,500 and 10,000 yards range respectively. Burne found the smaller gun to be just out of range of his 12-pounders, but said that he could reach the big Creusot. All the other naval guns joined in a concentrated bombardment on the offending 'Long Tom', which had the effect of putting it out of action until 5 pm when a large puff of black smoke signalled its reappearance on the scene.

During the late forenoon the Boers ran up some field guns and pom-poms into some dongas and prepared pits about 4,000 to 6,000 yards in front of Burne's guns. He managed to find the range quickly, with such effect that they retired, which earned him the congratulations of the Commander-in-Chief.

Apart from these few successes, however, the naval guns spent a baffling day trying to locate and destroy those of their well-hidden enemy, who, firing from a distant ridge or crest, would retire behind it after every few shots and so be immune from any effective reply. It has to be said that the sailors did not obtain much satisfaction. Indeed, the Boers seemed to dominate the scene with their artillery, switching their concentrated attacks from the captured ridge to the field batteries and then to the naval guns, even taking an occasional shot at Buller's command post in the rear, as and when they pleased.

After the war Ogilvy presented a paper which, among many other matters, described the difficulties encountered in dealing with concealed enemy guns firing smokeless powder, such as he experienced at Vaal Krantz. The Boers were so cunningly clever at this particular type of warfare that it required a 'Sherlock Holmes' approach to discover their guns' positions. On one occasion, Ogilvy recalled, General Buller was concerned about a high-velocity Boer gun which was causing serious problems to his infantry. He was told that the gun he referred to was behind a certain hill, and, though able to enfilade the attacking infantry at around 6,000 yards range, was perfectly protected from our artillery fire.

'How do you know the gun is there if you cannot see it?' the General asked.

'Look through the glass. Do you see those six trees across the neck?'

'Yes.'

'Well, there were seven there last night, and if you look very carefully you will see that every effort to obliterate the evidence of the removal of the seventh has been made, such as removing all branches, putting earth on the fresh-cut stump, etc. Further, if you watch very carefully you will notice a slight haze every now and then, and always, about sixteen seconds afterwards, there will be a shrapnel bursting amongst the troops you refer to.'

On another occasion a beautifully concealed gun position was discovered by the track through the dew-covered grass in the early morning, made by the gun's crew going down for water.

Many methods were tried to conceal guns, but their positions were usually given away by the dust thrown up by the rush of gas from the muzzles when fired, hence the mention of the need to watch for the 'slight haze'. Sometimes Ogilvy tried wetting the ground in front of his own guns so as to reduce the amount of dust thrown up, but scarcity of water often precluded this. Wherever possible, he placed his guns on a reverse slope, out of sight of the target, and directed the firing with a telescope, No. 1 on the gun laying on a visible object and working his deflection scale and sight as ordered by the observer, who noted the fall of shots, the details being entered in a book by the midshipman of the gun when the range was found. Thus: 'Pom-pom by Bloy's Farm – Aim at top of right tree on Two Tree Hill – 1,000 yards, 10 knots right deflection.'

Burne's crews had several narrow escapes on the forward slopes of Zwaart Kop, one in particular being memorable, when a 6″ shell landed a few yards to their front, gouging a great groove in the ground before bouncing over their heads without exploding, showering everybody with clods of earth and clumps of turf. Some of the sailors carried the 100 lb shell up the hill to present it to the General and his Staff, but it seems that they were 'rather shy of it', although a commemorative photograph was taken.

Meanwhile Lyttelton's men, still holding their captured ridge, had been subject to two attacks in attempts to re-take it from them. They had successfully repelled these each time with their bayonets, but were now getting battle-weary and needed to be retired, having several casualties. General Clery sent Hildyard's Brigade of East Surreys, Devons and West Yorks forward to relieve them during the night, and these, in turn, needed to produce their bayonets to withstand successfully another effort by the Boers even as the last of Lyttelton's men were straggling back over the Tugela.

In the morning of 7 February it was seen that the Boers had been busy again under cover of darkness. The observation balloon reported that they had dug better trenches and sangars nearer to Vaal Krantz and increased their artillery strength considerably. The British positions on the ridge of Krantz Kop had also been strengthened and, although the Boer bombardment, when it began again, was much more intense, the defenders felt its force less than on the previous day because of their improved shelters.

This balloon was the second to be used by Buller in the war. The first had been damaged by shrapnel at Spion Kop and torn to shreds against the rocks. Now, at Vaal Krantz, the reserve balloon, operated by the Royal Engineers, had also come under fire the previous day and had to be unceremoniously withdrawn to a safer position, towed along, still inflated, by its control rope by a galloping team of Horse Artillery, bouncing along crazily, crashing repeatedly against the ground and up into the air again behind the limber to which it was attached, with its empty basket swinging madly from side to side.

After studying further reports on the nature of the Boers' defences from the rescued balloon, which suggested that, even if he took Vaal Krantz, the enemy would be able to enfilade his army all the way to Ladysmith, as the road 'bristled with defences', Buller decided that the operation should be abandoned. Thus the Battle of Vaal Krantz dwindled into a stalemate of little historical significance, and on the way back the mandatory thunderstorm broke over the Naval Brigade.

England and Hunt, with their 4.7s, joined the others at Springfield, and by noon on Sunday, 11 February, under a now blazing sun which brought a haze of steam from the rain-soaked veldt, making the kopjes look like gigantic glistening heaps of hot butterscotch fudge, they were all back on Gun Hill at Chieveley, except for Burne with his 12-pounders, which had been left at Springfield Bridge as a safety measure, along with some Horse Artillery, Dragoons and Hussars, Imperial Light Infantry and the York and Lancasters.

The sailors, after three days of marching, of hauling and serving their guns, were totally exhausted and 'slept where they stood'.

According to Boer accounts, over 5,000 British shells had landed on Brakfontein and Vaal Krantz during the action. Seldom can more shots have been fired with as little effect.

For the third time the gate had felt the horns of the khaki bull, but had not yielded. But the darkest hour often comes just before the dawn, and this was to be the nadir of British fortunes during the war. The string of their reverses since October, 1899, from Stormberg to Magersfontein, to Colenso, to Spion Kop, and now Vaal Krantz, was long. And still Ladysmith, Kimberley and far-off Mafeking were as firmly entrapped as ever.

But by a coincidence, at the very moment that Buller's forces were trudging back to Chieveley, Roberts and Kitchener were making encouraging headway on the western front at Modder River Station, and the erratic Sir John French, with his soon-to-be-outmoded cavalry, was about to have one of his good days.

CHAPTER 15

JACK RACES TO PAARDEBERG

Roberts arrived at Modder River on 9 February and immediately entered into conference with Methuen behind tight security. By now, nearly two months after the Battle of Magersfontein, the spot had struggled to recover some of its idyllic charm, although the steadily growing city of white tents, piles of military supplies, lumbering wagons and thousands of men and horses did little to add to its natural beauty.

Roberts' plan was to play to one of the weaknesses of his opponents, their belief that the British would be loath to pursue the action beyond a short distance from the railway. The wires between Cape Town and Modder River had been very busy as Roberts issued instructions pending his arrival up-country, which were to the effect that the front was to be broadened considerably. In accordance, Methuen had moved the Highland Brigade, under their new commander, General Macdonald, together with the 62nd Field Battery, Royal Artillery, sixteen miles to the west of Modder River Station, to Koodesberg Drift, and at the same time General Broadwood, with some mounted infantry and Royal Horse Artillery, had moved out to Sunnyside, a small village north-west of Belmont. This not only broadened the front, as per plan, but also gave the strong impression that Roberts was going to attempt a breakthrough by making a roll to his left.

By now, with the Sixth Division under General Kelly-Kenny, and the newly arrived Seventh Division, Roberts had an army of something like 35,000 troops assembled at Modder River, which included what was probably the largest force of cavalry ever put into the field – French's 4,000 horses.

The two new Navy 4.7s that Roberts had ordered had been landed at Port Elizabeth on 31 January and arrived on the train at Modder River Station on 3 February just as Bearcroft's men were giving the Boers at Magersfontein a dawn bombardment. Commander Grant divided his new crew into Dorises and Barossas, and gave them each a gun. The Dorises quickly christened their 4.7

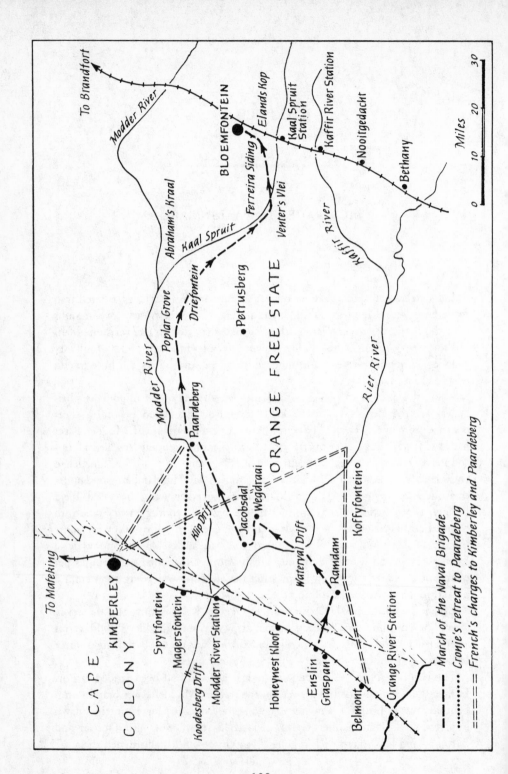

'Little Bobs' and nailed a horseshoe on the carriage for luck, while the Barossas called theirs 'Sloper'. These two, who were to proceed on many an independent mission, became known as 'Grant's Guns'.

But there is far more to a naval brigade than just a few men and a gun, and, in preparation for the long campaign to come, they moved fifteen miles down the line to Enslin to organize the rest of their equipment. In a day or so they were up to full strength, with thirteen wagons, two water carts, 284 oxen and a 'motley, laughter-loving crowd' of forty-two native drivers.

Meanwhile the nightly conversations with Kimberley continued by means of the *Doris*'s railway-truck-mounted searchlight at Modder River siding. The ensnared Rhodes was becoming ever more tiresome, complaining that the Boers were now shelling the town with a great 6 inch howitzer, and threatening Roberts that if he did not make the relief of Kimberley his first priority, then he, Rhodes, would surrender the town to the Boers. Colonel Kekewich, normally unflappable, uncomplaining and patiently optimistic, but being given a miserable time by Rhodes' constant carping, cabled Roberts on 9 February that he feared a public uprising unless relief came within a few days. On the night of 10 February, therefore, he was doubtless heartened to receive Roberts' morse message via the clouds, 'We are coming.'

Sadly for the sailors, it was not part of Roberts' plan for them to be a factor within the Kimberley relieving force. This was to be an operation which rested purely upon speed, mobility and surprise, which are not easily achieved with heavy ships' guns in kopje country. This was to be a job largely for the cavalry, with massive infantry support. At 3 am on the 11th General Sir John French struck out from Modder River in a southerly direction, leaving his tents standing in their orderly rows, gleaming white in the moonlight, to deceive the enemy. They travelled light, Boer-style, with just the clothes they wore and five days' rations.

They trotted through the dawn mist, hugging the railway to give the impression that they were being pulled back to Enslin. Then, at Honeynest Kloof, French swung to his left, i.e., to the east, and clattered into the collection of hovels known as Ramdam, just over the border in Orange Free State at about midday. Bivouacking here, they were joined next day by the Sixth, Seventh, with Roberts himself, and Ninth Divisions, each heralding its approach with a huge cloud of dust on the horizon to the west. Thus Roberts had effectively moved his base to Ramdam, leaving only the First Division at Modder River to keep an eye on Cronje, who was still clinging to the conviction that the British would never stray far from the umbilical cord of the railway.

Still at Enslin, only five miles from Ramdam, the Naval Brigade learnt that, although they would not be going right into Kimberley, they were to be by no means idle. Bloemfontein was to be their goal. In fact, Roberts was about to attempt a double trick which would, if successful, out-Boer the Boers with its cunning. He had feinted to the west of the railway, then marched out south, only to swing east, all with the rapidity of which he had made his name at Kandahar. Now he was about to strike north, without losing the slightest momentum. Speed, and more speed was, as ever, Roberts' strength.

Astonished and terrified burghers abandoned their farms in utmost haste as the 'rooinek' army advanced. Pots of coffee were found on kitchen tables, still hot enough to provide a cup for a thirsty Tommy. In one house warm shaving-water and an unwiped razor told a tale of panic.

The Naval Brigade drew three days' provisions and a generous supply of ammunition was loaded onto the wagons. Each man packed a light 'steaming bag' and the White Ensign was lowered from the telegraph pole where it had fluttered for the past week. At 4 am on the 12 February, followed by their water-carts and ambulance wagons, they too set off to invade the Orange Free State in the wake of the army, which they did by rolling unopposed through the huge hole that French's men had made in the barbed wire fence marking the border.

A buzz went round the crews. Some 'lower-deck lawyer' had said that, as they were now on active service in a foreign country, their pay was increased automatically by one shilling and sixpence a day.

Apart from scattered clumps of giant cacti and dusty blue-green wild tobacco, the landscape here was a flat and featureless desert. Even the great broad tyres of the gun carriages did not prevent them from sinking deep into the dry red sand. Each gun was hauled by thirty-two oxen, but even that amount of muscle, accompanied by much loud cursing and lashing from the native drivers, was not enough to extricate the heavy pieces from some of the worst spots, and the crews, helped by dozens of soldiers, would need to heave on the long drag-ropes in order to get along. Frequently even the trek chains broke under the strain and needed emergency repair with stout wire cable.

They reached Ramdam at 9.30 am and rested there while Kelly-Kenny's Sixth Division tramped through in an endless cloud of dust. Lieutenant Dean's naval guns had been attached to Kelly-Kenny's force and would eventually play an important part, racing far ahead of the other units of the Naval Brigade.

French had already departed from Ramdam in the middle of the night, flying northwards at top speed, hampered more by the slow-moving transport columns of the British infantry than by the Boers. Neither did the Riet or Modder rivers present any serious obstacles, and by nightfall on Wednesday, 14 February, French was north of both, outflanking the Boers' trenches well to the east of Magersfontein, where they were preoccupied with the artillery bombardment which had been launched, according to plan, by the forces remaining at Modder River Station.

He set the Lancers and Scots Greys at the thinly held Boer line at Abon's

110

Dam, galloping straight through it in an almost bloodless charge, and without slackening pace, like a giant ploughshare thrust the enemy aside. All that now remained in front of Kimberley was a five-mile-long plain, dotted with wild quince and babel thorn. Pausing only to water their mounts at De Villiers Farm, French's cavalry charged on, straight across the border, and back into Cape Colony and the besieged town that sat almost on the line.

So hard was the five-mile gallop in the fierce heat that many of the cavalry's horses, green and unfit so soon after their sea voyage from England, actually collapsed and died. The toll was so heavy, in fact, that the cavalry division could not thereafter be considered as a fully effective fighting entity in Roberts' army. Nonetheless, Kimberley had been relieved after 124 days, and with little bloodshed.

With the arrival of French's troopers the whole town went into party mood. Union Jacks were waved, music played, people danced, people sang, and 3000 women and children poured out of the deep recesses of the diamond mines where they had been sheltering from the intensified, but mercifully final, bombardment from 'Long Tom'.

At home, when the news broke of Kimberley's relief, the excitement was instant and unbounded. As the glad tidings spread through the streets, offices, pubs and shops like a forest fire, exuberant shouts went up as normal proceedings came to a momentary halt. The news was received at the London Stock Exchange at six minutes past ten and instantly posted up, whereupon everybody dashed out of the building to run back to their offices, imparting the news to passers-by as they went. At Liverpool Assizes a murder trial being heard by Mr Justice Grantham was interrupted while the judge, apparently unable to contain himself, told the jury that French was in Kimberley and the twelve good men and true broke into an instant bout of cheering. And it was announced by the Post Office that, with immediate effect, telegrams could now be accepted for Kimberley, South Africa, at sender's risk, not exceeding twelve words.

Thirty-five miles away to the south, among the kopjes at Ramdam, Commander Grant's gun crews were not yet, of course, fully acclimatized to the summer heat, here on the fringes of the Kalahari desert, having only recently arrived from the relative coolness of Simonstown. They began to suffer as the run rose each day and were grateful to find a 'pan' or pond at Ramdam in which to cool off. There was very little water in it at this time of the year, but the cooling effects of its muddy bottom were enjoyed by the sailors, wallowing hippopotamus fashion.

They waited here for the rest of the 9th Division to join from Modder River, before pushing on to Waterval Drift on the Riet River. They made the fifteen-mile trek in six and a half hours. The sun was baking hot and all arrived very weary. Men literally crawled into camp, dead beat, and the ambulances were kept very busy with the many cases of heat-stroke. Even the oxen were overcome by the effects of the sun's heat. Their tongues were hanging out, their sides heaving and their breathing was accompanied by 'deep and sorrowful sighs'.

Crossing Waterval Drift with such heavy guns was a difficult task. There were steep banks leading down to the river bed and, to make matters worse, the road was atrocious. The Royal Canadian Regiment was ordered to assist the sailors. First, the oxen were unshackled and taken over, and then, with drags and check-ropes hooked to the gun-carriage axles, they were slowly and safely lowered down to the water. Then, with a mighty 'two-six-heave!' the guns were taken over by British and Canadian manpower, according to one eye-witness, 'as if they had no weight'. A few hours' sleep after supper on the far bank, then the oxen were in-spanned and the Brigade set off again at 1 am under a full moon in the bracingly cool night air. They had got as far as Wegdraai Drift by the morning and bivouacked there, weary again, having covered twenty-seven miles in twenty-five hours, including the three-hour delay at Waterval Drift and their couple of hours sleep.

It was also at Waterval Drift that Roberts made one of his rare mistakes. The crossing of the Drift, undertaken by the Navy under great difficulty, was an even slower and more laborious task when it came to be done by a three-mile-long transport column of heavy wagons that was being severely tested by a cascade of bullets and shells. Christiaan De Wet had found them. De Wet, the immaculate marauder, arch guerrilla of an army of guerrillas, was to prove a thorn in the side of the British for a long time to come, even for many years after the end of the war. Short, stocky and dapper, with a big gold watch chain across his waistcoat, a briefcase in his hand containing war correspondence and plans, and a pair of binoculars slung round his neck, he looked more like a London stockbroker about to steal a few hours at Ascot than the brilliant Boer bandit that he was.

De Wet's speciality was to operate on a roving commission, and with French advancing on Kimberley, he had simply followed his instincts and taken his small but highly efficient and mobile band of burghers into the kopjes to hide and hunt for likely prey. And now, at Waterval Drift, he had found a juicy target – Roberts' baggage wallowing in the middle of a difficult crossing. The rocky bluffs flanking the Riet provided the perfect setting for an ambush and De Wet utilized them to the full, spewing Maxim and Mauser fire down on to the helpless wagons.

From Roberts' point of view he was engaged on an important mission, the relief of Kimberley, the success of which depended entirely on speed. To make any kind of stand to fight De Wet would delay him. He could not afford to be held up for a minute, and so, making a snap decision, he elected to abandon many of his laden supply wagons at this point so as to enable his infantry to press on ahead.

Nº 1 in D Nº 2 in E FLAT Nº 3 in F

Sung by MR MAYBRICK.

THEY ALL LOVE JACK

BALLAD,

THE WORDS BY

F. E. Weatherly,

THE MUSIC COMPOSED & DEDICATED TO

KENNETH L. WATERLOW,

BY

STEPHEN ADAMS.

Price 2/ net.

THEY ALL LOVE JACK, IS ARRANGED AS A WALTZ, ALSO AS LANCERS BY LIDDELL. 2/ EACH, NET

BOOSEY & CO.

LIMITED

EDITIONS HAWKES   BOOSEY. HAWKES BELWIN INC   BOOSEY & HAWKES. LTD   BOOSEY & HAWKES Australia LTD
16 RUE DU FAUBG ST DENIS   43-47 WEST 26TH STREET   295 REGENT STREET   PALINGS BUILDINGS ASH STREET
PARIS 10E   NEW YORK CITY   LONDON W 1   SYDNEY

THEY ALL LOVE JACK.

When the ship is trim and ready,
    And the jolly days are done,
When the last good-byes are whisper'd
    And Jack aboard is gone;
The lasses fall a-weeping,
    As they watch his vessel's track,
For all the landsmen lovers
    Are nothing after Jack.

    For his heart is like the sea,
    Ever open, brave, and free,
    And the girls must lonely be
      Till his ship comes back;
    But if love's the best of all
    That can a man befall,
    Why, Jack's the King of all,
      For they all love Jack!

Where he goes their hearts go with him,
    E'en his ship he calls her "she,"
Up aloft that "little cherub"
    Sure a maiden she must be.
And as o'er the sea he travels,
    The mermaids down below
Would give their crystal kingdoms
    For the love of Jack, I trow.

    For his heart is like the sea, &c.

When he's sailed the world all over,
    And again he steps a-shore,
There are scores of lasses waiting
    To love him all the more;
He may lose his golden guineas,
    But a wife he'll never lack,
If he'd wed them all, they'd take him,
    For they all love Jack!

    For his heart is like the sea, &c.

F. E. Weatherly.

THEY ALL LOVE JACK

Words by
F. E. WEATHERLY

Music by
STEPHEN ADAMS

*The Public Performance of any parodied version
of this composition is strictly prohibited.*

Printed in England

On Friday, 16 February the sailors marched the five miles into Jacobsdal, a Boer supply depot which had been taken by Roberts' troops three days earlier, still accompanied by the Canadians, who tramped alongside the guns, joining in the chorus of 'They All Love Jack', one of the popular songs of the day. There were no pubs in the town and the Boers had not left much food, although they had left plenty of the typhoid-stricken burghers from the Magersfontein trenches, who recieved all possible help from the British doctors. But there were plenty of sheep, one or two of which 'just followed me back here, Chief', and just enough rum for their tots. Some of the stokers had discovered a cache of potatoes, which were 'borrowed', and a hearty meal was soon prepared and consumed with relish, while they waited for the rest of Bearcroft's guns to catch up from Modder River Station. Disappointed at not getting a chance to see Kimberley after all their efforts to relieve it, these had set off for Jacobsdal on the 17th, leaving much of their personal gear behind, so as to make for light and speedy travelling, arriving there the next day to join with Grant's Guns.

General Cronje had hurriedly left his trenches at Magersfontein as soon as Kimberley was reached by the British. But where was he to go? Cronje's immediate subordinates, De Wet and Ferreira, both had ideas contrary to his own. As we have already seen, De Wet had already melted into the mountains to embark on his guerrilla campaign. Ferreira retired northwards alongside the railway and just sat there, playing a waiting game and reserving his options while he watched developments. To the west and north-west stretched miles of baking arid desert. And then there was Bloemfontein, capital of the Orange Free State, to think about. Unless he moved quickly, Bloemfontein would be wide open for the British to take more or less unopposed. His flight must be eastwards to save Bloemfontein.

The Boers were experts at making hurried departures from a camp, but here they broke all records. In a flash, 4,000 men had woken up, risen, saddled up, loaded up and mounted, leaving behind nearly all their personal belongings in the Magersfontein trenches that had been their home for so long, and fled towards Bloemfontein. Cronje, the old fox, managed to wriggle his way, unheard and unseen, through a fortuitous gap just ahead of Kelly-Kenny's Sixth Division as it rested between the kopjes on its way north to consolidate the gains that French had made. That he was able to do this, on a bright moonlit night, with a five-mile-long train of plodding bullock wagons, says little for the alertness of the British scouts.

Roberts set Kitchener and Tucker after him, one on each side of the tree-fringed Modder River, with Lieutenant Dean's naval detachment with their 12-pounders in support. And French, with most of his own cavalry mounts wrecked, useless and some even dead from exhaustion after their frantic charge to Kimberley, requisitioned fresh mounts from the Diamond Fields Artillery

10. General Joubert and his staff in their laager outside Moddderspruit.

11. A Naval 4.7" gun inside Ladysmith.

12. One of the Navy's 4.7" guns crossing Paardeberg Drift.

13. The Boers' attempt to dam the Klip River destroyed by Midshipman
Carnegie's 12-pounder, fired from Caesar's Camp.

14. A khaki-painted Naval 12-pounder and crew from Ladysmith.

15. Nelson's HMS *Victory* salutes the arrival of HMS *Powerful* at Portsmouth.

16. "Home from the War".

17. HMS *Powerful's* Naval Brigade raise a cheer at the Banquet given by the Mayor and Corporation of Portsmouth, who appear dumbfounded.

and De Beers and was now charging hell-for-leather across the featureless scorched-brown veldt to overtake and head off Cronje at Paardeberg.

The Naval Brigade had little respite at Jacobsdal. Roberts had Cronje on the run, and he had to be caught and brought to book before he reached Bloemfontein. The sailors were ordered to move out at 9.30 pm, only a few hours after arriving in the town, and with the complete complement of four 4.7s, two 12-pounders and marine escort, following the 82nd Battery Royal Artillery with whom they had now become firm friends and would be for many a mile to come, they trudged off into a starless, moonless, pitch-black South African night.

The night was so dark and the choking clouds of dust thrown up by the wheels and tramping feet was so thick that the guides had great difficulty in keeping the lumbering limbers and wagons on the track. Surgeon T. T. Jeans, of HMS *Monarch*, wrote in his diary:

In front of the naval guns, under the white dust cloud, were the two batteries. The rumble of their wheels, the jangle of harness and accoutrements, and the dull thud of hundreds of horses' hooves, half-muffled in the soft sand, interminable and continuous. We could see the indistinct figures of men, with their greatcoat collars turned up over their ears, and many with woollen nightcaps on their heads, nodding and swaying from side to side as they clutched reins or limber rails in their sleep. Our own long-chased guns, white with dust, rolling along two abreast behind the labouring oxen, their big wheels churning the dust like waterwheels. In front of each, a bluejacket guide plodded wearily along, wading through the soft sand. These two might have been asleep, so apparently aimlessly did they stagger; yet over and over again they would, with a wave of the hand to the right or left, guide the guns from danger, the little Bushman leaders of the ox-teams following their every motion.

In the middle of the night they passed an eerie sight. It was a long line of ambulance wagons, each with a Red Cross flag, full of huddled figures, looking like a phantom desert caravan in the murky gloom as it made its way back behind the lines, almost silently, full of men wounded in the running fight with Cronje's rearguard.

Short halts were called at intervals to allow the convoy to close up. Even if only for a few minutes, everybody slept. Now the bright moon had emerged to make night like day, and it was cold. Still and silent, dozens of figures lay on the ground to sleep, while the horses and mules stood gazing at whatever wisps of vegetation they could find.

The march was halted at 6 am at Klip Kraal Drift to rest and take breakfast. During the morning Lord Roberts and his staff cantered up, immaculate on their giant chargers. The Field Marshal said to Captain Bearcroft, 'I want the Naval Brigade to push up another ten miles. I have Cronje surrounded and I want to give the Navy a 'show.' Clearly French had made it to Paardeberg before the Boers, and was now behind them, acting as the other claw of Roberts' pincer.

Though eager to obey, Bearcroft had to wait a while to let his oxen finish grazing, and they moved off in the early afternoon. The dust was the worst yet, and the roasting sun seemed to burn right through their straw hats. Their feet sank ankle-deep into the scorching sand, their eyes were bloodshot, their lips were cracked and bleeding. The little water that remained in their bottles became too hot to drink. The men on the limbers suffered the worst, from the dust thrown up by the guns' wheels into their eyes. They needed to hold on to the crossbars, which exposed their hands to the sun, causing many to incur serious burns. Stones or potholes in the track would cause the limber-pole to swing across suddenly, like the boom on a yacht, and often, in their exhausted slow-to-react state, they were caught unawares and were knocked to the ground.

On 20 February, after a good night's sleep, they were on the march by 9.30 am and after five miles arrived at Roberts' main Headquarters in the shadow of a kopje on the approaches to Paardeberg. Here they were in sight of Cronje's laager, where he was trapped, with French at his rear. For some inexplicable reason Cronje had decided to stop, dig himself in at Paardeberg Drift and fight it out with French and Roberts. He had not needed to be caught with French at his back. He could have abandoned much of his heavy baggage, which was being dragged along by cumbersome bullocks at about twelve miles per day, and put on enough speed to carry himself to safety. Without even doing that, he could have easily elbowed aside French's woefully depleted and exhausted cavalry, then made to rejoin either Ferreira or De Wet. As it was, he elected to fight, and only a day or so after leaving one set of trenches at Magersfontein the burghers were digging frantically into the banks of the Modder at Paardeberg to make another.

Orders came from HQ for Grant's Guns to advance immediately to a range of 3,000 yards from the laager, with its three Krupp guns and a pom-pom, and to bombard it. To close the range as instructed, the Doris's and Barossas rumbled their long-barrelled khaki-painted 4.7s through the canvas town of tents where Roberts' huge army was drawn up awaiting the battle. Tommies poured out of their tents to whistle and cheer the sailors on. 'Give 'em some lyddite, Jack!' one was heard to shout, and a forest of hands patted the bluejackets' shoulders as they rolled forward.

They got to the banks of the Modder, with a mile still to go on the other side. It was armpit depth, and both men and animals had to struggle to keep their feet as they crossed the Drift. As they advanced, now on the north bank, they came under pom-pom fire and were fortunate indeed to avoid casualties as they set up their guns. Grant recorded that they opened fire at 4.30 pm and expended thirty-seven rounds during that afternoon, but the Boers' artillery only replied against the Royal Artillery batteries and the infantry lines, seemingly ignoring completely any presence of the Royal Navy in the field, which apparently caused Jack Tar to take offence.

The remainder of the Naval Brigade was not quite as fortunate. Their position was still south of the river, but only 1,300 yards from the nearest Boer trenches, and there were several concealed snipers even closer than that, one of whom shot a bluejacket dead.

Starting at 8.30 the next morning, Grant put in a full and successful day's bombardment of the Boers' supply wagons. Many of them were burnt or destroyed, turning the horizon into a sea of flickering flames, black, white and brown smoke, regularly interspersed with the green smoke of a salvo of lyddite. In the evening a thunderstorm extinguished most of the fires, leaving a gruesome scene of charred wreckage and dead and mangled animals. Just to the rear, aloft, swinging in the wicker basket under his balloon, the observer swayed and dipped and reeled, calling and waving the shots with his flag in between bouts of retching with air-sickness. And another bluejacket was shot dead by a sniper.

Water supply became a problem. The Modder had been intentionally polluted upstream by the Boers and was full of decomposing bodies of oxen and horses. The water was as thick as ship's cocoa, and christened 'Dead Horse Soup' by the men. Even boiled with a pinch of alum to clear it, it was not easily, or wisely, drinkable. Food was scarce, since Roberts had abandoned the supply column at Waterval Drift, and the meat of the trek oxen was so tough that it had to be ground through a mincing machine and then made into soup. Fortunately there was a large flock of sheep grazing in the rich pasture near where the oxen had found good grass, and again, like those at Jacobsdal and many other places later, they seemed to have an affectionate attachment to Royal Navy stokers, whom they would 'follow home' quite frequently, or tend to 'stray' so far from the main flock that nobody could tell who the real owner was and, 'I couldn't let a poor sheep wander about lost, could I, Chief?'

And so it continued, with the shells from the naval guns crossing the Mauser bullets of the Boer snipers in midair. There was no let-up apart from the usual Sunday morning hymn-singing from the Boers, and at night the cries of wounded and dying animals could be heard from the river bed. It was a sad and pitiful experience for those within earshot. On the Monday the Royal Artillery brought up a pom-pom and four big 6-inch howitzers in support of the naval guns. Thus augmented, the British shells filled the air with rasping screams, until a terrific explosion was heard. Surgeon Jeans thought that a magazine had blown up and hurried to the top of a kopje to see. He wrote in his diary: 'The whole laager was filled with the oily green curling lyddite smoke, and when this blew away they let fly another salvo, the four shells falling in a line across the laager at regular intervals. The sun had just set, and in the gloom the flames of the tremendous explosions seen through the green smoke made it a most ghastly spectacle, and we felt, for the first time, exceedingly sorry for the foolhardy people below us.'

Throughout the war there had been mutterings, not only from the Boers but also from several other quarters sympathetic to their cause, notably Germany, about the use of lyddite. Lyddite, named after the little town on the fringe of Romney Marsh on the south Kent coast where the army had its testing ranges, was composed chiefly of picric acid, gun cotton and gum arabic. The patent was purchased by Armstrong & Co. in 1888 from its inventor, a Frenchman, Monsieur Turpin, who had called it melinite. Needing a hard surface on which to land in order to achieve an explosion, it proved to be very effective when used against the Boers in their rocky eyries in the kopjes of South Africa. Its power was such that a 4.7" lyddite shell could kill anybody within a radius of 75 yards of its bursting, but on the other hand it proved almost useless when used against dispersed troops in open country, because the blast diffused rapidly away from its centre. Britain was criticized for the use of a weapon whose destructive powers were considered outside the bounds of acceptable etiquette. Furthermore, it was not really fair to send sailors ashore to fire it against simple farmers. There had been no objection, mused a *Times* corresspondent, when France had used lyddite's cousin melinite in Madagascar only two years before. And at Paardeberg the Naval Brigade continued to pump it into the Boers' wagons.

Lord Roberts, in his bed with a chill, twenty-five miles back in Jacobsdal, had appointed Kitchener as battle commander. This was a humiliating experience for poor Kelly-Kenny, and the two were at loggerheads throughout the fighting. Kelly-Kenny had planned to encircle the Boers with his infantry and let the artillery bombard them into submission, but Kitchener overruled him, ordering immediate full-frontal infantry attacks on the Boer trenches.

Kitchener had not been at Modder River, or Colenso, or Magersfontein. He had not experienced the task of attacking trenches occupied by superb marksmen armed with long-range smokeless magazine rifles. His tactics, unsurprisingly, were to prove disastrous. Battalion after battalion was thrown at the Boers – the 1st Welsh, the 1st Essex, Hannay's Mounted Infantry and the West Ridings, the East Kents, the King's Own Scottish Borderers and the Gloucesters, the Argylls, the Seaforths, the Black Watch and the Gordons of the Highland Brigade, the Oxfordshire Light Infantry, the 1st Royal Canadians and the Shropshires, even a half-company of the Cornwalls who were guarding the baggage. All these advanced into an inferno of Mauser bullets and the thud-thud-thud of pom-poms.

Then an unexpected turn of events occurred. Christiaan De Wet, still sartorially immaculate and now the proud possesser of the 140,000 tins of biscuit, meat, milk and various other rations that Roberts had abandoned at Waterval Drift, had followed his ears towards the thunder of the big guns. With only three hundred burghers, and more or less unopposed and unnoticed during the late afternoon, he had taken a kopje commanding the whole south-east ridge line. With De Wet blazing away at the British lines below, this would have provided an escape-hatch through which Cronje would have wriggled should he have chosen, but only a handful of his men did so. The old fox stayed in his sandy lair, looking sad but determined, and holding Mrs Cronje's hand, according to a Boer prisoner, whilst 4000 of his faithful followers continued to exact a fearful toll on Tommy Atkins with their Mausers for three more days.

And for those three more days De Wet stayed defiantly on his ridge, despite Kitchener's attempt to shift him with constant artillery fire, until at last his burghers began to melt away, as was their habit after any lengthy stalemate, leaving the kopje deserted.

Meanwhile the Naval Brigade and the heavy Royal Artillery guns had been steadily pounding Cronje's baggage wagons into destruction. Many of their horses had died in the terrifying non-stop barrage, and now their corpses were to be seen, bloated in the sun, beside the charred remnants of the wagons.

That night the final infantry advance was made. At 3 am, with the bagpipes wailing, the Gordon Highlanders advanced towards the laager, exchanging murderous fusillades with the entrenched Boers. By daybreak Cronje had realized that his position was hopeless. His men, with most of their personal belongings now being picked over by British troops miles away in the Magersfontein trenches, were starving. His supplies and his horses had been destroyed. He was completely surrounded. White flags of surrender began to wave from the warren-like trenches in the banks of the Modder. It was 6 am on 27 February. The anniversary of Majuba! Roberts, by now recovered from his chill, ordered, 'Splice the mainbrace'.

After any battle the scene on the field is grim, but this one was particularly nightmarish. After Spion Kop, Paardeberg was the bloodiest battle of the entire war. The dead, dying and wounded on both sides lay among the blackened and twisted iron-work of the burnt-out wagons and charred heaps of supplies, scattered over an area of half a mile. The British doctors, led by Surgeon C. M. Beadnell, RN, of the *Powerful* went into the laager, searching among the scattered clothing, harness, empty shell cases, Bibles, cooking pots, broken boxes and dead animals to dispense whatever humane assistance they could, but the stench was so sickening that even the strongest stomachs were turned.

Some of the Boer livestock found itself changing sides after Paardeberg. The Naval Brigade adopted three motherless chicks, who rode all the way to Bloemfontein in a kettle. At each halt they would come out and peck around for scraps until they were tired, when they would go and stand by their kettle, waiting to be put back in. A stray dog adopted the sailors, rewarding their

121

kindness with hares and other small game which it would catch on hunting forays across the veldt. And there was a goat found wandering about the laager which was recruited into naval circles, and which was apparently quite content on a diet of old newspapers and tobacco!

Paardeberg losses were ninety-eight British officers and 1437 men, and the Boers lost six guns and 4100 prisoners, including Cronje himself. The Boer losses in terms of men killed was astonishingly light, which statistic must pay tribute to their skills in remaining invisible to their enemies. The British victory was earned at a fearful price, and was only earned at all because they had immobilized their opponent and destroyed his food supplies.

The Boer prisoners were marched back to Modder River under the guard of the City Imperial Volunteers, to be taken by train down to Cape Town. Cronje, together with his wife, 'a thin decrepit old woman, in a rough straw hat and dirty old black dress, without a cloak or shawl', and their grandson, was provided with a cart drawn by six horses for the journey. At Cape Town he was placed aboard HMS *Doris*, where Admiral Harris allocated him one of the flag officers' state cabins, although it was soon decided that he and his entourage should be packed off aboard the SS *Milwaukee* to spend their captivity on the island of St Helena, thus paying him a similar compliment to that paid to Napoleon Bonaparte.

CHAPTER 16

'LOLLIES ERE LONG'

Ladysmith was now in its fourth month under siege. At the beginning of their ordeal, supply officer Colonel Ward had estimated that they had enough food for fifty days. They had now doubled that time, and were still alive – just.

Since the raid on Caesar's Camp on 6 January the Boers had made no serious attempt to take the town by force of arms. They had maintained their 'starving out' tactics, sitting patiently in the kopjes around the town and tossing sporadic shellfire into it just to keep the screw tight.

The shortage of food had taken its toll on the fitness and strength of every one of the defenders. Cheerful letters home became rarer, simply because they had become more difficult to write. Games of football became fewer and shorter. Lambton himself was given to recurring bouts of sickness. Troops who three months ago had been glowing with health and vigour had now grown so skinny and feeble that it was noted in the Official History that, 'Even the short marches entailed by the relief of the outposts were already as much as many of the soldiers could manage.'

And Halsey had another mouth to feed beside his own. He had adopted a terrier pup that had been born in the corner of their mess-tent one evening during dinner. It is clear from his letters that she had won his heart. 'Such a nice little beast, but she eats a lot of my rations ... she has become part and parcel of my life up here. . . . If I ever get out of this place I shall never be able to leave her behind now . . . She is called Victoria after the battery.'

Lambton's men suffered an unnecessary loss on the 22nd when Able Seaman Payne and Stoker Wheeler were both killed. A local parson had an unexploded Boer 6-inch shell and persuaded the sailors to take the fuse out to make it safe. In direct disobedience of their Captain's orders that such shells should not be touched, the men agreed, and the shell burst while they were attempting to defuse it. One of them was blown to fragments, and the other had to have both legs amputated on the spot. It was the 'most awful sight imaginable' and the man died eight hours later, still unaware that he had lost his legs, and continually asking if his chum had been hurt.

Morale, already in the depths, plummeted to a new low after Spion Kop. Buller had heliographed before the battle that he was confident that he would be in Ladysmith before the week was out. The Royal Engineers' observation balloon could be clearly seen, circling above the distant skyline like a vulture looking for a meal. HMS *Terrible*'s railway-truck-mounted searchlight played in the sky every evening from Chieveley, tantalisingly close but yet so far, dotting and dashing its messages of hope. All Ladysmith's expectant eyes strained towards the south, Cove Redoubt being a favourite vantage point from which to watch for the first khaki figures to appear between the near but yet so distant kopjes. And when the Boers were seen to be evacuating Spion Kop, amid the sickly-green lyddite smoke and great fountains of brown earth splashed up by the shells from the Navy's 4.7s far back on Mount Alice, many Ladysmithers rushed down the hill to break the exciting news that Buller's troops were on their way in. But then the British withdrew, while the Boers rallied and reoccupied the mountain with their village of white tents. Many said that was the worst day of the whole siege.

The food problem grew ever worse. In the end, General White had no alternative but to order the slaughter of some of the cavalry horses. This had involved no small measure of soul-searching. To the British mind the consumption of horse-flesh was not far removed from cannibalism and many a trooper sobbed tears of true sorrow on the day that the first of the horses went to the engine shed-cum-slaughter house to be converted into sausages, soup and a new concoction that had been given the name 'Chevril', a parody on the trade name Bovril.

The sick and wounded had first call on the supply of milk, and their numbers were rising steadily, with a dozen people dying each day from enteric fever. Lambton's men did not escape. 169637 Able Seaman Dunn, HMS *Powerful*, died of enteric on 13 February.

Joubert denied General White's early request for evacuation of the women and children, and the sick and wounded, but he did agree to the setting-up of a hospital camp for the latter, subject to parole being given that all who were dispatched there would take no further part in the war. This was done at Intombi Spruit, in no-man's-land, just outside the south-eastern perimeter on a tongue of unhealthy and swampy land between the Klip River and the railway line. It was a hotchpotch conglomeration of tents, makeshift shelters and awnings, which started off containing 300 beds, and was staffed by thirty doctors, 120 trained medical assistants and fifty-six Indian bearers.

Later Mother Marie des Anges, leaving her convent in the town to be bombarded by the Boers, took her nuns out to Intombi to help with the nursing, but gradually they too fell sick. And when the doctors themselves succumbed to dysentery and the fever the townswomen of Ladysmith took over, awaiting with brave faces each daily white-flagged train from the town with its cargo of sick, wounded and dying.

Eventually Intombi became a hellish place, infested with snakes and scorpions and the stench of dysentery and death. As conditions worsened and the siege wore on the 300-bedded camp was to be crammed with 1400 patients, rising to 2000 by the end, and the staff had shrunk to fifteen nurses. This was all in addition to the three Field Hospitals in the town itself. Altogether, in the four months' duration of the siege, the Hospitals and Intombi Camp handled 10,688 cases, and 551 people died of disease, most of them in the final seven weeks when the typhoid epidemic was rampant.

The Boers, too, were hit by the dysentery epidemic and on several occasions sent a delegation into the town under a white flag to beg some chlorodine, which was given to them readily, as a precaution against it spreading even more. Such was the etiquette of war.

The Boers tried to dam the Klip River to the south-east of the town in an attempt to flood the inhabitants, but each time the work neared completion their efforts were frustrated by the accurate shells of the naval gun on Caesar's Camp under Midshipman Carnegie, who took great delight in destroying their handiwork with potshots from his 12-pounder.

Lionel Halsey sent another batch of letters out by runner, including one to his mother saying that he had now heard that his brother Arthur was with Buller's forces; 'I am looking forward to the day when the Relief Column comes in – what a fight it will be. I hope I shoot straight that day. . . . I sent a message to headquarters with a request that it might be heliographed to Estcourt to Arthur, and the Chief of Staff has just written me a most civil note saying that he has sent the following for me: "To Lieutenant Halsey. All well – wire home – from Lieutenant Halsey."

Lambton's Naval Brigade suffered not only from a shortage of food, but, just as importantly, from a shortage of ammunition. After the first two days of the siege, when the air was full of screaming steel and almost a third of the total supply of shells expended, he imposed a strict ration of two firings per day, and by the end of the year had reduced it to one. Just before Christmas Lionel Halsey had managed to persuade Lambton to sanction the firing of a dozen shells in an effort to silence the 'Long Tom' which continued to harass them from the top of Bulwana, and of course there had been the skirmish at Wagon Hill/Caesar's Camp which had meant that several more had been spent. All in all, the situation was becoming critical, with only about 100 rounds of ammunition remaining for the 4.7s at the beginning of February.

Buller remained convinced that he had the key to Ladysmith, even after Colenso, Spion Kop and Vaal Krantz, though he had tried it in the lock on all of those occasions, only to find that it did not fit. Which lock to try next? He had tried a full frontal assault. He had tried a roll to the west twice. And failed each time. Perhaps, like a drunken man fumbling unsuccessfully to open his front door on a foggy night, he had come to the wrong house?

After Vaal Krantz Buller returned to his fortified stationmaster's house headquarters at Frere to plan his next move. The first necessity, he concluded, was for even heavier calibre artillery. Percy Scott was sitting in the 4 pm train at Durban station, waiting to depart for Pietermaritzburg, where, in his capacity of Town Commandant of Durban, he had an appointment with the Governor of Natal, when Buller's telegram was handed to him.

'Clear the line. Urgent, No. 383. Have you a six-inch gun on carriage that I could move a mile or so across the flat? If you have, telegraph in my name to Admiral, and ask if I may have one for a few days. Utmost importance. If possible, I want it Monday, 12th, and you to work it, – Buller.'

Scott wired back: 'General Buller, Chieveley. Six-inch gun on mobile mounting will leave here on Sunday night. – Percy Scott.'

The problem then facing Scott was how to fulfil his promise. He sent a steamer and a lighter out to the *Terrible* in Durban Roads and signalled to her to send a 6″ gun ashore. Then he remembered that at Pietermaritzburg there was a pair of wheels that had been discarded because the tyres were too narrow for a 4.7. By 10 pm he had the wheels from Maritzburg and the gun from *Terrible* in the factory. The dockyard workmen toiled all night putting broader tyres on the wheels and forming an axle tree and trail, and on the Sunday morning 200 men were landed from *Terrible* to drag the big gun down to the beach for some test firing. It worked perfectly.

Thus Scott displayed his usual alacrity in compliance with requests for his ingenious assistance. The 6″, with an overall weight of 11 tons, was entrained for the front, where it arrived on the 12th as requested, and Buller ran it up on to Gun Hill. An extra draft of Terribles were sent up from Durban to man the big gun. They were Lieutenant Drummond, in command, Midshipman Skinner, Petty Officers Connor and Carey, and the captain of the gun, Petty Officer Allen, plus fifty seamen and stokers.

On the same day, 12 February, Scott sent another party of Terribles ashore at Durban to proceed into Zululand with a couple of field guns to augment the forces guarding against possible Boer raids across the far north-eastern border of Natal. Lieutenant Dooner, with Midshipman Kirby, Petty Officers Neil, Sparks, Bicker and fifty seamen and stokers travelled by rail up the coast as far as the terminus, then marched the last 28 miles into Eshowe to join the forces already there. By all accounts it would appear that their journey was comparatively uneventful, but the episode is included for the sake of record.

Back at Frere Buller continued to ponder. Of equal importance to heavier artillery, he assessed, was his need for reinforcements, and he cabled Roberts accordingly, only to receive an out-and-out refusal. This seems to have spurred him, or perhaps more accurately, needled him, into action.

He had tried the left flank, he had tried the centre. But what about the right flank? To his right the Tugela swept in a serpentine writhe to the north, cutting its way through a deep six-mile-long gorge between the kopjes, taking it on a course to the rear of the eastern section of Botha's trenches. This meant that, for a change, at least some of the Boer defences would have a river at their backs, rather than have their usual luxury of a river between them and their attackers. And a fast-flowing river with a waterfall in a deep gorge at that.

That was it! It had been staring him in the face all the time – the Tugela. Here he had them trapped! Back them up to the river and the line would surely crack. The river at the Boers' rear was the real key to the lock. But even now that he had located the key, the lock itself would need to be lubricated with some up-to-date military thinking.

Between Buller and the gorge of the Tugela stood several craggy outcrops. The range of hills grew craggier as they spread eastwards from Spion Kop and here they were at their craggiest. Hlangwane, Green Hill, Cingolo and Monte Cristo were their names, the last-named rising a thousand feet above the plain, and they were cleft with rocky ravines and cliffs, adorned with knotty woods and tangled undergrowth as thick as knitting, and bristling with thorny mimosa. The Boer trenches were spread across the two westernmost kopjes, Hlangwane and Green Hill.

Just four miles to the north of Chieveley stood Hussar Hill, which was, in truth, the forward prominence of a ridge running due north to join up with Green Hill in the centre of the section, and, unlike its neighbours to the north, was devoid of any craggy features whatsoever, or indeed of any cover at all.

In the early morning of the 14th a small raiding party seized Hussar Hill, opposed only by a handful of surprised Boer pickets. Over the next two days Buller placed thirty-four heavy guns, including Ogilvy's battery of 12-pounders, on its summit. Quickly throwing up redoubts of earth-bags around the guns, for they were being subjected to ferocious and uncomfortably accurate shellfire, they began a blistering creeping barrage that skimmed the heads of Hildyard's and Barton's advancing infantry, the shots falling nearly as close ahead of the soldiers as the raindrops that dripped off the peaks of their helmets. Behind this protective veil of exploding steel, and spurred by the wail of the bagpipes of the Scots Fusiliers, they gingerly picked their way forward onto the ridge itself and onwards around the crescent line to Cingolo.

The gun causing the main discomfort to Ogilvy's crew was being fired from near Bloy's Farm, and here was a chance for the new boys to show their mettle. The six-incher fired its first shells in anger from Gun Hill, at a range of 16,500 yards, and Allen hit it with his third shot. It was not heard again. Later on, in the evening, with another superb shot, Allen knocked out a Boer searchlight which was proving troublesome.

All day long the big guns kept up their relentless rate of fire while the infantry inched forward under the screaming umbrella of shells. One by one, the hills fell to the British, first Cingolo and then Green Hill. That only left Monte Cristo.

On Sunday the 18th came the struggle for Monte Cristo itself, one of the last tumblers in the lock, at the same moment as Kitchener was sending his infantry to be butchered at Paardeberg.

Monte Cristo was the top prize of the day. To take it would be to turn Botha's left flank and open up the way to slide behind Hlangwane and snip it off from the Boer forces on the north of the river, like a surgeon removing a polyp. Take it they did, and with all haste, Ogilvy and his guns, closely escorted, set off from Hussar Hill to march through the night to Monte Cristo.

Arriving there just after dawn the next morning, they needed to enlist the help of the Devonshires to haul the 12-pounders up to the summit, but once there they were able to take in, at last, a breathtaking view of their objective, Ladysmith, and the full layout of the siege surrounding it. Now they were nearly close enough to fire on the Boers who were firing on the town. In particular, there were three 45-pounders only 5,000 yards away across the Tugela, and Ogilvy had caught them in the act. He quickly found the range and poured several common shell and shrapnel shells in them, until, with unbelievable reliability, the usual thunderstorm broke with such ferocity that the whole panorama was shrouded in an opaque mist of precipitation which allowed the Boers to withdraw safely and escape further punishment.

Later in the day the 4.7s were also moved over to Monte Cristo, which involved about the toughest ten-mile trek they had yet faced. Making only about one mile per hour, the oxen bullied their way through some hellish country. Trees and stands of cactus were broken off by the sheer weight and momentum of the guns, leaving glaring stumps in their wake. Huge stones were simply bounced over, and dongas were taken at the rush 'down and up'. And all the while the sun shone down unmercifully. It was so hot that the oxen, as is their wont when they are thirsty and overtired, simply went on strike and refused to pull the guns another step. Drag-ropes were the answer, and with the help of a hundred borrowed soldiers from a regiment which happened to be resting nearby, the sailors manhandled the 4.7s up the hill to join Ogilvy and the rest, and immediately opened fire.

On the 19th British soldiers strolled into Colenso without a shot being fired and without seeing a single Boer. This had the immediate effect of pushing the railhead forward, and the speed with which trains reappeared was remarkable. Within a very few hours train after train was snorting into Colenso station bearing men and supplies of all descriptions, particularly ammunition for the guns.

By the 20th Buller was able to stand on top of Monte Cristo, gazing at the country ahead through his telescope and watching his infantry, fifteen battalions of it, swarming forward far below. The Boers had fled back across the river rather than be trapped against it.

On the 21st came happy news for the relief force. Some of the Free Staters in the Boer ranks were hurrying westwards to help defend their country against Roberts' invasion, and the Boers were also evacuating some of their heavy-gun positions, presumably in order to pull them back for safety. This made it a simple task to take Hlangwane and to throw a pontoon across the river near Colenso, across which the major part of Buller's forces tramped the next day.

Among the first across the Tugela pontoon was Lieutenant James with the *Tartar*'s guns, who came under very heavy fire from what was assumed to be Botha's reguard. James himself had a close brush with danger at this point, when his horse was shot dead underneath him and he was lucky to escape unhurt.

All day long and well into the next Buller's forces marched and rolled and plodded over the pontoon under stubborn shelling from the forward kopjes. When the first 4.7, weighing nearly six tons, went to cross, the pontoon started to crack and the gun was hurriedly drawn back, but not before one ox had fallen into the swollen Tugela and was swept downstream towards the waterfalls. It plummeted over the falls, a drop of over thirty feet, but was rescued apparently unscathed. The bridge was clearly untrustworthy, so the oxen and mules had to be removed and the wagons dragged backwards from the steep donga leading down to the river. The guns themselves were taken from their carriages, placed on wagons and taken across, and the operation undertaken in piecemeal fashion. Nevertheless, the problem caused a twenty-four hour delay and it was not until dawn the next day that the Naval Brigade were all on the north bank.

All the time the Boers were frantically bringing up reinforcements. They had at least three 40-pounders, twelve 15-pounders and several other smaller guns, including some of Long's pieces which they had captured two and a half months before at Colenso.

Now the Naval Brigade was joined by Lieutenant Melville of HMS *Forte*, with two 12-pounders. A few bluejackets were wounded at this stage, although only two seriously, namely Able Seaman Helman, of Lieutenant England's 4.7 crew and Thomas Tunbridge, Captain Jones' coxswain, who was struck on the thigh by an unexploding shell which removed most of his leg.

Midshipman Hutchinson of the *Terrible* was especially lucky when no less than three shells burst within feet of where he was standing during the course of the action without causing the slighest of scratches.

Buller's plan to attack on the right flank under an artillery barrage had slipped, somehow, to the left into a central head-on infantry approach. He had intended to bypass Colenso altogether, yet now here he was, right in the middle of the place. If he maintained the course on which he was now set, with only Lieutenant Burne's guns, now at Colenso, plus the new 6-inch and Lieutenant Wilde's 12-pounders at Gun Hill to give them cover, he was heading for the same likely fate he would have suffered if he had not withdrawn at Vaal Krantz. The two roads from Colenso to Ladysmith were steeply terraced on both sides nearly all the way and, just as the balloonist had reported at Vaal Krantz, they were bristling with defenders. Indeed, what James and Melville had been facing was not a rearguard at all, but 5,000 burghers who were snugly ensconced behind the rocks and in the crevices of the first line of kopjes north of the river, waiting for the onslaught.

In a drive to bring the attack back on to its originally intended course, on the 23rd and 24th first General Wynne with the 11th Brigade and then the impatient General Hart with his 5th Brigade of Inniskillings, Connaughts, Dublin Fusiliers and Imperial Light Horse, advanced to try and bludgeon their way north-eastwards along the north bank of the Tugela, battling to take each kopje in turn, only to be cut to pieces by the Mauser rifles and Maxims trained on them from the looming slopes. Predictably, the butchery was fearful.

By the evening of the 24th, although Wynne had taken the first two hills and Hart was engaged on the slopes of the third, which was to become known as Hart's or Inniskilling Hill, the fighting had continued for two days, and darkness fell again. The fighting had been at such close quarters, and the toll of casualties had been so high on both sides, that the dead, dying and wounded were crammed together on the ground. All night long the agonized cries of the wounded rose from the slimy mud where they lay. When a truce was called the next day to bring in the dead and wounded the stretcher-bearers had difficulty in placing their feet between the bodies without treading on them as they picked their way among the prostrate forms, 'fallen like waxworks in strange attitudes', and peered into each staring pair of eyes to see whether any life remained.

Except for the reckless Hart, who had charged so far ahead with his Irish Brigade that they had been cut off and were still pinned down on his Hill, Buller now called his army back across the river. No wonder they dubbed him the Ferryman of the Tugela! He had now crossed and re-crossed it four times!

Over the next day and a half, the sappers worked at a desperate pace to dismantle the pontoon bridge just north of Colenso and move it further downstream to sit under the mouths of the massive artillery juggernaut of over eighty guns which had now gathered on the brows of Hlangwane and Monte Cristo. They were anxious to get the job finished, because the following day,

27 February, had a very special significance. *It was the anniversary of Majuba Hill!*

Ripples of excitement swept through the British ranks as the guns opened up with a deafening roar, which seemed as if it would shake South Africa to its very roots, at 7 am on the 27th, and Barton's Brigade, followed by Walter Kitchener's and Norcott's, tramped across the new pontoon to assault Pieter's Hill, Railway Hill and Terrace Hill respectively.

All day long the crashing thunder of the guns rolled, echoing and re-echoing against the kopjes, as Buller's new technique, the creeping barrage, practised so well the previous week, was now put into relentless effect. All day long the infantry charged into a curtain of exploding earth and rocks just ahead of them, only to see it lift in the nick of time and move another few yards further on, ready for them to charge it again. Here the khaki bull was charging not a gate, but a friendly matador's elusive cloak of lyddite, embroidered with shrapnel, which its horns were never quite to reach. All day long the brave Boer defenders danced and dodged from trench to trench, from boulder to boulder and from crevice to crevice, bobbing up to fire their Mausers at an advancing Tommy, bobbing down again to avoid some shrapnel, but nonetheless retreating all the while. All day long the Boers' big guns fired defiantly from the ridges of Grobelaar's Hill.

And all day long the Naval Brigade kept up a withering rate of fire; laying, loading, firing without pause, it seemed, for breath, as the sweating stokers bore shell after shell to the crews. In the background, adding its deep bass voice to the booming orchestra, came the periodic bark of the big 6-inch back on Gun Hill. But it was the 4.7s, according to George Crowe, who deserved most of the credit for flushing the Boer snipers from their hiding places. One of them, at 9,000 yards range, placed no less than three shells straight into a Boer gunpit in rapid succession, completely destroying the gun and killing its crew.

Captain Jones, describing the actions of the two 4.7s commanded by Lieutenant Anderton of the Natal Naval Volunteers, wrote:

Two 4.7 inch guns, with platform mountings, came across from Chieveley. We mounted one on a hill to the right of Hlangwane, just finishing by 5 am. I left the other till night, not wishing to do it in daylight, as we were only 2,300 yards from the enemy's highest position on the range. It was very heavy and tiresome work in the dark, and the glimmer of a lantern to the front always produced some sniping. On this, as on every other occasion, Baldwin, the senior Gunnery Instructor of HMS *Terrible*, showed himself to be an invaluable man ... During the night we mounted the other platform gun, finishing by 3 am. Sniping was worse than ever all night, when the Engineers rigged a sand-bag defence for them. I remained with these two guns during the fighting on that great day, 27th, and not

131

only saw every detail of the fight from relatively quite close to, but also the finest shooting from one of them that I have ever seen in my life.

Once mounted, and at the ranges at which they were required to fire, the platform has a great advantage over the wheeled mounting. Having once got the range, of course you can put as many shots in as you like, and as quick as you like. A man from the *Philomel*, Patrick Casham, was the captain of the gun, and a born shot.

At about 5 pm, with the infantry having taken Pieter's and Railway Hills, leaving only Terrace Hill to conquer, the British artillery ceased fire, as planned, except for the wheeled 4.7s of England and Hunt and Ogilvy's four 12-pounders, which continued to sweep the crests and beyond so as to harry the retreating Boers.

Inniskilling Hill still held the brave but foolhardy Hart and his Irishmen. They had worked their way upwards, leaving a grim trail of dead and wounded, until only the last ridge remained in Boer hands, and the Irish were not only pinned down again but in danger of being slaughtered by enfilading fire from their left. But the Lancashires were following up in support and a lyddite shell burst directly in the Boer trench. As soon as the smoke began to clear, the glinting bayonets of the Lancashires could be seen through the haze, charging upwards to carry the ridge.

At that the whole army, which had just received word of Cronje's surrender at Paardeberg, jumped to its feet as privates waved their helmets on their bayonets or simply threw them into the air. Generals slapped each other on the back and shook hands. Everybody seemed to realize at one fixed moment that victory was theirs.

According to J. B. Atkins of the *Manchester Guardian*: 'Cheer answered cheer, backwards and forwards across the river till all cheers came from the same cheer, and Staff officers forgot that they were not as ordinary officers and threw up their helmets and shook hands with one another.'

The last hour saw the Naval Brigade lay down some of the most accurate, intense and rapid fire from heavy guns that many had ever witnessed. Through the crackle and the roar could be heard Commander Limpus's calm and flat tones as he directed *Terrible*'s two 4.7s: 'England – up ten yards – right three. Hunt – down five yards – left two.'

One of Ogilvy's guns was clocked at 190 rounds in the final fifty minutes of the action, and the others were not far short of that rate. Small wonder that Lieutenant Burne was to say that he would be prepared to bet heavily on a Royal Navy gun's crew of 'handy men' to beat any crew in this world for all-round service and quick shooting. Here was the master of the creeping barrage in action. Ogilvy was landing his shells so close ahead of the advancing infantry that one watching senior army officer voiced his concern for their safety, and had to be reassured by Lieutenant Lees, the naval ADC who was 'spotting' the fall of shot, that the soldiers were in the safest hands.

Buller, in his dispatch dated 14 March, 1900, reported:

The fire of the naval guns here was particularly valuable, their shooting was admirable, and they were able to keep up fire with common shell long after the Royal Field Artillery were obliged to cease their shrapnel. Indeed, Lieutenant Ogilvy, of HM Ship *Terrible*, kept up fire on the largest sangars till the infantry were within fifteen yards of them. His guns must have saved us many casualties. No one who watched the operations can have the slightest doubt that artillery, co-operating with infantry in an attack on a prepared position, ought to have a considerable proportion of common shell.

At daybreak on the 28th it was apparent that most of the Boers had evacuated their positions during the night. All that was to be seen of them were the back of a few dusty wagons moving northwards, pursued by a stream of Lee-Metford rifle bullets from the West Yorkshires on the crest of Pieter's Hill.

Perhaps it was a mistake in that it added to the eventual length of the fighting, but Buller forbade any full-scale pursuit of Botha and his commandoes. His attitude was, as one correspondent put it, that his aim and objective was to reach Ladysmith and the least contact he had with any Boers on the way the better.

But it was now downhill all the way. The townspeople of Ladysmith were woken by the bark of Lambton's 4.7s and 12-pounders, now in full voice after many weeks of ammunition rationing, giving a gala performance of farewell to their erstwhile tormentors. They took a fiendish delight in having a final word with 'Long Tom' as the burghers on Bulwana raised a large wooden sheer-legs in preparation to move the big gun. Halsey's 4.7, on Cove Redoubt, hit it spot on, and the whole emplacement vanished behind a billow of smoke, to accompanying cheers from the onlooking soldiers.

By this time Halsey, who had celebrated his 28th birthday the previous day, was the only Royal Navy Lieutenant on his feet. Egerton and Stabb were dead, and Heneage, Hodges and Tyndale-Biscoe were all in hospital. With Captain Lambton himself not yet recovered from another bout of sickness, much extra responsibility fell on Halsey's shoulders. Indeed, it meant that he was often in command of the complete naval brigade and it was fortunate that, with all the sickness around him, he escaped its worst clutches, which he thought was due to his 'rattling good constitution'. His most serious bout of illness seems to have been the couple of days when he was forced to direct his guns from the depths of an armchair alongside the parapet of 'Princess Victoria', nursing a temperature of 102°.

With all these additional burdens to bear, it is not surprising that the patience even of the stalwart Halsey was becoming a little frayed. His superior officers, his brother Arthur and General Buller all came in for a broadside of uncharacteristic tetchiness. He wrote to his mother on 27 February, clearly totally unaware that Ladymith was about to be relieved, just after having taken lunch with General Hunter at Headquarters:

> They are still eating of the fat of the land, and he still has lager beer left. I had a bottle, the first drop of intoxicating liquor I'd had for weeks and weeks, and if I'd had a glass of wine on top I should have been quite muzzy I think, but that beer was good. I also had a cigarette, which he had got through by runner from Buller's Chief of Staff.
>
> I heliographed to A. [brother Arthur] to send me some smokes a fortnight ago, but they haven't turned up. I expect he jibs at the price of the runner, but if he could send me 5 lbs of Baccy, I could keep 1 lb and sell the rest for at least £5 a lb, and the runner would be only a fiver, if that, and letters that could be sent by him would be well worth that to me.
>
> No birthday presents yesterday, needless to say, but I know you all at home drank my health and thought about me.
>
> I never think now about when Buller is coming in, and don't expect him till I see him, as he has been so near and yet so far, so many times now.
>
> Love to Father and all from
> Your affectionate Son, Lionel.

In the early evening of the 28th Lord Dundonald, with Colonel Gough (whose brother was among the besieged) and a few mounted colonial troops from the Natal Carbineers and the Imperial Light Horse rode into the battered, now world-famous, tin-roofed little town, carefully in line, two abreast, so as to avoid any future dispute as to who had been the first to relieve it.

'Who are you?' inquired a picket. 'The Ladysmith Relief Force,' came the reply.

After 112 days Ladysmith had been relieved and Majuba Hill avenged. And then, as if by some preordained magic, there was another thunderstorm.

The Naval Brigade of the relieving force consisted of thirty-nine RN officers and 403 ratings, plus three officers and fifty ratings of the Natal Naval Volunteers. Between Colenso and Ladysmith they fired 4,000 rounds of 4.7 ammunition and 12,000 from the 12-pounders.

It was quite an eventful week for the Philomels down in Durban. The Ship's Log records that on Tuesday, 27 February, they dressed ship and cheered when news broke of Cronje's surrender at Paardeberg. Next day they dressed ship all over again and cheered to celebrate the Relief of Ladysmith.

And on that day, at Colenso, Staff Surgeon Lilly, HMS *Forte*, set off at 8 am to ride into Ladysmith, crossing the railway at Pieter's Station, and then on to join the now safe road up from Colenso. He had expected there to be some sullen residual opposition from the heavy Boer artillery, especially from 'Long Tom' on Bulwana, but there was nothing but an eerie silence as the Boers dragged their guns away to the north and the haven of the Biggarsberg Mountains.

Before departure on the ten-mile ride Lilly and the rest of the Naval Brigade had crammed their haversacks with whisky, tobacco and whatever other delicacies they could lay hands on, intending them for their long-lost comrades of the *Powerful*. But they had not realized that their route would take them through the hospital camp at Intombi and the sights of suffering that they saw there filled them with pity and horror. Even Lilly, a hardened medical man, was taken aback and allowed his haversack to be plundered of its contents long before they reached Ladysmith.

Drawing nearer to the town, they passed the spot where the Boers had repeatedly tried to dam the Klip River to cause flooding, which had provided Midshipman Carnegie with opportunities to practise his gunnery. The scarcity of ammunition had placed strong demands for accuracy on his part – not one shell could be wasted – and he had performed well to frustrate the Boers in their plan. It was estimated that no fewer than half a million sandbags had been used in the abortive construction, and, as Lilly rode past, he noted hundreds of spades, pickaxes and new bags scattered all around in a scene that told of the hurried departure of their owners.

As it happened, his professional eye was pleasantly surprised to find the Ladysmith Brigade in finer fettle than he had expected, and a very cordial day was spent with Lambton and the Powerfuls, with much back-slapping and laughter.

Of the sixteen officers and 267 ratings under Lambton's command, the casualty toll had been one officer killed, one died from disease and one wounded, plus five men killed, twenty-five dead from disease and four wounded. The Boers had proved to be less of a dangerous enemy than enteric fever, which was to claim another victim later, when the popular Fleet-Paymaster Kay died on the voyage home.

Lieutenant Burne, ordered back to Colenso by Buller on 27 February, was to stay there for another week after Ladysmith was relieved, as parties of Boers were reported to be roaming the countryside to the west. He and his Terribles must have been itching to get into the place that they had come so far to see and relieve, but his diary gives little indication of this:

Thursday – 1st March: Burne rides around Colenso, noting the roofless houses and general desolation, with everything smashed to pieces. The stench from the bodies of dozens of dead horses is unbearable. He notes how well the Boers had protected themselves with comfortable bomb-shelters dug into the rear elevation of the kopjes, and the trenches, over mile long, deep and sand-bagged, now full of empty cartridges and broken bottles and odd bits of abandoned personal belongings, some of which he collects as souvenirs. He concludes that the British shelling had done practically no damage at all to the trenches themselves.

Friday – 2nd March: It is very hot. He starts to feel ill, and is in agony with an attack of colic. His men give him hot tea and mustard and water, which makes him feel better.

Saturday – 3rd March: He still feels ill, spends all day resting under an ammunition wagon, but is 'much revived' by some champagne which his best bluejacket, House, gets for him from his friend, Major Brazier Creagh, at the hospital.

Thursday – 8th March: He draws his guns up to leave Colenso for Ladysmith at 5.30 am, accompanied by the 73rd Field Battery. Still feeling ill with dysentery, he cannot ride his horse and so gets onto a wagon. In Ladysmith Lambton's men have now departed and Burne finds Ogilvy and the Naval Brigade encamped at the convent.

Buller delayed his entrance to the town until 1 March. It seems that it was done with an absence of theatricals. White met him in the street, they shook hands and went back to Convent Ridge for a glass of the champagne that had been carefully hoarded for the occasion.

The grand ceremony took place three days later when Buller led his troops in a victory parade through the town. He rode down the long, straight, dusty main street at the head of the long, long column, with the Dublin Fusiliers in the place of honour immediately behind him, between the clapping, cheering rows of exultant people, black, white and brown faces, off-duty soldiers, Indian dhoolie-bearers, townsmen and women, Zulus, shopkeepers, children and gaunt but happy Devons who lined the route, many with faces awash with tears as they presented arms to the passing General, with bayonets gleaming in long ruler-straight lines.

But for all the glory of the occasion, the robust figures of the relievers showed sure signs of the hard fight they had undergone. Their uniforms were torn by weeks of clambering up and down rock-strewn kopjes, pushing through thickets of thorny mimosa, wading through drifts, marching for many miles and sleeping rough, sometimes on hard ground, sometimes in mud. Boer bullets had rent the tunics of many, and the toes of some could be seen through yawning boots. One or two had even discarded torn khaki trousers and donned replacements of blue or brown, presumably acquired from the body of a dead Boer somewhere on the veldt.

But the people didn't care. They just cried and laughed alternately. Young and old, men and women, boys and girls, all laughing, crying, dancing and crazily cheering at the same time. Here and there a hand would reach from the crowd to slap a Tommy on the back, and, overcome with joy, in between hugging each other, respectable ladies hugged the nearest dust-cake tunic. Flags waved. Bagpipes skirled. Drums thudded. Nobody who was there was ever going to forget this day for the rest of their lives.

General Sir George White rode forward, surrounded by his staff. Poor White had taken a large part of the blame for the siege at the outset. In sixteen weeks he seemed to have aged sixteen years. A far cry from the upright Scots Guard in his portrait, he was now stooped and hesitant, no doubt still suffering from the effects of the fever, as he trudged up the steps of the Town Hall to address the crowd that had assembled there. There must have been times when in the darkest days of the siege, as he promised the hungry children of Ladysmith 'lollies ere long', he had come to doubt his own words even as he said them.

But now all their privations were over. Forcing a wan smile, he told everybody that they had been fortunate in having the services of Colonel Ward, who had eked out their scant resources so miraculously that he could claim to be the best Supply Officer since Moses, but for all that he was dreadfully sorry that he had been forced to place them on such meagre rations.

'But,' he said, 'I promise that I shall never do so again.'

And far away in Simon's Bay the big 9.2s of HMS *Powerful* crashed and boomed out a Royal Salute.

CHAPTER 17

POWERFULS IN POMPEY AND WINDSOR

The mercy of the relief was to be short-lived for both White and Buller. Soon the knives were out for their reputations. Strangely, the rank and file of their forces and the public at large displayed a general affection and respect for both these senior officers which was not reflected among the upper echelons of the officers who had served with them. Rawlinson, Lyttelton and Hamilton all waged an anti-Buller crusade.

Lord Roberts, who was an old friend of White from their times in India, but held him responsible for the siege situations, now denied him any positions of real responsibility. All that was offered him was to remain in Natal in command of a division. This humiliation was mercifully curtained by another outbreak of fever which beset him and he was invalided home.

For all the euphoria in Ladysmith, it was still a dangerous spot, ridden with enteric fever. Throughout the siege it had killed 541 of the defending forces, which easily beat the total of 244 credited to the Boers. Of the naval brigade alone, the disease was to claim twenty-seven victims.

All the bed-ridden sick and wounded patients, including Lieutenant Heneage and eighteen men of the naval brigade, were sent down to Durban at the very earliest opportunity to drink in the clean seaside air, and the rest of the garrison was packed off to higher ground in accordance with usual summer practice. Some of the fever-sufferers were never to recover. It was a cruel fate, to have come through the siege only to die after its relief. *The Times* reported: 'The Admiralty announces that Stoker David Paton, 282960, of Her Majesty's Ship *Powerful*, died of enteric fever at Ladysmith, March 5.'

Lambton's brigade of Powerfuls did not linger long in Ladysmith after the arrival of the relief column. A few days in which to enjoy the now plentiful beer, jam, cake and several square meals with unlimited bread and potatoes, not forgetting the unmitigated breakfast bliss of Quaker Oats, and they were ready to depart.

Midshipman Sharp records that a Thanksgiving Service was held on 4 March, and they turned over their faithful 4.7s 'Lady Anne' and 'Princess Victoria', together with their remaining ammunition of only 42 rounds, plus the three 12-pounders to the Royal Artillery. [An account appeared in one of the newspapers which blamed Lambton's shortage of ammunition during the siege on Captain Percy Scott. Scott hastened to set the record straight, after the war, saying that he had suggested that Lambton be given 5,000 rounds of 4.7 ammunition, but was overruled by Admiral Harris, who would agree to only 500. Scott pointed out that, as a 4.7 could easily fire ten rounds a minute, this meagre ration could be expended by the two guns in less than half-an-hour's action, but to no avail. Seasoned arguer that he was, a trait that was to put him at frequent odds with his superiors for most of his career, Scott quoted Harris's orders from the official telegram book which clearly puts the blame on the Admiral.]

Then on 7 March the Powerfuls collected their mail – some people having over 100 letters to read – and their Christmas presents of pipes and tobacco, and those who were fit enough to travel set off for the station behind the pipes of the Gordon Highlanders. Buller was there with his staff, as well as a large crowd of assorted friends to see them off at 9.30 am.

They stopped at Intombi Hospital to pick up some walking invalids, but the track between there and Colenso was impassable because the bridge over the Tugela had been damaged in the fighting and that part of the journey had to be made by road. It took them all day to reach Colenso, ten miles away. Everywhere the roads were strewn with dead horses, mules and bits of shell case. At Colenso, where the vultures had long since picked the bones of Colonel Long's lost artillery horses clean and the summer sun had bleached them white, they rested for two hours until their train arrived.

Being still officially sick, Sharp was sent direct by train to join the transport SS *Columbian* at Durban for passage to Simon's Bay, where HMS *Powerful* waited to take them home, but the rest of the brigade were received at Durban station next day with great ceremony, and both officers and bluejackets were treated to a slap-up luncheon by Sir Percy Scott.

Lambton still being less than 100% fit, the duty of reply to all the congratulatory speeches fell to Lionel Halsey. He wrote a last letter to his mother, from aboard the *Columbian* dated 10 and 11 March, 1900:

The story of the Relief of Ladysmith is now a thing only to be remembered as a dream that, for the first 3 or 4 days, was hard to realise. It came as a real surprise to everyone on 28th February exactly 17 weeks after being invested – Arthur rode in from Melthorpe next day, much to my delight and surprise, and I saw him every day till we left the last Wednesday, but I have been so busy. . . . I am the sole officer left for duty and I had to

139

turn over all our big guns to the R.A. and I found the mustering of stores, spare parts etc., and the red tape and the paperwork perfectly awful. . . .

The Baccy I am appreciating, it is good, but the other things namely socks and Balaclava helmet, which Arthur said he had sent on, never fetched up – Cicely's wedding cake I have not devoured yet, but am going to today. . . . I hate these awful receptions and dread them, but I fear we are in for many more, but the Skipper is much better and won't be able to get out of many more I hope, I think he was rather mean to leave me in the lurch in Durban! Much to my astonishment, the banquet did not overcome any of our men – and they marched down the hill awfully well after it – I thought they would all be very intoxicated, not having tasted liquor for 5 months before. . . . Goodbye, I am so thankful to be clear of Ladysmith.

Believe me ever,
Your affectionate Son,
Lionel.

After their splendid lunch they marched through the town, headed by the band of the *Terrible* playing 'A Life on the Ocean Wave', to board the *Columbian*. The Tartars, back in harbour after a patrol up the coast to Delagoa Bay, had been given a 'make and mend' that afternoon, but were required to form a guard of honour as the Ladysmith Brigade arrived at the jetty. They sailed at 6 pm.

As the *Columbian* slid smoothly out of Durban towards the Indian Ocean, she passed a party of men under punishment breaking rocks with sledge-hammers on the harbour mole. Among them was a familiar face. It was the marine bandsman who had stolen Midshipman Sharp's suits in the *Terrible* nearly five months before.

Rejoining *Powerful* on 12 March, returning to earth as it were, one of Lambton's first tasks was to record in the ship's log that during the course of the Siege of Ladysmith he had lost a 6lb sledge-hammer, a five-eighths spanner, a one-gallon oil can, one bucket, ten shovels and three coal sacks.

At 3 o'clock on the afternoon of the 15th Rear-Admiral Harris came on board to inspect the naval brigade, and as soon as he had gone ashore Lambton weighed anchor and sailed for home, leaving behind two of his Ladysmith stalwarts, Lieutenant Hodges and Gunner Sims, in hospital at Simon's Bay. Sickness and tragedy were to overtake them again after a week at sea when Fleet-Paynmaster W. H. F. Kay, the popular father-figure and Mr Fix-it of the siege, died of enteric aged 52. They buried him on Ascension Island, where they dropped anchor on 26 March.

If the relief of Kimberley had caused excitement among the British public, the relief of Ladysmith, subject of the blood-and-guts glamour piece of the three sieges, can be said to have been a source of unmitigated joy, and the homecoming of the saviours of the town was awaited eagerly. *The Times* reported: 'The First Lord of the Admiralty will pay an unofficial visit to Portsmouth in order to be present at the arrival of the *Powerful*, cruiser, Captain the Hon. H. Lambton. It is understood that the vessel is steaming at only twelve-and-a-half knots, which will enable her to reach Portsmouth about Easter.'

Pausing at Las Palmas for coal, she steamed into Portsmouth Habour on 11 April. The scenes of welcome were unprecedented in their patriotic emotion as she secured to the South Railway Jetty that afternoon at 4.15. Tugs whistled, hooters blasted, and of course the air was full of cheers and waving flags.

Nelson's *Victory*, still afloat in those days, was dressed overall. A hundred years before she had been one of the biggest warships in the world. Now she was dwarfed by the four huge grey funnels as *Powerful* slid past, and can be seen in a photograph to be nodding her lofty wooden masts towards the young giant on a convenient roll from the gentle bow-wave.

Next day Lambton gave eleven days' special leave to the Naval Brigade, discharged eight more men to hospital, eleven for court martial and twenty-five whose 'time had expired'. The special leave gave a welcome opportunity to see families and sweethearts. Their menfolk had been at the centre of world attention for over five months, and now Maudie, Clara and Ethel, in London, Birmingham and Pompey, wanted to have a word or two with them in private. No doubt the eleven days flew away in a trice and when they returned for duty, leaving at home the Chinese silk, Japanese fans, carved elephants and chopsticks, the Powerfuls found that a tremendous round of pomp and ceremony was about to begin which was to put them, yet again, in the limelight. So much so, in fact, that some commentators took the view that the men were being used as circus performers in a way which was scarcely fair after their ordeal.

Back at Portsmouth, Lambton found a telegram from Copenhagen, signed by Alexandra, Princess of Wales, who was only a few months away from becoming Queen of England:

> My heartfelt welcome to you on your return from your heroic defence of Ladysmith. Pray also convey my warmest wishes to the officers and men of the *Powerful* who so gallantly and bravely supported you in your grand and noble work. Long live the handy man! Hope all well on board.
> Alexandra.

The *Powerful*'s homecoming had certainly taken a grip on the public imagination, especially and naturally in Portsmouth. That it was momentous enough to close streets, railway stations and, astonishingly, even H. M. Dockyard itself, could be seen when it was announced on Tuesday, 24 April:

In order that dockyard workmen may have the opportunity of witnessing today's demonstration, the establishment will be closed at 4.30 this afternoon, and to avoid any confusion inside the dockyard during the muster of the brigade the yard will be closed to visitors at noon. Traffic in the vicinity of the Town Hall, where the dinner is to be held, will be stopped at 4.45, and later on Portsmouth Town Railway Station will be closed to in-coming and out-going passengers.... The Lord Lieutenant and the Mayor will drive with Captain the Hon. H. Lambton to the Town Hall. The Naval Brigade, under the command of Lieutenant L. Halsey, will leave the dockyard at 5.45 and march through Queen Street, Edinburgh Road, and part of Commercial Road to the Town Hall. The thoroughfares to be traversed are decorated with unprecedented profusion, and every window on the line of route has been appropriated. The whole of the troops in garrison will line the roads, and at the square in front of the Town Hall, there will be an inner line of boys from the training ship *St Vincent*. Soon after 6 the Mayor will arrive at the Town Hall, where he will be met by the Corporation, and will welcome the Naval Brigade. It is expected that the dinner will be over about 9 o'clock, and the Brigade wil then return to the dockyard, taking such a route as will enable them to pass the Seamen and Marines Orphan Home. The procession will be headed by three local Volunteer Bands and 100 torch-bearers. Special arrangements have been made by the Railway Companies for visitors to leave the town.

On the evening of 30 April the whole crew of *Powerful* was entertained at a smoking concert by Mr Pink, Mayor of Portsmouth, again at the Town Hall. If a contemporary painting of the occasion is anything like accurate, it must have been a riotous event. The bluejackets at the long tables are clutching their glasses in horny fists held high above their heads and cheering each other to the rafters, whilst the distinguished members of the top table, resplendent in the evening dress of the period, are standing stiffly and solemnly, trying, it would appear, to hear the words of the toastmaster above the din.

The high point of the welcome-home festivities was the inspection of the naval brigade by Queen Victoria at Windsor Castle which was scheduled for 2 May. The only one of Lambton's Lieutenants not to be present was Hodges, still laid low in his bed. Heneage, Gunner Sims and even young Midshipman Chichester were all back on duty, the latter having written to his mother from Cape Town on 21 March that he was recovering well and had been out rook-shooting before boarding the liner *Orotava* to come home.

Also joining the Ladysmith Brigade for the presentation to the Queen were Major Urmston, who had commanded the Royal Marine detachment on the Kimberley front, Lieutenant Jones, RM, who had been wounded at Graspan,

Lieutenant Briscoe, a retired officer of the Royal Marine Artillery who had volunteered his services to Lambton in Ladysmith, and Ogilvy, now a Commander, who had been promoted out of the *Terrible* for his distinguished services.

All through the previous day Lambton had the Brigade practising their drill alongside *Powerful* on the South Railway Jetty, ready to put on a perfect performance in front of the Queen. Dawn arrived on the big day and a special train was sent into the dockyard, on to which the twenty-two officers and 286 men walked directly from the ship, unobserved by the public.

In Windsor the *Times* special correspondent described the scene:

Longer ago than I would willingly computate with precision it was my lot, in the most humble of military capacities conceivable – that is to say, as a schoolboy cadet keeping the streets – to be a witness of the arrival of fighting men returned from a campaign in foreign parts. They were the 60th, returned from Ashanti, and they looked ragged, dirty, yellow, sallow and altogether miserable. It was, therefore, entirely without any anticipation of pleasure that I came to Windsor this morning; and the feeling that the spectacle might very lightly be a painful one was accentuated and even exacerbated by things heard. It was said, even by men who ought to know, that the men were worn to a shadow; that the triumphal progress projected for them through Windsor today and through London next week was in the nature of a mistake; that they were, so to speak, being butchered to make an English holiday. But the plain fact, when it came before one, was in diametrical opposition to what had been said. The greater part of the spectators who watched the Naval Brigade detrain at Windsor today united in confessing that they wished they felt half as well and half as strong as the bluejackets looked, and there can be no question about it that no spectator enjoyed the day's proceedings half as much as the men whom the crowd had collected to honour.

Let an effort now be made to convey an impression of the scenes which have taken place here today. Imagine first Windsor ablaze with summer-like sunshine, with flags flying everywhere, with crowds assembled from many quarters and composed very largely of ladies in the brightest of summer dresses at every place where there seemed to be a chance of seeing anything. Through those crowds, and from the Great Western Station, drives the Duke of York with Sir Charles Cust, as yet in plain clothes. The crowds grow thicker. The morning wears on. It is time to go to the South-Western Station. Here is the band of the Grenadier Guards, under Mr A. Williams, and here is the Major, Mr Barber, with a huge bouquet, composed for the most part of orchids, which is intended that Captain Lambton shall carry away with him and present to the Queen in due

143

course. Outside is the expectant crowd, and outside also are one or two Royal carriages ready to take distinguished visitors up to the Castle. Then, up into the station glides the gaily decorated engine, on the front of which is the design of a gun roughly outlined and the legend 'Welcome to the Heroes of Ladysmith'. Then the Grenadier band strikes up 'Rule Britannia', and there is a brief interchange of civilities between Captain the Hon. Hedworth Lambton and the Mayor – that is to say, the Mayor welcomes Captain Lambton in his own name and in that of the Corporation of the Royal Borough, and Captain Lambton acknowledges his kindness, adding that it is seldom that a Naval contingent has the honour of being received at Windsor, and the bouquet is offered but not accepted. After all, the idea of a Naval Oficer in full dress marching up the streets of Windsor with a fountain bouquet in his hand is inconceivable. Far better is the bouquet with the Mayor in a brougham, and it is no more seen, or, if it is seen, it is no more noticed.

Then the men, bluejackets and marines, red and blue, detrain with their guns; and they are a revelation. One had sympathized before with these 300 poor fellows, some from Graspan but most from Ladysmith, who were being made into a spectacle. But their appearance speaks volumes either for the health-giving properties of the South Africa climate or for the intervening sea voyage, for – again by universal consent – they are as healthy and stalwart a body of men as ever were seen; not over-burdened with flesh, but fit to fight again tomorrow. They have their guns with them too, a 12-pounder painted in khaki, and a couple of Maxims, of which the shields are pitted with bullet-marks. So, amid loud cheers, they rolled rather than marched, with rifles at the trail some of them, and others hauling their 12-pounder or their Maxim as the case might be, up the hill towards the Castle. And it was a lovely spectacle. In the background are the towers of Windsor, with the Royal Standard streaming on the breeze and in the sun; below is the steep acclivity of the street thickly lined on either side, and there are shouts that one almost seems to see, and in the middle are the sailors dragging their gun as cheerily as if it were Jubilee Day. And all the while in front of them the band of the Grenadiers plays first 'A Life on the Ocean Wave' and next 'They All Love Jack'. And they all do; at least they all look like it, and shout as if they did. All the way up the hill and along the High Street and up to the turning into Long Walk the story is the same. It is one long and grand acclaim, one blaze of colour, one flutter of handkerchiefs and of flags.

Inside the Castle the proceedings are more formal, but not less significant. The group which the Naval Brigade encounters there includes Mr Goschen, Lord and Lady George Hamilton, who look upon a son, a

Midshipman, in the entering Brigade; Viscount Carson, M.P., the Earl of Kintore, Admiral Sir Michael Culme-Seymour, and last, but by no means least, Sir George White, in full uniform and wearing the Grand Cross of the Royal Victorian Order, and Lady White. The brigade comes in through the George IV Gate, turns to the right and lines up. Then the Duke of York, in his naval uniform and wearing the Order of the Garter, and Prince Louis of Battenberg, in his naval uniform and wearing the Order of the Bath, walk up to the officers and there is a short conversation, and at last, at 25 minutes past 12, comes the climax.

From the private entrance appears a carriage and pair conveying the Queen, who is looking wonderfully well. With her are Princess Christian and Princess Henry of Battenberg. Behind the carriage walk the Duke of York, Admiral Sir Michael Culme-Seymour, and his staff captain, and the Equerries in Waiting, Colonel Legge and Captain Ponsonby, and then comes a second carriage conveying Princess Victoria of Schleswig-Holstein and Princess Louis of Battenberg. The Royal salute is given, the band plays 'God save the Queen', the inspection begins, the carriage goes very slowly and deliberately, and the Queen clearly takes the greatest interest in the proceedings. A march past follows, and an advance in review order, and then Captain Lambton calls for three cheers, which are given, and given indeed. The great quadrangle rings to the echo.

Next the officers are presented, and they form a cluster round the carriage. To them, the Queen says, 'I wish you all heartily welcome on your return home after the great trials you have so nobly borne, and I thank you warmly for the great services you have rendered to your Queen and the Empire.' And Captain Lambton, in a voice to which at any rate Ladysmith has done no sort of harm, answers that he does not consider that the Naval Brigade has done anything very wonderful at Ladysmith, and that what they have done is nothing to what they are prepared to do at any time for the Queen. So, the dramatic part of the scene is almost over save that, before the men are dismissed, the Earl of Kintore presents Mr Lawrence, M.P. for Kimberley, and his wife and his two sons, who had all been there during the siege. Of the sons, indeed, one had fought. Then the sailors and Marines march out in fours and the Queen causes her carriage to be stopped to take one last look at them, and that is the end.

It is the end, that is to say, of things seen, the end of a series of very stirring spectacles. Afterwards the men were entertained in the Castle riding-school at a substantial dinner, and drank the Queen's health in port from the Queen's cellars, and were presented with cigars, and the officers lunched with the Household. And then, a few minutes after 4, with little

Union Jacks, which they had taken from the table, in their straw hats, the bluejackets swung down the hill again and into the train, and off to Portsmouth.

The Queen drove soon after the inspection to the riding-school where the seamen and Marines were being entertained at dinner, and when the sailors and Marines saw her Majesty, who did not alight, through the open door, they rose immediately from their seats and cheered.

Midshipman Sharp had been the youngest and most junior officer present. He was therefore the last to be presented and stood quite close to the Queen while waiting his turn. Recalling the experience, in the mid-1960s at over eighty years of age, he said that for the rest of his life he had always remembered her voice very clearly. Indeed, in those days of pre-radio, he was one of the few commoners to have heard it.

But it was not all over for the Powerfuls. Five days later, on 7 May, they had to haul their guns again, this time through the streets of London after being inspected on Horse Guards Parade. Already it was a sell-out. The Admiralty announced, nearly a week beforehand, that all seats in the stand on Horse Guards, price five shillings (25p), had been sold and that no more were available.

They arrived at Victoria Station at 10.45 am and marched to the Admiralty by way of Victoria Street and Whitehall. After the inspection the First Lord of the Admiralty entertained Lambton and the officers to luncheon at his residence, while the sailors and Marines took dinner in the new Admiralty building.

Then, at 3.30, they set off again, rolling their 12-pounder and the bullet-pitted Maxims past the stony one-eyed stare of Nelson himself in Trafalgar Square, down Northumberland Avenue to the Embankment, along to Black-friars Bridge and Queen Victoria Street and into the City, the streets lined all the way with the, by now, familiar crowds waving and cheering from the pavements, upstairs windows and any other convenient vantage point.

At the Royal Exchange they paused for refreshments kindly provided by Lloyds of London, who also presented the officers with cigarette cases and the men with tobacco boxes. Then it was down King William Street and over London Bridge to the station, to where their special train had steamed round from Victoria to take them them back to Portsmouth.

Lieutenant Hodges, whom Lambton had left in hospital in South Africa, just failed to make it home in time for the presentation to the Queen and the triumphant marches through Windsor and London. His home town was Dorchester, and when he arrived there on the evening of 10 May, he found the town was *en fête* in his honour. He was chaired through the flag-decorated streets, amid rowdy throngs of inhabitants of that usually quiet town, to the municipal building, all to the accompaniment of incessant pealing of the church bells. The Mayor of Dorchester presented him with a bouquet. Unfortunately it is not recorded whether, unlike Lambton at Windsor, he deigned to accept it.

CHAPTER 18

THE OTHERS

HMS *Terrible*, of course, still had to keep her appointment on the China Station, and her men with the Natal Brigade were recalled to rejoin her. They departed from Ladysmith on 11 March, leaving the Fortes, Philomels and Tartars, under Captain Jones, with two 4.7s and four 12-pounders, to continue the pursuit of the Boers with Buller's forces.

Lieutenant Burne of the *Philomel*, still very groggy with dysentery and feeling unsafe to ride his horse, rode into Ladysmith in a wagon on 8 March. There he was heartened to have read to him the telegram from Queen Victoria: 'Pray express my deep appreciation to the Naval Brigade for the valuable service they have rendered with their guns.' But his condition worsened and he was forced to go into the Field Hospital. To add to his unhappiness, he learned that he was to lose his Terribles: 'To add to my sorrow all my good men of the *Terrible* are starting off to rejoin their ship. I feel it to be a great blow, after all my trouble and training, that my *Terrible* bluejackets are to go. Good fellows.'

Buller was at the station to see them off on the special train. 'Good-bye, Terribles, and good luck to you all – hope you have a pleasant commission in China,' he called as they slowly steamed out of Ladysmith.

It took eighteen hours for the train to reach Durban on the congested line, where everything was urgent and everybody was trying to go everywhere at once in the aftermath of the siege. There they were rejoined by their colleagues from the Zululand expedition. The townspeople gave them an uproarious reception, entertaining them at a sumptuous noonday banquet calculated to leave them with happy memories of the town.

In his capacity as Town Commandant, however, Scott, was unable to leave until his replacement, Colonel Morris, arrived, therefore it was not until the 27th that *Terrible* at last weighed anchor and proceeded on her way to China.

Ogilvy, promoted to Commander for his distinguished services in the field, had returned to England to take up another appointment. Assistant Engineer

Roskruge had been invalided home. Midshipmen Hodson and Boldero had been left in hospital, as were eighteen bluejackets. Midshipmen Sharp and Chichester had transferred to *Powerful*, although the latter was still in hospital. And four men had lost their lives.

Terrible seems to have made her way across the Indian Ocean in a fairly leisurely fashion, taking a month to reach Singapore via Mauritius and Colombo. Enteric fever still pursued the Terribles of the Natal Brigade across the Indian Ocean. The Secretary of the Admiralty announced, 'the death of Able Seaman George Lewin Gould, 176069, of enteric, on board her Majesty's ship *Terrible*, at Singapore on May 2.'

Singapore gave them a wonderful eastern welcome. On 29 April *The Times* reported that: 'Her Majesty's cruiser *Terrible* arrived here on Friday. A luncheon was given today to the Captain and Officers. Tomorrow afternoon 400 seamen will land and be publicly entertained at dinner in the drill hall. Afterwards they will march to the theatre, where a company of amateurs who have recently produced a comedy in the town will repeat the performance for the men of the *Terrible*. Singapore is brilliantly decorated.'

And on 2 May, the same day that Lambton's men were hauling their 12-pounder through the streets of Windsor, on their way to the Castle, 'The *Terrible*, cruiser, Captain P. M. Scott, C. B., will leave at daylight tomorrow. The Marine Club is sending off biscuits and other delicacies, and half a pound of cavendish tobacco for every man of the crew.'

It was a five-day steam to her new home of Hong Kong and, now world-famous, she was given a predictably vociferous reception at the 'Gibraltar' of the Far East. Cheers were raised on all hands for Captain Scott, his officers and crew, accompanied by the waving of handkerchiefs, the tooting of whistles and the firing of crackers. The *Terrible* steamed majestically ahead, and two long lines of launches closed in and accompanied her to her buoy. At the Kowloon Dock the crew of HMS *Orlando* were assembled. This was the ship that Midshipman Sharp, ex-Ladysmith Siege, now home in England, was originally supposed to have joined, and as the *Terrible* steamed by they raised a cheer which for the moment drowned even the tooting of the launches and the banging of the crackers.

Hong Kong was in party mood. The festivities, with receptions, banquets in the City Hall, smoking concerts and general merry-making, went on for four days.

Soon the *Terrible*'s guns were to go ashore again, this time to deal with the trouble in North China when Peking, came under siege. Several members of her South African naval brigade were soon to find themselves doing it all over again.

Kimberley and Ladysmith had been relieved, but, amid all the euphoria, many had tended to forget that there was indeed another story, or rather the continuation of the same story, still going on in South Africa. A writer to *The Times* gently reminded the public of this:

The British public are justly very proud of the doings of the Naval Brigade that lately returned from South Africa, but the large majority of the people in England do not know there is a still larger Naval Brigade on shore in South Africa with Lord Roberts' force, composed principally of officers, seamen and marines from the flagship *Doris* and the *Monarch*; most of whom have been over six months on shore, and fought at Belmont, Graspan, Modder River, Paardeberg, and all the operations under Lord Roberts since Cronje's surrender. Their 4.7 inch guns ('Joe Chamberlain' among them) enabled Lord Methuen to hold the Modder River, just as the *Powerful*'s guns kept the Boers in check at Ladysmith. They took part in the celebrated march from Poplar Grove to Bloemfontein, guns and all, 64 miles in 73 hours, and the equally creditable march to Kroonstad since. Their losses have been very heavy, those among officers being Captain Prothero R.N., and Lieutenant Jones, R.M.L.I., wounded; Major Plumbe, R.M.L.I., Captain Senior, R.M.A., and Midshipman Huddart, killed. Three midshipmen died of enteric fever, two were invalided from the same cause, and one with dysentery – 7 out of the 123 midshipmen landed. The men have also lost heavily in proportion; in fact more so than any of the other Naval Brigades in South Africa, and they still have much hard work before them before entering Pretoria with Lord Roberts. There is also a Naval Brigade with Sir R. Buller.

CHAPTER 19

THAT OLD PIG AT BLOEMFONTEIN

The surrender of Cronje at Paardeberg had been a major step forward for Roberts, but there still remained much to be done, as the writer was correct to point out. First, there was Christiaan de Wet, the bold and elusive Boer-pimpernel, the arch exponent of a guerrilla-style rearguard action, to catch.

The Boers had polluted the water in the Modder with dozens of dead horses and mules before retreating towards Bloemfontein. The stench of their decomposing carcasses had become overpowering in the windless late summer heat, so water being a necessity, Roberts moved his forces five miles upstream. It was his good fortune that this move took him in the direction which he wished ultimately to follow, i.e., nearer to Bloemfontein. The information feeding back from his scouts was that the Boers had retired to a ready-prepared line of defence in the kopjes before the Orange Free State capital, on a front of about ten miles, at a place called Poplar Grove.

One commodity that the British did not lack, and which de Wet had not laid hands on at Waterval Drift, was ammunition. Wagon after wagon trundled into the new camp, laden with lyddite, cordite and black powder, just as a series of electric storms hit the area. There was much concern as to the consequences if any of the wagons were to be struck by lightning, which hurled great jagged bolts at the landscape all around, but there was nothing to be done about it except to keep the wagons spaced apart and to pray. Luckily, no such catastrophe arose.

On 5 March Grant's Guns were ordered forward to mount an isolated kopje about 7,000 yards from where the scouts had spotted the Boers' gun emplacements on what was christened One Tree Hill. It was difficult terrain up which to haul the heavy guns, and first of all, taking care to keep well down out of sight of the Boer lookouts, the sailors had to spend the whole day rolling big boulders to one side and smaller ones into the potholes so as to make a passable track up the near side of the hill. By evening, with every man heaving on the drag-ropes or manning the spokes of the wheels, they had taken 'Little Bobs' and 'Sloper' up to a level just below the crest so as to leave them out of sight until morning.

Next day, at 4 am, the guns' crew fell in, ran the two 4.7s into position and sent an opening shot crashing through the dawn silence. It landed about halfway up One Tree Hill and received absolutely no response at all from the Boer gunners. Lord Roberts himself was standing nearby, watching the fall of shot, and personally directed the next few salvoes. One of the shells landed in the middle of a colony of anthills, throwing up great fountains of earth, whereupon no less than 200 Boers emerged from their foxholes, which had been set, evidently, among the anthills, and scampered away beyond the ridge, followed by bursts of 4.7" shrapnel fire.

As they fled the Boers came into the range of Bearcroft's 12-pounders on the other side of the Modder. These had been moved into a forward position and now shelled them with lyddite. This did bring a reply from the Boer artillery, in the shape of a large Krupp gun which until now had maintained silence from its hidden emplacement on One Tree Hill. The 12-pounders had been caught in the open, and now another Krupp opened fire on them from the other flank, catching them in a fierce crossfire.

Grant's guns turned their attention to the Krupps, in defence of the 12-pounders, which also replied to the Boers' fire with all the venom they could muster. The Boer gunners, severely outnumbered, fought bravely all day to cover the withdrawal of their transport wagons, but both their gunnery and their ammunition were poor that day, and eventually they were forced to abandon their guns and retire.

The Battle of Poplar Grove, if indeed it could be called a battle, had been almost bloodless, although it was an undoubted victory for the British, forcing the Boers to retreat further and capturing their two Krupp guns.

The fighting had taken place about twelve miles from Poplar Grove itself and the column was marched there to rest for two days. It was a long, hot, eight-hour slog to haul the guns into town. The wheels sank into the soft red sand, both men and oxen were distressed by the ferocious heat, and they had all been on their feet since 4 am. They arrived exhausted and hungry, dining on tinned sardines and biscuits with scrapings of jam, washed down with generous draughts of the sweet Poplar Grove well water, before sinking to the ground to sleep.

Four more officers, all from HMS *Doris*, arrived from Cape Town to reinforce the Naval Brigade at Poplar Grove. They were Major S. D. Peile and Lieutenant A. H. French, both of the Royal Marines Light Infantry, and two Midshipmen. The first of these was Lionel Lloyd, who succumbed to enteric fever almost as soon as he arrived. He was sent back to Kimberley, where he died on 28 April.

The other was to become famous in later life, commanding the British Mediterranean Fleet, over forty years later, in the Second World War, becoming Chief of the Naval Staff, and eventually First Sea Lord. He was Andrew Browne Cunningham – ABC.

In May, 1898, as a shilling a day cadet (in addition to which his parents were required to pay the Admiralty £4 3s 4d per month), Cunningham had taken passage from Southampton to Cape Town in the same mail steamer as Admiral Harris and his flag captain, the bearded giant Captain Reginald Prothero, all on their way to take up their new appointments on the Cape of Good Hope Station, also Cecil Rhodes, whom Cunningham managed to defeat in the final of a shipboard chess tournament. However, he was gracious enough to admit that the millionaire appeared to have dined well before playing the match.

Cunningham found Prothero an intimidating character, with his gruff manner and big black beard, but nonetheless, following his rating as midshipman within a few weeks of joining the *Doris*, and a resultant 9d per day increase in pay, his Captain saw fit to certify that he had conducted himself 'with sobriety and attention to his duties', in the required phraseology of the time.

Prothero certainly put his midshipmen through some tough training. Often he would wait for a strong south-east gale to blow up off the Cape before ordering them into the ship's cutters for sailing drill. So it may have been somewhat of a relief when, in October, 1899, Prothero himself joined the other members of the *Doris's* ship's company to go ashore with the naval brigade for the advance on Kimberley, as did Major Plumbe of the Royal Marines, Midshipman Huddart, and eventually Commander Grant, of Grant's Guns.

On the other hand Cunningham was itching to get ashore himself, and up to the front with the guns, and the time he spent kicking his heels aboard the *Doris*, even in the absence of Prothero, became a source of frustration. In a letter to his mother, he complains that another midshipman, younger than himself, had been selected to go.

At Graspan, it will be remembered, Plumbe and Huddart had both been killed, along with Commander Ethelston of the *Powerful*, and Prothero himself had been wounded. These losses were to provide Cunningham with the opportunity he craved. Plumbe's replacement was the easygoing Major Peile, just out from England, and just before the Royal Marine officer was due to go ashore to join Bearcroft's brigade, Cunningham managed to persuade him to agree to take him along as his ADC. There remained the problem of official permission to leave *Doris*. There was no time to put his request through the usual channels in accordance with service etiquette as Peile was due to depart in a couple of hours. Plucking up courage, and bluffing his way past the sentry, Cunningham went to Prothero's cabin. The Captain, just out of hospital and still recovering from his wound, was asleep in his armchair. Cunningham, startled by his own bravery, made a noise to awaken him. For this the boy received a fierce glare, but managed to stammer out what he wanted.

'Wait outside,' grated Prothero, and when Cunningham was summoned back by the sentry, the Captain handed him a note to give to the Admiral's secretary.

Cunningham always said thereafter that the bravest thing he ever did in his life was to beard Prothero the Bad in his lair! But the result was that he boarded the train that day at five o'clock with Major Peile, Lieutenant French and Midshipman Lloyd, wearing the white uniform that he had carefully dyed with coffee to give a close resemblance to khaki, and, after a journey of several days by train and ox-wagon, they caught up with the naval brigade at Poplar Grove the day after the battle.

Then followed the long chase of the Boers. Some of the most gruelling stints of the whole campaign were about to be demanded of Bearcroft's crews. Roberts, still maintaining his reputation for speed, did not intend to give the enemy time to catch their breath now that he had them on the run, and the pace was hectic. Marching only in the cool of the evening and through the night and snatching only a few hours sleep during the middle of the day, the naval brigade and their guns made thirty-four miles in the first twenty-six hours.

Cunningham was lucky to be given a stray horse that had been caught roaming loose on the veldt, which saved him much fatigue, but it was blind in one eye and therefore had to be steered on a course 90 degrees from the desired direction of travel. He was not much of a horseman, however, and indeed it was not much of a horse, being sick with glanders to boot, and the two soon parted company.

The Army started off again in pursuit of De Wet at sunrise on 10 March. All day long they tramped out of Poplar Grove and it was not until 3 pm that the Naval Brigade took up their usual position behind the 9th Division at the rear of the column, save only for the 6-inch howitzer battieres, ammunition, baggage and ambulance wagons. Already they were beginning to feel the effects of the loss of so much food in the supply wagons captured by de Wet and had been placed on reduced rations. It was beautiful cattle country, however, and the oxen, horses and mules ate very well on the plentiful lush green grass along the way.

It was a sparsely populated district. Indeed many farmers had gone south as refugees. It was not until evening came and darkness fell that they passed the first inhabited farm. The house had lights in the windows and curtains that twitched as the inhabitants looked out, apprehensively, to see what was going on and, more particularly, to see to which side the thousands of thudding feet belonged. They halted at 10 pm to snatch some sleep until 2 am, when they moved off again. It was a treacherously bad road on which to take heavy guns in pitch darkness and they were glad when the camp-fires of the 9th Division came into view, just before dawn, at Driefontein Dam.

They were only allowed a rest of four hours before setting out again because it had been rumoured that the Boers had brought up some 'Long Toms' just ahead of Roberts' advanced troops. This meant that it was vital to get the long-range guns into place in order to deal with the menace. But they did not see a single Boer all day and arrived at Doornboom in the late afternoon, where Roberts had amassed about 18,000 British troops.

Monday, 12 March brought the usual dawn start, with miles of mules and ox-drawn wagons, tramping men and officers on horses moving out of camp and the naval brigade falling in near the back of the column.

By now some of the infantry were looking bedraggled, which was not surprising considering that many had fought and trudged their way from as far back as Belmont, now nearly four months ago and many miles behind them. Surgeon Jeans, of HMS *Monarch*, wrote in his diary:

> Their clothes in rags and their boots worn out, the soles tied on with string, and some even walking with their puttees wrapped round their feet, they went limping by. Their faces were black with the sun and sand, bearded and parched; their lips were swollen cracked and bleeding; their eyes were bloodshot, but their heads were held high, and they had that grim determined expression which success, and the knowledge of their power and strength alone could bring, and carry them, with empty stomachs, through the terrible marches under the burning sun by day, and those as terrible bivouacs in the rain and cold by night.

By the time they reached Venter's Vlei, about twenty miles from Bloemfontein, more and more divisions had joined Roberts' force, so that now it numbered about 30,000. News came through that the town had been evacuated and that French's cavalry had cut the railway both north and south of it. To do this French had had to race ahead across the veldt on the poor horses he had borrowed from the Diamond Fields Artillery back in Kimberley. The hard riding had broken many of them, bringing collapse and even death from exhaustion.

It was at about this point that Jeans noticed a peculiar difference between the Army and the Navy technique when on the march. The Royal Artillery soldiers would march, all in step, with military precision beside their guns, leaving the driving to the Africans, it being no business of theirs. But Jack, by now, had learned from the drivers how to drive oxen, using whips and imitating the strange African sounds for orders to stop, start or turn, and so on. In return, Jack had taught the drivers many naval expletives, most of which are not even understood by non-naval British people. The drivers had become quite fluent and the air was thick as they exercised their extensive but salty vocabulary. The funny part was that they seemed never to be able to master the skill in arranging the various adjectives in the right order, which sounded quaint to an officer accustomed to hearing it done properly by the members of *Monarch*'s lower deck.

They had done a lot of chasing, but very little fighting, by the time they reached Ferreira Siding, only four miles from Bloemfontein, and Jack was finding it frustrating. But here was a large deserted farm, and a mass foraging expedition after dark brought a bumper harvest of potatoes, tomatoes, mealies and huge pumpkins. These were practically the first fresh vegetables that many of them had tasted for six weeks, and they all slept with full stomachs that night.

All day long they had swept to the south of the Modder, which had the effect of turning the Boer flank of entrenched defences to the north-east, forcing de Wet to retreat yet again. In fact, unbeknown to the British, he had done more than just retreat. Up in the kopjes he had gathered his commanders around him and ordered them to grant their men ten days' leave!

The way into Bloemfontein was now open, thankfully at the price of very little spilled blood. The following telegram was received at the War Office in London at 7.30 pm, 14 March:

Bloemfontein, March 13, 8 pm.

'By the help of God, and by the bravery of her Majesty's soldiers, the troops under my command have taken possession of Bloemfontein.

The British flag now flies over the Presidency, vacated last evening by Mr Steyn, late President of the Orange Free State.

Mr Fraser, member of the late executive Government, the Mayor, the Secretary to the late Government, the Landdrost, and other officials, met me two miles from the town and presented me with the keys of the public office.

The enemy have withdrawn from the neighbourhood and all seems quiet.

The inhabitants of Bloemfontein gave the troops a cordial welcome.

Roberts.

The Times correspondent wired his report to London:

The Free State, in spite of urgent representations from the Transvaal, decided yesterday to surrender the capital, Mr Steyn leaving secretly at 6.30 for Kroonstad, the new seat of Government, via Winburg, without replying to Lord Roberts' demand for surrneder within twenty-four hours.

The keys were given up four miles out at 11 o'clock today.

Lord Roberts, heading a cavalcade a mile in length, descended the southern slopes beside the railway and entered the city at 1 o'clock, meeting with an enthusiastic reception. There were renewed cheers as the procession passed into the market square. A great reception was given to the British Commander by the members of the club. Going to the Government buildings, Lord Roberts took possession of Bloemfontein in the name of the Queen. After inspecting President Brand's statue, Lord Roberts turned to the left, crossed the river and entered the grounds of the Presidency amid great cheering and singing of 'God save the Queen'. A Union Jack, specially made by Lady Roberts, was hoisted at 1.30 in the grounds.

The Boers and their sympathizers have fled. Mr Steyn's brother entertained General French at his farm yesterday, and Lord Roberts had breakfast there today.

That the brother of one of Robert's chief adversaries should be so willing to entertain him might, at first sight, be thought somewhat strange. Perhaps the answer rests in the comparative lack of enthusiasm for the war that prevailed generally within the Orange Free State.

English was by far the most prevalent language in the town, which at that time boasted a population of around 3,500. Of these there were scarcely more than 900 Dutch-speaking Boers, and even the 1,500 Africans nearly all spoke a kind of 'pidgin' English. Of the remaining 1,000 or so, who represented the non-Boer European community, many were British and most of the others spoke at least some English.

An English visitor to Bloemfontein just before the war noted that even the local Boer farmers expressed 'kindly feelings towards the English' and 'having come fresh from the Transvaal, with a tolerable knowledge of the Boer cruelty towards the Africans, spite and fraud towards the Uitlanders, and sullen vindictiveness towards the English nation in general, I found residence in pretty, peaceful Bloemfontein and association with friendly Free Staters very attractive.'

By virtue of a communications blunder by somebody in the 'back office', the Naval Brigade's arrival had not been reported and they missed the promised honour of taking part in the ceremonial entry into the town. Nonetheless, orders were received to march there on 15 March and the sailors spent the previous day on what the Navy calls a 'make and mend'. Traditionally, this was a day set aside every so often for the old-time handy sailors to make or mend clothing. In more modern times, in practice, it became little more than a day off. Jack was not necessarily allowed ashore, but would spend the day on board the ship at leisure. On 14 March, 1900, in Bloemfontein, a 'make and mend' for the Naval Brigade certainly retained its original strict meaning. They spent the day washing and mending their trek-worn and torn uniforms, tidying up unkempt beards, or some even shaving off altogether. And there were several layers of sand, dirt and dried sweat to scrape and rinse from their bodies.

Writing later, Surgeon Jeans remembered how reassured he had felt to be, at last, near a railway, and to know that it connected him to supplies of stores, food and medicine, and, in particular, whisky. 'There it was,' he said, 'its rails glistening in the sun, going serenely southward, as if the life of an army was not entirely dependent upon it.'

At 5.30 am the next day, on a bright cool morning, they inspanned the oxen and rolled the 4.7s and 12-pounders off on the last four miles into town, bivouacking on a grassy area just south of the old fort, near the Free State Arsenal and the lunatic asylum, which was being used as a military hospital, whence Midshipman Lloyd was confined immediately on arrival, suffering from enteric fever.

Then, Jeans went on to recall, he had an experience which was to remain in his memory for many years to come. It was sitting down to dine at the English Club, his first whisky and soda for several weeks, snowy white table linen, clean plates and an abundance of food. As with all hungry people, the temptation to gorge themselves persisted, and several tongues needed inspection by unsympathetic medical staff over the next few days.

Bloemfontein, with its surrounding countryside of billowing pastures full of grazing sheep and cattle, was a pleasant place in which to rest after their gruelling slog through dusty deserts and muddy waters, and over the rocky kopjes of the Orange Free State.

When it came to be reckoned up, Grant's Guns' crews and their oxen had hauled their 4.7s and 12-pounders over 157 miles from Enslin in thirty days. In that time they had paused only to do battle with the Boers at Paardeberg and Poplar Grove, and to catch their breath afterwards. All in all the 157 miles had been covered in only 76 hours actual time on the move.

Now they were able to relax a little, and the next fortnight, during which time the seamen and stokers from the *Powerful* went back to join their ship, was maily spent playing football, painting the guns a 'bilious yellow', ready for inspection by Lord Roberts, and embroidery. Sailors were very good at embroidery in those days. On many an English parlour wall, opposite the carved ebony elephants from China on the mantelshelf, hung a framed work of embroidery, usually with White Ensigns and Foul Anchors as prominent features, and often centred with the photograph of an absent sailor. For all the horniness of the calloused hands, they were nimble with a needle when it came to darning a sock or doing a little embroidery during the off-duty hours in the middle of the ocean. Here in Bloemfontein, in the middle of an ocean of grass, they turned their hands to embroidering the upturned brims of the new soft felt hats with which they had been issued, with either an Admiralty foul anchor for the sailors or a bugle for the Marines, in place of their tattered straw hats and helmets. This distinctive badge was about the only distinguishing feature which set the Naval Brigade apart from the soldiers, now that they had discarded their thin cotton clothes and been issued with khaki serge tunics. The South African winter was setting in and the nights, especially, were growing cold.

Like all good things, however, this lazy time came to an end when there was a slight scare from the direction of Sannah's Post, when General Broadwood's forward column blundered into trouble by getting himself surrounded by a posse of burghers near the Bloemfontein Waterworks. It was thought that de Wet might be about to mount a serious raid on Blomefontein itself, and as a precaution the guns were taken to the top of a kopje two miles north of the town which was to become known as Naval Hill, 'a name which it will probably bear for all time', which was a correct prediction, because it still does, ninety-seven years later. This hill was an ideal camping-ground, commanding as it did a view of the entire panorama to the north. So Bearcroft moved his Brigade there, alongside their guns. Jack soon made himself comfortable in his new home and had all the paths into camp clearly marked with whitewashed stones. The bluejackets were very proud of their handiwork with the whitewash brush, and one described it as making the place look 'like a fucking coastguard station' and 'so homely'.

While the sailors busied themselves with their embroidery and whitewashing, the officers enjoyed many a convivial dinner party at the Club, smoking afterwards outside on the moonlit veranda, listening to the nightly tattoo of the pipes and drums as the Highland Brigade played in the town square.

On 18 April the Royal Garrison Artillery relieved the Naval Brigade on the now muddy Naval Hill, and the 4.7s and 12-pounders were brought down in readiness to advance again, eastwards and northwards in a sweeping lunge.

During their stay in Bloemfontein enteric, dysentery and camp-fever had all taken their toll. 'Few are likely to forget,' wrote Surgeon Jeans, 'the long string of stretchers which passed through the camp, morning after morning, and wended their way down to the field hospitals, with their burdens of fever.'

Eighty-nine casualties left the Brigade in this way at Bloemfontein, which, coupled with the departure of the Powerfuls, resulted in considerable underman-ning. Captain Bearcroft was compelled to reorganize his crews, which he did by allocating one of the 4.7s to the Royal Marine Artillery escort, who thus found themselves promoted to the role of gunners. The loss of so many men to disease had an understandable effect on the morale of the others and it was no wonder that everybody displayed an eagerness to get under way again.

By 2 May they had all gone except two 12-pounders, which were left behind with their crews to guard the town. These included Midshipman Cunningham, who was furious. He had needed every ounce of his courage when he bearded

159

Prothero the Bad on board the *Doris*. He had trekked hundreds of miles to catch up with the action, just missing it at Poplar Grove. He had missed the ceremonial entry into Bloemfontein. And yet again, it seemed, he was going to be denied the prospect of some real excitement, now that it had at last arisen. 'I have had some very bad luck,' he wrote to his mother, 'all thro' that old pig Bearcroft who has left me behind here.'

CHAPTER 20

TO THE FOOT OF MAJUBA

Over in Natal Buller elected to get on with the war, letting all the vociferous criticism by his staff officers and other rivals at the War Office bounce off his ears without response. There would be plenty of time for him to have his say when it was all over.

Retreating from the Ladysmith perimeter, the Boer generals had dug themselves in along the line of the Biggarsberg Mountains, sixty-odd miles to the north. With Buller in Ladysmith, they had no doubt also been acutely aware of Roberts' presence in Bloemfontein and of his reputation for making lightning long-distance strikes. As they saw it, there was the distinct possibility that they could find themselves trapped in a pincer-like grip, and had pulled back beyond its immediate reach.

After Ladysmith had been relieved, and the Powerfuls and Terribles had departed, the residue of the Naval Brigade consisted of the Philomels, Fortes, Tartars and Natal Naval Volunteers, numbering in all ten officers and ninety men. These were just sufficient to man two 4.7s and four 12-pounders, the other guns having been turned over to the Garrison Artillery.

Captain Jones set up his new camp just outside the northern perimeter of Ladysmith and rested there until 19 March when he trekked on north for sixteen miles to Elandslaagte to join the main body of the British column. They pitched camp between the railway station and the Sunday River, right by the station master's house where the Boers had caroused with their British prisoners on looted whisky five long and weary months before, only to feel the unmerciful steel of French's Lancers and Dragoons on the morrow.

Jones placed himself under the command of General Clery and awaited orders, but absolutely nothing happened until 10 April. No orders to advance or retire. No sound or sight of the Boers. Nothing. Buller was certainly taking his time building up his strength before pushing on. And the Boers appeared to have gone asleep.

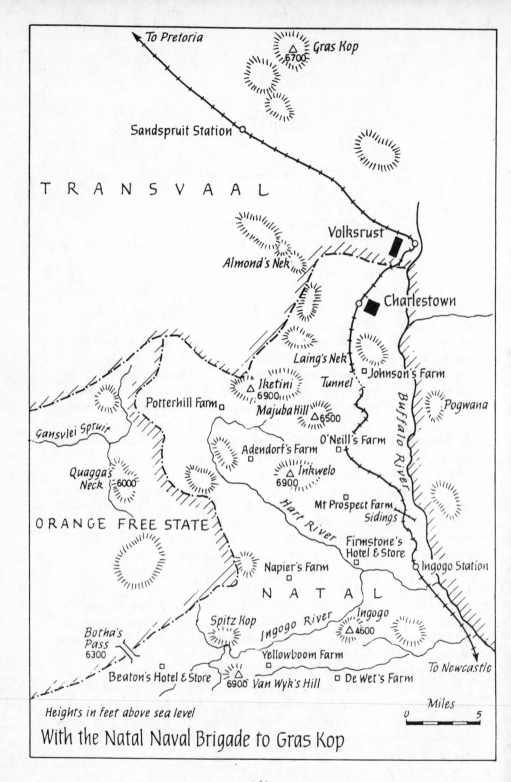

To Pretoria

△ Gras Kop
6700

Sandspruit Station

T R A N S V A A L

Volksrust

Almond's Nek

Charlestown

Laing's Nek

Johnson's Farm

△ Iketini   Tunnel
  6900

Pogwana

Potterhill Farm

Majuba Hill △ 6500

Gansvlei Spruit

O'Neill's Farm

Adendorf's Farm

Quagga's
Neck   6000

△ Inkwelo
  6900

O R A N G E   F R E E   S T A T E

Buffalo River

Hart River

Mt Prospect Farm
Sidings

Firmstone's
Hotel & Store

Ingogo Station

Napier's Farm

N A T A L

Spitz Kop

Ingogo River

Ingogo
△ 4600

Botha's
Pass
6300

Yellowboom Farm

To Newcastle

Beaton's Hotel & Store

△
6900   Van Wyk's Hill

De Wet's Farm

Heights in feet above sea level

Miles

0   5

With the Natal Naval Brigade to Gras Kop

162

Then at 8 am that day all hell broke loose. Maxim and Krupp fire suddenly erupted from several different gun positions around the British encampment. This was unusual, because the British had long since become accustomed to trying to persuade the Boers to return their fire, and so reveal their positions, rather than open the action themselves. Now, the 'khakis' found themselves surprised and unprepared. The Boer shells were arriving fast and furious among the naval brigade wagons.

The African drivers behaved with admirable coolness under the shelling. They ran to round up the oxen, which had been grazing peacefully in the rear. Then, rapidly inspanning them, they hauled the guns into their emplacements. The sailors, many groggy from the effects of dysentery and fever, raced to bring all six guns into action with practised speed, managing to knock out one of the big Krupps and contain the fire of the other guns.

The Naval Brigade losses in this skirmish were worse than in any of the fighting south of Ladysmith. One Boer shell destroyed a wagon and killed two Philomels, wounding two others. The body of one of the dead was completely pierced by a shrapnel shell case. And there were several lucky escapes that morning. Some bluejackets saw a fragment of shrapnel flying towards an officer and shouted to warn him. He jumped aside just in time, as it grazed his leg. One of the gun limbers was smashed when a shell hit it full on, and another shell perforated a box of 12-pounder ammunition, cutting all the cordite cartridges in two.

The log of the *Philomel* records that on 31 May, 1900, at sea off Delagoa Bay, an auction took place, in accordance with naval tradition, of the effects of 124780 Petty Officer W. Brock, Able Seaman J. Wilkes and Able Seaman F. Parkinson, and a similar one on 5 July, 1900, of the effects of Able Seaman R. Belcher. These were the men who had been killed in the action at Elandslaagte and others who had succumbed to disease. In the Royal Navy it is customary for dead men's effects to be auctioned among their crew-mates and the proceeds sent to the widow or next of kin. Understandably, these occasions are fraught with emotion, and the sense of esprit de corps is at its keenest. It is usual for amounts far in excess of true value to be raised.

The Naval Brigade received a commendation from General Clery for the steadiness it had displayed under some of the heaviest of fire. This was especially pleasing, in that many bluejackets in the guns' crews had not seen action before, having been held in reserve 'down the line' and only having just been brought up to the front.

Poor Lieutenant Burne, still suffering from dysentery, had missed the action of 10 April. After struggling to his feet to join his bluejackets in giving three hearty cheers to the released Ladysmith Brigade under Lieutenant Lionel Halsey as they passed through Colenso on their way down to Durban soon after the siege was lifted, he was ordered into Ladysmith himself. But he was still very weak and he was obliged to take himself to the Field Hospital on 10 March, where he stayed for the next fortnight. During this time there was a fearful hailstorm, with hailstones as big as golfballs, which blew down some of the hospital tents, stampeded all the horses, and hastened the death of several enteric patients by soaking them in their beds.

After another fortnight's convalescence at a friend's house near Maritzburg, he rejoined the Philomels at Elandslaagte, still a stone under weight. But Burne was not the only one of Jones's slimmed-down naval brigade to go sick. Lieutenant James of the *Tartar* went down with fever on 20 April and his guns were placed under Burne's command. Then Burne's servant, Gilbert, became dangerously ill and was shipped home. Even Captain Jones himself was afflicted by jaundice within a few weeks, and took to his bed. Indeed, most of the Brigade seemed to be a little off-colour.

After the 10 April outburst all was quiet again until the 21st, when the look-outs spotted some Boers trying to encircle the British positions by occupying some small kopjes on either flank. Soon afterwards two big guns opened up from about 4,500 yards, catching the encampment in a dangerous crossfire but no damage was done. The naval guns were now positioned on top of the hill on which the Battle of Elandslaagte had been fought. It was an emotive experience for the sailor-gunners, as they stood to their guns, surrounded by both British and Boer graves and the remains of hundreds of dead horses and cattle. The 4.7s replied quickly with some accurate shooting which knocked out one of the attackers and silenced the other.

The firing was kept up all day, there being distinct activity observed in the distant kopjes, and as night fell the Boers set fire to the grass across a front of about four miles north of the British camp. A night attack was fully expected, but it did not come. Then they 'went to sleep' again for nearly three weeks while everything was being prepared for Buller's advance.

At last it came – the order to advance. On Wednesday, 9 May, Buller started to move his troops forward. Now was the time to make the holiday they had enjoyed over the past two months pay a decent dividend. The Boers, of course, had had ample time to dig themselves in, making their positions up in the Biggarsberg range very secure indeed. Some stiff fighting was going to be necessary if they were to be shifted, and shifting them was going to be necessary if Buller was to carry the operation into the Travsvaal itself.

For two days the British infantry, wagons and baggage, rolled north out of Elandslaagte in a twin-pronged advance. Buller himself took the eastern flank, sweeping across Sunday's River, through Helpmaakar to Dundee, while Hildyard's Division worked round to the west, protecting Buller's left flank, through Wessel's Nek and Waschbank and up over the beautiful Pass of Glencoe to Glencoe itself.

Now that he was about to move off after such a lengthy halt, Lieutenant

Burne found his bad luck still pursuing him. First he needed to carry out some urgent repairs to his rolling-stock, in that many of the wooden wheels had shrunk from the tyres owing to the hot dry weather they had experienced. Second, while in the course of overseeing his guns being brought down from Elandslaagte Kop in preparation for marching off, his horse bolted and he was thrown heavily on rocky ground, damaging his shoulder, concussing him and cutting his temple to the bone. Thus another casualty was added to the list and Burne's guns were placed under the temporary command of Acting Lieutenant Steel of HMS *Forte*, who had himself barely recovered from a bout of enteric.

The Naval Brigade, with Captain Jones still laid low with jaundice and Burne heavily bandaged, stitched and feeling 'altogether unlovely', finally set out on 17 May to follow Hildyard up the Pass of Glencoe, passing many abandoned laagers which showed recent signs of occupation. Indeed, some of the campfires were still smouldering.

There was to be much heavy work for the oxen and guns' crews, extending over several weeks, but they soon settled down into a regular routine. After a day of struggling through thick dusty sand, sometimes a foot deep, the countryside became pleasant and pretty, and, although there were one or two difficult dongas to cross, (one ox had broken a hind leg by catching it in the trek chains while going down a particularly steep bank and had to be shot), there was ample grazing and sweet water in the many spruits. The oxen needed at least a couple of hours at grass in order to feed adequately, and in any case could not graze while still in-spanned with their yokes. Therefore a good rest was usually taken during the middle of the day, with the animals turned loose.

The weather had become bitterly cold and, although the sailors had their tents, Buller forbade them to be pitched for some reason, which meant many uncomfortable nights spent trying to sleep outside, exposed to the elements.

They pressed on past Glencoe and had nearly reached Danhauser when a galloping messenger, his horse bathed in a lather of sweat, came up from the rear to inform Captain Jones that Buller required the Naval Brigade wagons to return to Glencoe to bring up additional supplies. The Commander-in-Chief was concerned about the limited amount of rations his column was carrying to provide for such a large number of troops. This gave a welcome break, because many repairs needed to be carried out, and Jones arranged for this to be done in nearby Dundee, which abounded in blacksmith's and wheelwright's shops.

Burne noted in his diary:

Tuesday, 22nd May. Busy getting my wagon wheels and guns right after their trek over the bad road, and obliged to send them into Dundee to be cut and re-tyred. I rode with Steel and Hunt to Dundee which is five miles off; it is a small and miserable place with tin-roofed houses, bare dusty surroundings, and awful streets. We saw poor General Penn Symons' grave with the Union Jack flying over it, and other graves marked with fading wreaths and wooden crosses. We had a talk with the Chaplain who said that the Boers had passed through on Sunday in full flight with their guns. We rode back from this desolate scene, amid the dust of ages and the smell of dead animals.

The hold-up at Glencoe also provided time for Surgeon Lilly to catch up with the naval brigade. He had been on sick leave and had walked all night, on his own, from Waschbank!

Each village the sailors passed through bore signs of wanton damage done by the Boers as they retreated, and the nearer they got to the Transvaal border so the destruction worsened. In fact, even before they had reached Glencoe Burne had counted twenty-eight railway bridges and culverts that had all been blown up. By the time the town of Newcastle was reached, overlooked by the impressive Drakensberg Mountains, very few houses had escaped damage of one kind or another, showing broken windows, doors ripped from hinges, furniture burnt or roofing torn off.

Some good news now filtered through the grapevine to reach their ears and boost their spirits. Roberts was across the Vaal River, into the Transvaal, and threatening Johannesburg, while General Hunter was pushing up through the Orange Free State on a parallel course to Buller. On the other hand, Buller's force was faced by 10,000 determined Boer mountain fighters, at Laing's Nek, on Pogwana Hill, and on symbolic Majuba Hill itself.

Jones had hoped to rest at Newcastle, where there was good water and grazing, but on his arrival he was given immediate instructions to cross the Buffalo River at Wool's Drift and proceed to and capture Utrecht. This meant that at last they would be inside the Transvaal. The crossing of the border lacked the excitement that many had anticipated. In fact, it was something of an anticlimax, because they were unopposed and not a shot was fired!

Bivouacking on the outskirts of the town, Jones heard that he would be able to buy fresh eggs and vegetables from the nearby Dutch farms, albeit at a price. This was a real luxury to men who had been feeding on nothing but compressed rations for months on end. He called at what he thought looked like a friendly farm, bought four fowls from the 'vrau' and was pleasantly surprised when she demanded only double the usual price. However, she would not allow him to take any water for his oxen or horses.

There was a parson, out from Utrecht, visiting the farm at that moment, and he told Jones, in no uncertain manner, that he did not believe it was within the bounds of the etiquette of war for sailors to be sent so far up-country to fight farmers!

After a hearty meal, Jones, still sick with jaundice, marched the rest of his bluejackets into the town centre, leaving two guns outside the town, under

Lieutenant Burne and Chief Petty Officer Munro, to guard the approaches. No fighting took place. The Landrost came out and surrendered the town's keys to General Hildyard, saying he had done the same thing in 1881, but the British had not occupied the town. History was to repeat itself, because, after posting a notice on the Church door to the effect that the town had surrendered, the British trekked back to Wool's Drift. Two days later found them north of Newcastle at De Wet's Farm, near the point of the long finger which northern Natal jabbed between Transvaal and the Orange Free State.

By now, Buller calculated, any reasonable Boer Commander must have concluded that his position was such that he could not hope to win the war. The Boers had retreated, retreated and retreated again. The British were pouring more and more men into South Africa. It was, he considered, an opportune moment at which to try to end hostilities by offering Botha terms for an armistice.

He placed two 4.7s and two 12-pounders on the slopes of Inkwelo, in commanding positions, and at perhaps a deliberately chosen spot, O'Neill's Farm at the foot of Majuba itself, where the convention of 1881 had been signed, Buller met Christiaan Botha, brother of Louis, on 2 June under a flag of truce.

Buller told Botha that he hoped to avoid further bloodshed by negotiation. He urged him to accept that his position was hopeless and to surrender his artillery. In return, Botha's burghers would be allowed to return to their farms in peace. Botha asked for three days' ceasefire while he consulted the other generals, during which time the British troops were not to move. This was agreed, but on 5 June he sent word that he could not accept Buller's terms.

Thus the violence was set to continue. The Boers were determined to fight to their last breath. It was clear that the end of the war had not come with the relief of Kimberley and Ladysmith. Far from it. These events had only marked the beginning of a long and exhausting guerrilla campaign that was to run and run.

CHAPTER 21

TRAVELLING LIGHT TO VILJOEN'S DRIFT

The Naval Brigade contingent of the Bloemfontein town guard, which included the peeved Midshipman Cunningham, was to remain in the town under the command of a Major of Marines and Lieutenant Colquhoun of the Royal Victorian Navy while Roberts pressed on with his advance towards the Transvaal.

The order came through at 1 pm on 2 May for the others to be prepared to move off at 5 o'clock. They needed little encouragement. All heavy baggage was to be left behind in Bloemfontein. They would be travelling light, taking 'steaming bags' only. And Roberts clearly intended for them to travel fast. Wagons were quickly loaded, oxen in-spanned, and they plodded out of the town at dusk, hauling their two 4.7s and two 12-pounders, now reinforced by the arrival of Lieutenant E. P. C. Back of HMS *Monarch*, and the appropriately named Paymaster W. B. Penny of HMS *Philomel*.

On this leg of their marathon advance they were to have the reassuring presence of the Bloemfontein-Johannesburg railway line alongside them as Roberts cut a swathe fifty miles wide through the Orange Free State. Perhaps rations would now become a little more plentiful and Surgeon Jeans would worry a little less about his medical supplies.

After half a mile, Number One 4.7 got stuck in a deep donga when trying to take a rather too clever short cut. The oxen had to be turned round and taken back to drag it out backwards. Then it missed a turning altogether and the rest of the brigade were baffled as to its whereabouts, until after an hour it reappeared, its crew red-faced, having gone two miles out of their way before wondering where the others were.

It was a bitterly cold night and they found it difficult to sleep when they bivouacked just short of the Modder River at about 1 am. Most of them were glad to be on the move again when they were given a shake at 4 am and prepared to cross the river.

'How many times had we crossed and re-crossed that dirty stream,' wrote Captain Leslie Wilson of the Royal Marine Light Infantry, 'Only once more were we to cross it, and that was on our way home!'

Roberts, after a short, sharp fight, had just taken Brandfort, a small seedy town with two hotels, one large church and a single street, and it was here that the naval brigade caught up with the main force the next night.

When Roberts carried out the major reorganization of his forces after taking Bloemfontein, the Naval Brigade had been assigned to General French, with the Cavalry Division. The naval contingent, while complaining little, found this to be a less than comfortable arrangement. From their point of view, therefore, it was fortunate that, when Captain Bearcroft was on his way to report his arrival in Brandfort to Roberts' Headquarters, he should happen to meet General Pole-Carew.

Pole-Carew was extremely popular with the sailors. He had been the 9th Brigade commander almost since they left the Orange River, but now commanded the 11th Division. Bearcroft managed to persuade him that the 11th Division needed more heavy long-range artillery, and, in turn, Pole-Carew was able to convince Headquarters. The result was that the Naval Brigade was transferred to the popular General's command and everybody was happy.

Fifteen miles further up the railway Bearcroft's men were enjoying a couple of hours' rest later that day when they were rudely disturbed by the arrival of an army provost sergeant and two troopers. A local farmer had angrily reported that the sailors had stolen and eaten twenty of his sheep and was demanding compensation. Nobody was allowed to move until the Naval Brigade camp had been searched, and seven carcasses were found near their wagons. Bearcroft, furious, ordered everybody to fall in. The whole brigade denied most vehemently that they had stolen any of the sheep. Bearcroft, now impatient as well as furious, threatened that unless the culprits stepped forward and confessed he would return every man-Jack to his ship and bring ashore some fresh blood. He knew that that was the quick way to arrive at the truth. Nobody in the Brigade would want to relinquish his place in it and, if any of them had stolen the sheep and not confessed the crime, the others would deal with the guilty parties in their own rough and ready way! Nobody stepped forward.

That was good enough for Captain Bearcroft. He believed Jack Tar. He informed the provost-sergeant that he suspected the carcasses of being a 'plant' and handed him £5 'compensation' to be given to the farmer with a curt request that the latter should be sent on his way.

Hardly had the provost departed when the boom of heavy gunfire was heard from up the line and Bearcroft was ordered to move with all haste up to the Vet River, about four miles distant, where the Boers were resisting.

At their flat-out speed of 3 miles per hour the Brigade charged towards the action. With such hectic urgency mishaps are always more likely to occur.

Crossing a drift, one of the limbers capsized, spilling its hidden cargo of tinned milk, jam and other delicacies which the crew had been carefully hoarding for a special occasion. And then one of the 4.7s became stuck fast in a quicksand and the sailors had to call for the help of a regiment of Guards, who were acting as escort at the time, to extricate it.

Eventually they came into action at 4.30 pm on the southern approaches to the Vet River, just behind the shorter-range guns of the Royal Artillery. For the next three hours Briton and Boer exchanged a deluge of heavy artillery fire. The way in which the Royal Artillery gunners conducted themselves, with magnificent discipline, serving their guns as calmly as if they were on a practice shoot, while the Boer shells fell fast and thick all around them, was a sight which impressed all who witnessed it. Finally, at around sunset, having inflicted no serious casualties, at least not on the naval contingent, the Boers elected to withdraw.

The following morning was spent in getting Roberts' complete army across the Vet River drift, and marching on to Smaldeel. This was a small but straggling village, whose only reason for existence appeared to be the fact that it boasted a railway station. Conversely, the only reason for the station to be there seemed to be that it was in the middle of a village. Enteric fever was still taking a heavy toll on their numbers. Several men were sent back to hospital from Smaldeel and one Royal Marine Corporal died.

It was to be nearly another month before Bearcroft's men saw any more serious action. The British advanced steadily and the Boers retired steadily, all the way up to the Zand River, where they made a half-hearted attempt at a rearguard action. The British guns fired a few rounds in reply to the Boer artillery, only to see them retire again almost instantly. Later the Naval Brigade learned that their last two shells had killed seven Boers and wounded several others, and that President Steyn himself had made a reappearance from hiding in an effort to lift the morale of his burghers. It was even rumoured that he had used his sjambok, or buffalo-hide whip, on some of them.

The buzz was that the Boers were digging in to make a determined stand at Kroonstad, an important railway junction, only fifty miles or so from the northern border of the Orange Free State with the Transvaal. But the buzz was wrong. When they got to Kroonstad on 12 May, keyed up for a fight, there was not a single armed Boer to be seen. They had retreated again.

Transvaal had a long perimeter to defend, far too long. So why defend it at all? On that basis De Wet had done his best to convince his Government that pursuance of a war based on guerrilla tactics was their only chance. They had agreed only reluctantly and half-heartedly. De Wet's point was this. Now hopelessly outnumbered by the British and depleted by the slow drift of burghers back to their farms for the winter, far better for the Boers to harass Roberts' long thin chain of communications, striking quickly and then melting away into the kopjes, than to try to meet the enemy head-on in open battle. Their fieldcraft, high mobility and initimate knowledge of the country would ensure that the British would never know where to expect them next.

There was plenty of evidence of recent Boer presence in Kroonstad, however. Roberts' speed of advance seemed to have put his enemies on the wrong foot yet again, in that the Boers had evidently not enjoyed enough time in which to finish preparing their trenchworks. Half-dug trenches had obviously been hurriedly abandoned, with shovels and mattocks simply dropped on the ground. If the British advance had not been quite so rapid, the rumours of an impending stiff battle would have been well founded.

Kroonstad was a fair-sized town, with an imposing railway bridge which the Boers' Irish Brigade, led by one Major John McBride, had as thoroughly destroyed as they had all the others between Bloemfontein and the Vaal as they fell back. They had also taken most of the available food with them, commandeering stocks held by the town's hotels. But in their haste they had left plentiful supplies of whisky behind in the various bars, and the hotels themselves had not been seriously damaged. As it was, Roberts rode into the town at the head of his army, to be greeted by the cheering English inhabitants as he received the keys to the Town Hall from the civic authorities. To add some pomp and ceremony to the occasion, Pole-Carew's 11th Division, which now included the Naval Brigade, were drawn up in review order, albeit somewhat travel-worn in apperance, to receive the little Field Marshal, accompanied by the fifes and drums of the Scots Guards.

The bluejackets and marines rested for over a week at Kroonstad. Three more of their number went back to the hospital with enteric, including the last Royal Marine subaltern. But there was a notable arrival. When some ammunition and supply wagons came up from Bloemfontein, under the command of a grinning Major of Marines, one of them was carrying a present of 50,000 cigarettes from the officers of the Mediterranean Fleet.

A couple of weeks later a train steamed in, carrying Midshipman Cunningham, who had been released from his frustrating sentence of inactivity in Bloemfontein. Lord Roberts was a personal friend of Cunningham's father, who was Professor of Anatomy at Trinity College, Dublin. The Field Marshal was fully aware of his friend's son's presence in South Africa and had enquired at the Kroonstad Naval Brigade camp after the boy's welfare. On being told that Cunningham was back in Bloemfontein, he ordered Captain Bearcroft to have him sent up to the front at once.

Cunningham wrote at once to his mother: 'I am off to Kroonstad by the next train which is a goods by the way. I am quite well and in perfect health.' He clambered into his goods truck, accompanied by a party of soldiers, and they chugged off, painfully slowly, because of congested rail-traffic and suspect lines. It took thirty-six hours to complete the 100-miles journey, and it was freezing cold, but he found the soldiers to be good companions who shared their food with him.

Arriving in Kroonstad, he discovered that the Naval Brigade had moved on a fortnight since, which set him off on a series of efforts to catch them up, only to miss them by a whisker every time. Indeed they had moved off, on 22 May to be precise, making the twenty miles to Honning Spruit that day, seventeen miles the next, and fifteen miles the next, which took them to Vredefort Road Station.

The marches had been long, but uneventful, apart from the usual difficulties in crossing the numerous drifts with heavy equipment. They were now using mules to haul the guns, and these animals are well-known for their uncooperative nature! Nevertheless, they all went along at a smart pace. The days were hot and the terrain was dusty, but it was freezing cold at night.

And now, with the South Africa winter well advanced, the troops were to find themselves still waiting for the thousands of heavy greatcoats which were somewhere between Southampton and Bloemfontein. Bivouacking on the open veldt, they would often wake in the mornings to find a layer of frost on their waterproof sheets, but even then there were one or two hardy characters who would persist in taking their customary early morning dip from an ice-cold bucket.

The northern border of the Orange Free State seemed as if it was never going to come into sight. They had seen no Boers, they had heard no shots, for several weeks now. Even the scouts ahead had seen little more of the Boers than the occasional smoke of a fleeing train rising above the kopjes, or sometimes a fleeting glimpse of distant galloping horsemen. Everything seemed so quiet. There were not even any buzzes about likely battles in the offing. It was a boring journey through boring countryside.

The grassy undulating country disappeared near the border, however, where it degenerated into a stretch of deep sandy desert. On Sunday, 27 May, the last four miles to the Vaal River proved some of the worst going they had yet encountered, with the sand over a foot deep in places. It is well versed that the last mile is the longest, and here was a prime example of the truth of that proverb. With aching limbs, they crossed into the Transvaal at 10 am at a place called Viljoen's Drift.

Surely the Boers would stand and fight on Transvaal soil? But no. Passing on through the town of Vereeniging, the trek continued as far as the Klip River, almost as casually as if they had been hauling their 4.7s through Hyde Park on a Sunday morning.

But the sentries and pickets were having to be ever more vigilant. Apart from the body of Boers ahead of Roberts' main column, commanded by Louis Botha, there were now the lightning commandoes of the two De Wet brothers, Christiaan and Piet, together with other Boer leaders who had recently reemerged from other fronts, such as Viljoen, Delarey, Prinsloo and the future South African Premier, Jan Smuts. Each composed of only a few hundred burghers, they had already started on their hit-and-run style of fighting, concentrating mainly on causing maximum destruction to the supply lines behind Roberts' Grand Army, which now numbered well over 40,000.

As early as 3 April, with Roberts still in Bloemfontein, Christiaan De Wet, with only 800 burghers, had attacked the British garrison at Reddersburg, taking 546 of the Royal Irish Rifles prisoner and causing the defenders to lose forty-five officers and men killed and wounded. He had then gone on to lay siege to the garrison at Wepener, on the Basutoland border, pinning down 1,900 of Brabant's Horse and causing 300 casualties between 9 and 25 April before fleeing from the relief force under General Rundle which plodded on to the scene.

Following the relief of Wepener, Rundle had continued to push De Wet northwards and eastwards, and, in an attempt to head him off, Grant's Guns had been detached from Bearcroft's main body when they left Bloemfontein and ordered due east with a column under Lieutenant-General Colvile.

'Little Bobs' and 'Sloper' had already been lowered by hand from Naval Hill, and the three officers, fifty seamen and stokers, three conductors, forty-two natives, thirteen wagons with 570 rounds of 4.7 ammunition, three carts, seven horses and 290 oxen marched, rolled and trudged off behind McDonald's Highland Brigade of Seaforths, Black Watch, Argylls and Highland Light Infantry and detachments of Royal Engineers and Royal Artillery. It felt good to be on the move again, but one worrying factor was that Surgeon Jeans had been recalled to Simonstown and they would therefore need to rely on army doctors for any medical attention, and these were not always close at hand.

For the first few days Grant's Guns followed the same routine as Bearcroft's men – early morning starts, freezing cold, midday breaks and bivouac camps. The roads were no more than rough and stony tracks, and there were many awkward drifts to cross, especially at Fairfield and Papjei's Vlei. The only excitement at this time came on the morning of 4 May, two days out from Bloemfontein, when they came to a big humpy kopje known as Baboon Kop and found the enemy well dug-in on its steep sides. For once the Mauser fire was no more than sporadic and 'Long Tom' seemed to be absent altogether. The 4.7s laid a heavy bombardment of lyddite on the Boer positions, covering the Highlanders as they attacked. But there was little inclination to fight on the part of the Boers. The British losses were negligible, and they took several prisoners, one of whom said that one lyddite shell had killed or wounded no less than thirty of his companions.

Spruits abounded in this district, woven across the landscape so profusely that to avoid them was impossible. Splashing their way through the interminable drifts, Grants's Guns arrived in Winburg on 7 May, two days after Hamilton had raised the Union Jack over the town. Here they stayed for two weeks, camped on the north-eastern side of Winburg, waiting for army reinforcements to be sent up.

On the move again, with the bad roads and numerous drifts continuing to slow their progress, there was no sign of Boer resistance until 26 May, when they caught sight of a body of burghers on a ridge at 3,700 yards dead ahead, but a couple of 4.7 shrapnel shells was enough to persuade them to retire.

It was a different story as they approached Lindley, however. Lindley had been proclaimed the provisional capital of the Orange Free State after the fall of Kroonstad, which itself had been declared the provisional capital after the fall of Bloemfontein. In the middle of a totally featureless stretch of flat treeless veldt, Lindley was a bleak place, with its tin roofs and tall church tower looking like the sails of a clutch of helplessly becalmed yachts in a waveless sea. But it had a symbolic importance for the Boers, and Grants's Guns were sniped at all day by skilfully concealed riflemen, as they tramped across the grassy ocean towards the tin-roofed armada.

Lieutenant Fergusson, HMS *Barossa*, recorded in his diary for 27 May, 1900: 'A very cold and windy day. Boers sniped at column all day. Ammunition wagon, laden with 5,000 lbs of ammunition, on a hard road, accidentally ran over the legs of an Able Seaman without breaking a single bone!' And on the following day: 'Ten degrees of frost at 8 am. Marched out at 9 am. Came into action in the middle of the forenoon. '

By now, of course, the naval brigades had taught themselves little tricks, many of them simple and/or obvious, but all designed to make life easier for themselves. These included a method of bringing a heavy gun into action rapidly. As soon as the order 'Action Front!' was heard, the 'voorloeper' turned his leading bullocks sharp round and doubled back. As the last pair turned, the wire span slackened, enabling it to be quickly unshackled. Therefore, because the gun was hauled with its barrel pointing for'ard (which was the trick), it was ready to come into action as soon as it was unlimbered. Furthermore, such a routine demanded less of a turning circle than if the gun itself had also needed to be turned round, which was an important advantage when advancing through broken, kopje-dotted terrain. Plus, of course, it took the bullocks to immediate relative safety at the rear of the action.

It should not be forgotten that most of the land between Bloemfontein and Johannesburg is at the 5,000 feet plus level, and although this was not anything like the altitudes at which Buller's forces had fought to relieve Ladysmith and beyond, the distances involved were far greater. The nights and early mornings were terribly cold. The wind-chill effect made them even colder, the wind-whipped dust stung the face like a back-handed slap, and there was little food or forage for men or beasts.

By the time they reached Heilbron on the evening of 30 May, with the Boers having landed shells with great accuracy amongst the Grant's Guns' wagons all day, they had marched 128 miles in eight days, with fighting on five of those days. They had lost forty-two oxen since Bloemfontein, fifteen on that day alone.

Midshipman Cunningham was still trying with all his might to catch up with the action. Missing the naval brigade at Kroonstad, he followed by train as far as Roodevaal which was the current railhead. There he ran across a party of Marines, commanded by Major Marchant of the *Doris*, who were waiting with empty wagons for supplies of ammunition. He waited with them, and the next day they all set off to catch the brigade, jolting and rattling the eighty miles up to Viljoen's Drift in four bone-shaking days. But again Bearcroft had gone – four days earlier.

CHAPTER 22

MAJUBA TAKEN

On the Natal Front, Buller, having had his terms for an armistice rejected, pondered his next move. To make any further advance of any consequence, he needed to force a way through the beautiful but imposing Drakensberg Mountains. He chose Botha's Pass as the spot at which to do it. This was not going to be easy, and heavy artillery, using the creeping barrage technique which had enabled the infantry to bludgeon their way through to Ladysmith from the Tugela, would need to play a major part if he were to succeed.

Captain Jones was ordered to ride over to Van Wyk's Hill, which faced Botha's Pass at about 7,000 yards' range, to reconnoitre for a likely place in which to position the naval guns. He deployed Halsey, with his two 12-pounders, to Yellowboom Farm, to the right of Van Wyk Hill, and Burne, with the remainder to the summit of the hill itself.

The route the guns would need to take to their new positions was fully exposed to the Boers' fire and Jones waited until dark before moving them. But on the way the Boers set fire to the two-feet-high grass of the mountain meadows. Terrified by a mile-wide wall of blazing grass, which made the night as bright as day, some of the oxen stampeded. Dragging two of the 12-pounders behind them, the huge beasts thundered into a drift, while the drivers looked on helplessly. Before they could be brought under control they had capsized both guns in the water. The crews managed to right them, but one had broken an axle and was abandoned, to be recovered later and skilfully repaired by the Royal Artillery armourers, carpenters and wheelwrights.

The big 4.7s were more difficult to get across the drift, but it was managed by dismantling them and taking the parts over in wagons. In the morning the steep rocky ascent of the hill had to be faced, but with sixty oxen for each gun and wagon, together with the applied brawn of the bluejackets on the drag-ropes, it was accomplished without mishap.

All was ready for action, with the naval guns mounted in the emplacements prepared for them by the Royal Engineers, and as dawn broke a sudden boom echoed around the kopjes as the first salvo of lyddite hurtled on its four-mile journey to soften up the Boer laager in the dongas on the approaches to Botha's Pass. The bluejackets were grateful for the exercise to help them keep warm. Many had been half dead with fatigue and from the extreme cold produced by the freezing winds on the 6,000-feet mountain top.

Lieutenant Burne recorded in his diary for 7 June:

> Sir Redvers Buller, quite blue with the cold, rode up about 9 am with his Colonial guide, and carefully surveyed the position through my long telescope ... After a good look round we could not see many signs of the enemy in front, and he was just going off to report this, but at that moment the spurs of the berg opposite to us became alive with them at 6,000 to 7,000 yards off; they came in a long line out of a donga and advanced in skirmishing order with ambulances in the rear and a wagon with what looked like a gun on it. I opened fire at once and put my first two shells at 6,000 yards right into some groups of horsemen; we saw them tumbling about, so after about a dozen shots from my gun off they went like greased lightning, seeming to sink into the earth and evidently quite taken aback to find we had a gun in such a position. In a few minutes not a sign of them was left, and the Commander-in-Chief riding up seemed much pleased and congratulated us on our straight shooting. ...
> Horribly cold! I slept in the open under a limber.

The bombardment of Botha's Pass itself started the next day. The first objective was to clear a way for the infantry to advance, and from 10 am a searching barrage was laid down on the slopes of Spitz Kop at about 3,000 yards.

The British infantry of East Surreys, West Yorkshires, South Lancashires and Lancasters began their general advance around noon, swarming steadily up, past Beaton's Hotel & Store on to the lower reaches of the Pass. The Boers played their usual game of holding fire until the attackers were within very close range. As soon as the first khaki figures appeared over the first ridge, they were met with a torrent of pom-pom and Mauser fire. The Boers had started several grass fires behind the trenches, each making dense clouds of blue-grey smoke to conceal their true gun positions from the British gunners, but this only served to unsight their own riflemen and the fires were allowed to die.

All day long Burne and Halsey lobbed their shells over the heads of the British infantry, clearing the trenches in front of them, and gradually the Boers were forced back. By sunset Botha's Pass was in British hands. The order to cease fire came at dusk. It was bitterly cold and a freezing fog had come down, but the bluejackets settled down to sleep under their wagons.

No sooner had they crawled under their waterproofs to try to catch some semblance of sleep in those atrocious conditions than the order came from Captain Jones to take the guns down the hill ready for the next day's march. The Dublin Fusiliers, who were currently acting as their escorts, were to help them, and the arrangement was that they should rendezvous with the soldiers at the top of a certain gully.

At 10 pm they waited at the appointed spot, but no Dublins. Jones sent out bluejackets in twos and threes in all directions through the freezing murk to search for them. The fog grew even thicker, with visibility down to a few paces, as the sailors dribbled back to report no sign of the missing soldiers. Captain Jones reported the situation to the General. He had no news either. They waited all through the night until well after daybreak, when the Dublins appeared at the bottom of Van Wyk's Hill, having been wandering around totally lost in the fog.

In the meantime, however, Jack had not been idle. In the absence of the lost Irishmen, a battalion of Dorsets was recruited to assist the sailors in getting the guns down. They had all been sweating through the night on the drag-ropes and check-chains, with every man needing to apply his full strength to control each heavy piece on its way down the three-quarters-of-a-mile-long gully. Then, after each 'package' had been safely lowered, they had to climb to the top again with their chains and ropes in order to start on the next. The complete job meant eleven such trips and it was very tiring work. All was safely at the bottom by 4 am, and the men, nearly asleep on their feet, sank to the frost-covered long grass to rest for a couple of hours until the order came to take the guns across a steep ravine.

On the way down one of the 12-pounders broke away and smashed a wagon to splinters and injured two of the oxen so badly that they had to be shot. It was at that point that the lost Dublin Fusiliers appeared out of the early morning gloom, 800 frozen, tired and ravenously hungry men. They needed to eat before they could resume their escort duties and a stand-easy was ordered while they were fed.

All was back in shape by mid-morning and, now rejoined by Halsey and his guns from their position at Yellowboom Farm, they marched to form part of General Coke's column in the long haul up over Botha's Pass and into Orange River Colony. They had broken through the formidable Drakensbergs. They had outflanked the Boers. But the latter still held Laing's Nek, which was, for them, an historic symbol. It had to be taken.

The hard stone-free roads in Orange River Colony were an undeniable luxury compared to what they had had to endure in Natal, mainly because, once clear of the mountains, the countryside opened out into the flat veldt. Here the oxen fairly skipped along at a steady three miles per hour and by dusk they had reached Gans vlei Spruit.

Many Boer ambulance wagons were hurrying hither and thither, all displaying prominent white flags, and most of the farms along the way were flying white flags from their chimneys. These were all left unmolested, under stern orders that there should be no looting. One farm did cause a problem. It contained many plump fowls and pigs, besides several large stacks of sweet-smelling hay, and was an obvious Boer supply depot, but it was protected by a large white flag and therefore immune from interference. But the oxen were half-starved. They understood nothing about white flags and the scent of hay in their nostrils caused many of them to break away in a wild rush towards the stacks.

Captain Jones made his peace with the farmer by buying some poultry at an enormous price, but even with those his food supply levels were becoming critical. The wagons contained only enough for about another three days.

Buller turned north-east after Gans vlei Spruit, in order to work round behind General Clery's Division, who were pressing towards Laing's Nek, and General Lyttelton's farther to the east near Utrecht. This would also bring him close to the railway again, which would solve the food supply problem. The next obstacle to be faced was Almond's (or Alleman's) Nek Pass, a narrow gap in a jagged line of cliffs facing Volksrust, and only three miles from the railway. The Pass appeared to be deserted as the navy guns approached it, but they had a warm reception from the 5-inch Creusot and pom-poms hidden on the slopes. A fierce fight soon developed and, although the Boers had not had time to dig themselves to their usual standard of security, nevertheless they were in an extremely strong position tactically, owing to the narrowness of the Pass.

For once Buller had outwitted his enemy. Even as the West Yorkshires, East and West Surreys, South Lancashires, Middlesexes, Dorsets, Dublins and Devons tramped away from Gans vlei Spruit, the Boers were busy digging trenches on Quagga's Hill, anticipating that Buller would strike there next. But this time they were wrong. Buller was fifteen miles away.

At dawn on 12 June the British artillery laid down a barrage which smothered the ravines and small kopjes before Almond's Nek, while 3000 yards from the Nek itself, still on the plain, the noise grew in a terrific crescendo as the Boers poured their pom-poms at the advancing infantry, and the Royal Navy and Royal Artillery guns plopped common shell lyddite and shrapnel just in front of the khaki line, slowly dislodging the Boers, who had, so far, not fired a single rifle shot.

At last the Mausers opened fire with a noise 'as if it were hail beating heavily on a tin roof' to join in with the bass voices of the heavy guns of both sides. Lieutenant Burne had a lucky escape when a large piece of still-smoking shrapnel imbedded itself in the ground not far from his left foot.

The Boers had concealed themselves on the terraced ridges of Almond's Nek, which were scattered with small boulders, making it ideal ground for the British to use lyddite shells. But the Boers were in a strong position and the British advance was held up.

At about 11 am Buller moved his artillery forward, now forty field guns in all, including the ex-Navy, now Royal Artillery, 4.7s from Ladysmith on the left, and a Royal Artillery howitzer battery in the rear, all to within 5,000 yards of the Nek. The Boers' gun positions were, as ever, difficult to spot, as they used smokeless powder, but, by means of much concentrated staring through the long naval telescopes, their guns were all silenced by one o'clock and the British infantry advanced up the Nek.

There followed a tremendous fight. The infantry came under very heavy fire and incurred many casualties in working their way along the right-hand ridge to outflank the enemy. The Boers put up a brave and stubborn resistance, but by dusk the Nek was in British hands when the East Surreys gained the summit with a deafening cheer that could be heard above the din of the battle, and the Dorsets fixed their bayonets with a rattle, to drive the last few Boers into retreat north-eastwards. Captain Jones remembered the moment when the sun went down on Almond's Nek that day, in a 'gorgeous splendour behind the hills, the whole range was in our possession and the Boers were in full flight, leaving the countryside in a blaze behind them, as usual.'

The only Naval Brigade casualty in the battle for Almond's Nek was the holed water cart.

On the march down to Volksrust all the houses and farms were flying white flags and all the men had disappeared, leaving the town full of women weeping as in mourning for the dead. In their hurried flight, the burghers had left behind piles of valuable booty in the way of food and forage, rifles and ammunition, and, not least, the grim legacy of hundreds of empty coffins.

Laing's Nek and Majuba – if there were any names that held a special place in the Boer heart, these were they. For Laing's Nek and Majuba read Trafalgar and Waterloo. For Laing's Nek and Majuba read Yorkstown and Saratoga. Laing's Nek and Majuba, where nineteen years before, the Boers had out-manoeuvred and beaten the Redcoats, and killed poor General Colley. Laing's Nek and Majuba, the words with which they had taunted Tommy Atkins for years, revenge for which the said Atkins had long vowed that he would take, and of which Master-at-Arms Crowe of the *Terrible* had reminded the bluejackets in his piece of doggerel as they crossed the equator on their way to war six months earlier. And it was not as if Laing's Nek and Majuba were merely places evoking nothing but sentimental notions. They were formidable military strongpoints in their own right. If Ladysmith was the 'Aldershot' of Natal, the Boers had transformed Majuba into another 'Gibraltar'.

But now, faced with Buller's massive army of khaki coats and heavy guns, hopelessly outnumbered, the burghers had no alternative but to flee from these places to regroup in the distant kopjes and live to fight another day. And so they had fled.

Lieutenant Burne recorded in his diary for Thursday and Friday, 14 and 15 June, 1900:

> At Volksrust resting on our laurels, and all in good heart, although feeling this bitter midwinter cold. General Hildyard sent for names to mention in his despatches and I believe I am one. As commanding the *Tartar* guns, I was also very pleased to be able to mention six of my men, and am full of admiration of the way in which my bluejackets have worked, shot and stood the cold and marching. To sum up our recent operations, they are:- March from Elandslaagte to Glencoe, re-occupation of Newcastle; crossing of Buffalo Drift and occupation of Utrecht; ascent of Van Wyk at night with guns; turning and capture of Botha's Pass; march through Orange River Colony and Transvaal in pursuit of Boers; taking of Almond's Nek and occupation of Volksrust and Charlestown, with the strong position of Laing's Nek turned and evacuated by the enemy who are in full flight. This is all very satisfctory and we hear of congratulations from the Queen and others to General Buller. The Boers have, with their usual cleverness and ability, got away their guns by rail, but we hope to get them later. We are now busy refitting wagons and gear for a further advance. I hope the services of the bluejackets in these operations, which have been invaluable, will receive the recognition they deserve in the end of the campaign.

He rode over to Laing's Nek the next day with Captain Jones and Lieutenants Hunt and Steel of the *Forte*. That the Boers had abandoned such a stronghold, apparently so readily, they found surprising. There were deep and narrow zigzagged trenches stretching over three or four miles, even into the surrounding foot hills of Pogwana and Majuba, which protected the Nek from every conceivable point of attack.

The railway ran through a tunnel under the Nek and the Boers had blown up both ends of it, leaving a dead horse in each, for some reason. They had also tried to dig down through the rocky slate towards the roof of the tunnel halfway along its length so as to explode it, but had been unsuccessful. The Royal Engineers, under Captain R. E. Headley, a well-known Somerset cricketer of the day, were hard at work repairing the damage so that a new railhead could be established north of the mountains.

The naval officers went on to climb Majuba, on horseback until it became too steep for the horses, and then on foot for the remainder. Clambering breathlessly up the last few feet and then on to the 300 yard wide plateau, 'in the footsteps of the Boer attackers in 1881' was an emotive experience. There they found the wooden-crossed graves, in a wire enclosure, of the twenty-two bluejackets of the Naval Brigade beside those of the Gordons and King's Royal Rifles who had died alongside General Colley. Colley himself was buried at Mount Prospect, four miles away, but an insigificant heap of stones marked the spot where he had fallen, with a sign, written in black lead, 'Here Colley fell'.

Burne picked some nearby ferns and wild plants as a memento and rode back to Volksrust with a headache from the steep climb and strong mountain air, finding orders awaiting them to march to Wakkerstroom, to the east of the railway, to add some beef to General Lyttelton's 11th Brigade who were being held up.

When they arrived they found an angry town. The civic authorities had surrendered the keys to Lyttelton, who had pressed on to Sandspruit. This had left the town unguarded and the Boers had returned to take revenge for the town's surrender by shooting the Landrost's son in cold blood. Following on to Sandspruit, the Naval Brigade were met by Lieutenant Lees, the Naval ADC, with more orders for Captain Jones.

He was to return to his ship with all the Fortes, and the Natal Naval Volunteers were to be withdrawn. The information was that Admiral Harris had wired to say that he needed the *Forte* men to proceed on an expedition up the Gambia, but Burne and Halsey were to be asked whether they wished to rejoin *Philomel* and send the *Tartar*'s bluejackets back to their ship or stay on. They both replied, without hesitation, that they would stop and see it out.

182

CHAPTER 23

MANY MILES FROM SALT WALTER

Now deep into the Transvaal, Roberts was forced to take some tremendous risks. He could not afford to leave adequate forces to guard his long and tortuous supply line, one single railway track now stretching through many miles of hostile territory, and at the same time maintain the impetus of his advance on Johannesburg and Pretoria. Moreover, that hostile tract of kopje-dotted territory was perfectly designed for ambushes, sabotage and guerrilla warfare in general. And the railway line itself was of no use to him without sufficient rolling-stock to carry the desperately needed supplies to the front. His troops were almost down to their last biscuit.

The taking of Johannesburg and Pretoria was a matter of urgency for Roberts, because Kruger was also totally reliant on a single-track railway from Delagoa Bay for his supply of war materials. British control of the goldfields of the Rand would put an instant tourniquet on this artery by denying him the means to pay his bills, and it would only be when Pretoria fell, the British anticipated (wrongly as it happened), that the Boers would sue for peace.

And so Roberts took the risk of leaving minimal protection on his supply lines in order to keep his advance rolling rapidly northwards. His battle plan was simple. Hamilton and French, with about 20,000 men, would swing to the west of the railway and approach Johannesburg from that direction, while the main force would drive straight up the railway and press in from the other side.

Supplies being of such crucial importance, as each ammunition wagon became empty it was passed over to the Service Corps and became a supply wagon. The Navy's large-calibre ammunition weighed heavily and only forty rounds could be carried per bullock wagon; therefore, when forty rounds had been fired, one wagon would be lost to the Brigade. Jack had saved, scrounged or purloined various little luxuries, such as tins of jam and other sweetmeats, and if the wagons carried on disappearing, he would soon have no transport for these. Therefore the practice was adopted of using a few shells from each wagon, so as never to have any that were completely empty and to enable the contraband to continue on its journey.

A fussy staff officer noticed that none of the sailors' fifteen ammunition wagons ever seemed to be available for the 'baggage' lines and reported this to General Pole-Carew. Pole-Carew, who was almost certainly aware of the subterfuge, confirmed that all the wagons were required for ammunition and should continue to travel with the guns, but the staff officer still reported it to Roberts. The Field Marshal carried out an informal snap inspection personally, and, on examining one of the 'ammo' wagons, found that the tarpaulin had slipped to reveal a box marked 'Van Houten's Cocoa'. 'Well,' he said, his eyes twinkling, 'they mark it very funnily!'

The intense cold continued as they reached yet another Klip River and went to cross the old wooden bridge. The Royal Engineers said that it was safe to carry the seven-ton 4.7s, and although the ancient woodwork creaked ominously, the bluejackets' gun got across safely. However, when the second gun, of the Royal Marines, was halfway over, the left wheel disappeared through the woodwork and became stuck, leaning at an angle of forty-five degrees. There was little Bearcroft could do but to order the bridge to be cut down. The big gun fell into the river with an almighty splash, but luckily the Klip had a hard bottom and the next four and a half hours were spent in righting it and hauling it from the water, helped by sixty-four oxen and several hundred soldiers.

Firing was heard from ahead, in the vicinity of Elandsfontein Junction, where Colonel Henry and his Australian Mounted Infantry had been dispatched to seize the town. Control of this spot would place many items of vital railway rolling stock in Roberts' palm. Henry met with stiff resistance and fierce skirmishing took place among the slate-grey heaps of spoil of the Simmer and Jack mines. This was the firing that the Naval Brigade could hear and they hurried to back up Henry's attack.

Smiling at the plight of the Marines with their gun suspended in midair over the Klip, the bluejackets tore off as fast as they could go, which was 3 or 4 miles per hour, hoping to see some action, but before reaching Elandsfontein Junction they were ordered to follow the Field Artillery back to camp. The army field gun was a lightweight compared to a 4.7, and the sailors, anxious to keep up with the Royal Artillery, were taking a short cut across a corner when the heavy gun became stuck in deep mud, three miles from the camp. The bluejackets, with no blankets and no food, were forced to stay there in the freezing cold all night, guarding the gun until extra oxen could be sent up in the morning. When they arrived, red-faced, back in camp they were welcomed by the derisive cheers of the Marines.

It was at Doornkop, on the fringes of Johannesburg, that the last full-scale set-piece battle of the war would take place. Somehow, it was fitting that it should be so. For it was here, on the exact spot where the Boer commandos

184

from Johannesburg and Lichtenburg under Viljoen and Delarey would make their last stand, that the pathetic champagne-sodden figure of Doctor Jameson, of the famous Raid, had raised his white apron flag of surrender five years before.

Bruce Hamilton's 21st Brigade, with the Gordons and the City Imperial Volunteers in the front line, faced the Boers, who were entrenched on a ridge. The Gordons, with that swaggering swing of the sporran for which Highland Regiments are world-famed, advanced in open order with cast-iron discipline as the Mauser bullets zipped past their ears, plucked at their kilts and thudded into ninety-seven of their bodies. As they gained the crest the order was given to fix bayonets. That was enough. The battle was won.

Within Johannesburg itself chaos reigned as the street-fighting started. But there was a certain incongruity about the scene because, while the bullets were flying in every direction and people were huddled together in shop doorways and under the railway platforms, women were screaming and men were falling dead, the mines and railways carried on working as if oblivious to the fact that a war was being fought about their ears. After a long trip across the open veldt, it all seemed very odd to be in this place full of tall smoking chimneys, bustling engines, revolving winding gear and giant heaps of spoil, with a battle going on.

In the end the civic authorities emerged under a flag of truce and promised Roberts that, provided the Boer army were allowed to retire intact, the Golden City would be surrendered. Giving them twenty-four hours to do this, and on the strict understanding that the gold mines would remain undamaged, Roberts agreed.

On 31 May a grand processional march through the town took place, with Roberts reviewing his forces, including the Naval Brigade, in the main square. The inhabitants, of a dozen different nationalities, turned out in dense crowds to give a generally warm reception, with only a few hostile shouts. Some of the biggest mines even stopped working to allow their employees to watch the occasion. Many remembered the day for the strange sight of sailors marching through their town so many miles from salt water.

The Navy's guns played very little active part in the actual taking of Johannesburg, but Bearcroft's 12-pounders had been sent forward, under the Gunnery Lieutenant, to provide support, if necessary, for the final assault. Somehow they had got hopelessly lost and actually returned to camp via a sector of the suburbs which was still in Boers hands at that point, thus undertaking an unwittingly dangerous adventure.

At the railway station the persistent Midshipman Cunningham squatted beside a small fire on the platform. It was about 8 am and, after an uncomfortable night's sleep, he was frying a couple of rashers of bacon for his breakfast.

After the hectic ride on the ammunition wagon up from Kroonstad to

Viljoen's Drift with Major Marchant and his party of Marines, they had hurriedly transferred their cargo of shells on to a railway truck which they were told was about to depart for Johannesburg, where it had arrived at about midnight on 2 June.

As he prodded his rashers around the frying-pan, Cunningham was approached by a naval officer (most probably Paymaster Penny of the *Philomel*), who told him that the guns had departed an hour since and intended to travel nineteen miles that day. He had missed them again.

CHAPTER 24

DE WET GOES ON THE RAMPAGE

As Cunningham crouched over his frying pan, pondering whether he would ever catch the victorious Roberts and 'that old pig Bearcroft', Grant's Guns were hard at work digging. They were in a ticklish spot. A breakdown of communications, so often the cause of military disasters, and for which General Colvile was to take the blame on this occasion, had landed them in the branch-line terminus of Heilbron, still thirty miles south of Viljoen's Drift and almost surrounded by Boers entrenched on high ground. They were short of food and ammunition, and De Wet, now the proud owner of fifty-five wagons full of warm clothing and food captured down the road in the course of the fiasco, was in a threatening position. It was vital for the British to hold Heilbron. Hence the digging of gun-pits to protect the invaluable 'Little Bobs' and 'Sloper'.

Helped by the Royal Engineers, the bluejackets sweated to sink two pits, each thirty-two feet across, in the stony ground. The work was so laborious that their picks needed to be re-ground twice a day! Into each pit was built two 'ready' magazines, six feet deep and roofed with railway sleepers, as a safety measure against a direct hit on the ammunition. A four-foot deep trench, ninety yards long, joined the two pits.

All through June De Wet was to pursue a successful round of rampage in the northern part of Orange River Colony and southern Transvaal. For him this was truly home territory. His own home and farm were in the Rhenoster valley and he knew every inch of the ground.

He destroyed several railway bridges and miles of line. He attacked a large British supply dump at Vredefort Road Station, which was only lightly guarded by a skeleton force of the Derbyshire Militia. Here there were hundreds of tons of ammunition, thousands of winter greatcoats and blankets, stacks of forage, many truckloads of beef, flour and biscuits, and 1,500 bags of mail. De Wet carried off all that was possible to carry and destroyed the rest.

187

Then he proceeded to tear up thirty miles of track, almost down as far as Kroonstad, and at midnight on 13 June raided the railway again at Leeuw Spruit Station, where there were two trains full of supplies standing in the sidings. Two hundred line-repair workers were sleeping in their tents nearby and could muster only nine rifles between them.

At the same time, an attack was made at Kopjes Station, where De Wet managed to take about forty prisoners before being driven off by a squadron of mounted infantry. Perhaps he would have attacked with a little more vigour, and in more strength, if he had known that Lord Kitchener himself was asleep in his personal carriage in a siding.

But at Heilbron, the Boers just sat there, watching menacingly, and nothing much happened. It developed into a very boring episode, lasting many weeks, with very little to break the monotony, although on 20 June they received orders to move out to cover a convoy escorted by Methuen. Three miles out of Heilbron, Grant could see Methuen's column about twelve miles off. A party of Boers were seen to be stalking the convoy, but they, in turn, were not as yet aware that they were being watched. Grant quickly brought his guns into action at about 9,000 yards and his first salvo landed directly in the middle of the surprised Boers, who mounted their horses in haste and galloped off in all directions.

The sailors returned to Heilbron to spend another five weeks of boredom until, in the knowledge that De Wet had built up a strong local force, Grant was ordered to evacuate his position on 27 July. They loaded the two 4.7s, their wagons and the oxen on to a convoy of several trains on a cold and miserable night.

It was a most unpleasant journey to Krugersdorp in the depths of winter, the motley collection of carriages and trucks being most unsuitable for the transport of men or beasts. Lieutenant Fergusson wrote later: 'It rained and blew and was very cold. An open bogey-truck, with an inch or so of coal-dust in it, which gradually turned into a black mud, can NOT be recommended as a comfortable conveyance.'

Within a few days Grant's Guns were to turn the tables on De Wet and embark on an epic pursuit of the slippery bandit. It was to be a chase covering many hundreds of miles.

CHAPTER 25

LONELY TARTARS AND PHILOMELS

It was strangely lonely for Burne and Halsey in Natal now that Captain Jones and his bluejackets had left to take HMS *Forte* up the Gambia after seven months of campaigning with them. The Tartars were assigned the relatively unexciting chore of guarding Sandspruit Bridge, along with the Dorsets, the 18th Hussars and the 13th battery Royal Artillery, under the command of General Brocklehurst. Burne's men spent the next couple of days working with the Royal Engineers, digging emplacements for their guns, while the officers did the rounds of their neighbouring units, introducing themselves to their new colleagues.

The honeymoon period did not last long, however, because they soon began to be regularly sniped from the surrounding hills and were ordered to make several sorties, escorted by cavalry and infantry each time, to punish their tormentors. On most occasions a couple of dozen shrapnel shells were enough to disperse the small groups of Boers, but soon full-blown commandos came into the reckoning, numbering some 2,000 men or more, as the burghers gradually reorganized themselves. In fact, on Friday, 29 June, the Naval Brigade were out on patrol with the 18th Hussars, in support of a Flying Column under General Coke, when the order came to retire in the face of overwhelming forces.

Burne himself had not been in the best of health for many months, ever since long before the relief of Ladysmith in fact. Another bout of jaundice put him in the Field Hospital for five days and, passing command of his guns to Lieutenant Clutterbuck, he was ordered down to Durban to recuperate in the warmer weather. After a thirty-six-hour train journey, mostly in open trucks, he booked himself into the Marine Hotel. A large packet of mail caught up with him the next day and he also found that two of his friends, Nugent of HMS *Thetis* and Major Brazier Creagh (who had supplied him with champagne when he was sick at Colenso) were also in town convalescing after various illnesses.

He was not to return to active service until 26 July. In his absence

189

Clutterbuck and the Tartars took part in several operations with the two 12-pounders east of the railway, including the capture of Wakkerstroom and Gras Kop, and it was there that Burne caught up with his guns after an agonizing ride in a Scotch cart from the railway to the top of the 6,000-foot hill.

Grass Kop was to remain the base of the Tartars for the remainder of their time ashore, while Lieutenant Halsey and the Philomels stayed at Sandspruit until 10 July, when they were moved by train to Standerton. From there, on 24 July, they marched to Greylingstad to cover the repair work to the railway line to Heidelberg. When this was complete one of Halsey's guns remained to garrison Heidelberg, while the other returned to Standerton.

On Gras Kop the Tartars soon made firm friends with their new neighbours, three companies of the South Lancashires. It was a superb lookout post, commanding a grandstand view in all directions and ideal for the reporting of enemy movements for miles around. But it was also fully exposed to terrible winds and rainstorms, causing some of the men to suffer sickness from exposure at such an altitude.

Notwithstanding the atrocious weather conditions on the summit of Gras Kop, they tried to make the most of it. The mountain slopes and ravines abounded in many kinds of small game, guinea fowl and partridge in particular, and numerous shooting expeditions were organized to provide food for the mess table. A gaggle of geese was 'rescued' from a nearby deserted farm, and these were posted as sentinels in the Tartars' 'farmyard' which was established just in front of the guns.

But it was the never-ending boredom, with nothing to do except gaze through a telescope to watch for any sign of Boer movements or to wander out and shoot some partridge, which called for discipline of another kind from that required to relieve Ladysmith. They were to stay there for three whole months.

CHAPTER 26

A TABLECLOTH IN PRETORIA

Roberts may have made a serious strategic mistake in letting Botha off the hook at Johannesburg. He had had the means to crush the main Boer force there and then, but possibly his decision was tempered by a desire to minimize bloodshed.

The immediate problem of food supplies was solved by the purchase, albeit at astronomical prices, of food and forage from Johannesburg stores and outlying farms. On Whitsunday, 3 June, just as Cunningham was getting his fire ready to cook his bacon, Bearcroft and the guns departed from the other side of town, at the rear of the army, hot-foot for their final goal of Pretoria. Now there was a certain jauntiness about them. Even the mules seemed to have a spring in their step. Surely, this would be the end. Alas, what an illusion!

The rapid advance of Roberts' forces had caused pandemonium in Pretoria. Oom Paul, now dismayed at his predicament, had fled on 29 May down the Delagoa Line to Watervalboven, with £2 million of Rand gold which he had filched before the British could get their hands on it.

Back at Johannesburg Railway Station Midshipman Cunningham finished his bacon, smacked his lips and, hoisting his baggage on his shoulder, set out to try and catch the Naval guns on foot. A long hike still faced him, but he was lucky enough to fall in with a couple of soldiers who had acquired, by some dubious means, a small cart and a pony. They gave him a lift and the intrepid trio raced the conveyance along at such a pace that the poor pony could go no farther when they were still a couple of miles short of Cunningham's target. On foot for the rest of the way, he eventually caught up with Captain Bearcroft, after a chase of 900 miles, at about 5 pm on 3 June.

He had made it in the nick of time. The battle of Pretoria was to start the following morning at 6.30, with Cunningham assigned to the 12-pounder battery commanded by Lieutenant E. P. C. Back of HMS *Monarch*.

The Naval Brigade had reached Six Mile Spruit, just south-west of Pretoria, at noon the next day when they heard the sound of heavy artillery fire up ahead and prepared themselves for battle. Over the crest of the next hill the town was in sight, with its famous forts on the right front. The Boers had positioned several guns on the low hills to the left and the naval 4.7s were quickly drawn up to go into action.

Louis Botha had entered Pretoria with a large number of burghers and deposed the Committee of Surrender, which had planned to hoist the white flag when Roberts drew near. He was now able to call upon the valuable assistance of the armed 'Zarps', the renowned no-mercy hard men from the Johannesburg Police. The defenders opened up with a torrent of pom-pom and rifle fire, and a bitter battle ensued in the suburbs.

Commander de Horsey, also of HMS *Monarch*, was injured in the foot by a pom-pom fuse and had to be helped from his horse, and two of the mules were wounded by the fierce and accurate Mauser fire from the Zarps, who were positioned behind a solid stone wall about 700 yards away.

The Zarps were particularly troublesome until the Naval Brigade and Royal Artillery smothered their stone-wall fortress with shrapnel shells, causing them to retire. From the hills to the left the Boers intensified their shelling, which now concentrated on the ambulances and baggage wagons behind the naval guns and did much damage. Bearcroft's 12-pounders shelled one of the forts, hitting it several times, only to learn that the Boers had evacuated it before the battle.

Eventually the Boer fire slackened and the British infantry moved forward to the stone wall where the Zarp snipers had been, with the 12-pounders drawing up behind them. The sailors continued to hurl their shells on to the Boer positions on the hills to the left until they had silenced the enemy guns there, and the infantry moved forward again.

A bold cinematograph operator asked the officer in charge of the Royal Marines' gun to let him know when the gun was going to be fired so that he could film it. Motion pictures were, of course, in their early infancy in 1900. He took great care in setting up the primitive contraption and waited for the word. Just as the officer was turning to him to give the nod to start filming a salvo of Boer shells flew close overhead with a rasping whine. The film-maker took to his heels and ran, all thoughts of his work of art having vanished. This caused much merriment among the sailors and Marines, because, although the cameras had been following their progress for some time, they had noticed that filming was usually only ever done when they were stuck in a drift or a donga.

At 10 pm Pretoria, now in a virtual stranglehold, surrendered and the next day a huge Union Jack was hoisted over the Raadzaal.

The Naval Brigade hauled their guns into town via a pretty valley just below the great Klapperkop Fort which loomed on the right. They passed great masses of empty cartridge and shell cases strewn around. There was plenty of evidence that there had been a stiff fight, with much damage done to various buildings, and several dead horses lying in the streets. But it certainly was a very pleasant town, with nice houses, well-kept gardens and streams bubbling along beside the roads.

Bearcroft's guns, now accompanied by Cunningham, joined the column to march past Roberts in the town square at 1 pm, with the Grenadier Guards lining the streets to keep back the crowds. On the way the Naval Brigade's mules went on strike and lay down in the road, refusing to get up and ignoring all the threats of the drivers. By the time the stubborn animals had been coaxed back to work a considerable gap had opened between them and the men in front. However, this served to create much more of a spectacle when the sailors and marines marched into the square to the blare of 'A Life on the Ocean Wave'.

The crews were dirty and dusty, even more than they had been at Johannesburg. Nobody had washed for some time and their clothes were as tattered as any tramp's. It was all very un-Bristol fashion and hardly fitting for the representatives of the Royal Navy and Royal Marines to enter an enemy capital in such bedraggled order, but it could not be helped.

The first priority was to clean up, and then for a slap-up meal, for they were all very hungry after much exertion and little food. Many months later Captain Wilson, Royal Marine Light Infantry, of the *Monarch*, said that he had eaten a memorable meal at the Grand Hotel in Pretoria that night, but, strangely, the thing that he recalled about it most clearly was not the food, but the lovely white tablecloth!

Now the war came to within a whisker of being over. With Roberts in Pretoria and sitting on the gold in the Rand, Ladysmith, Kimberley and now Mafeking all relieved, the Orange Free State lost, Cronje captured, Joubert dead and Kruger on the run, Louis Botha's first inclination was to lay down his arms and concede defeat. If he had done so at that point it would have been difficult, even for the most fervent Boer, to have criticized him. But then word reached him that De Wet was having much success in harassing the British supply columns south of the Transvaal border and was actually pinning some of Colvile's force down around Heilbron, which of course included Grant's Guns. And the news of the international strife in China, where HMS *Terrible*'s Naval Brigade was soon to go into action again was heartening from the Boers' point of view. They were confident that France and Germany would soon be involved against the British.

Furthermore, Botha's spies gave their opinion that Roberts' position was nowhere near as strong as appeared at first sight. He needed to devote thousands of troops to the garrisoning of Pretoria, Johannesburg, Bloemfontein and Kroonstad, and to generally 'holding the line', so that now his front-line force amounted to only about 16,000 men. And Botha and Delarey had 10,000 burghers astride the Delagoa Line just fifteen miles east of Pretoria, where it crossed Pienaar's River, near Eerste Fabriken, just six miles on the Pretoria side of a long crescent-shaped kopje known as Diamond Hill.

8 June was a day of armistice and a conference between Botha and Roberts was scheduled for the 9th. Early in the morning of the 9th, however, Botha sent word that the conference was cancelled and that he did not wish to discuss matters any further. He had decided to fight on.

Botha's decision provided Roberts' with an obvious objective. He had to sweep the Delagoa Line free of all Boer forces, then block its entrance to the Transvaal at Komati Poort. Wasting little time, he attacked on the 11th. By then the Naval Brigade had established their camp at Silverton, also on the Delagoa Line, about eight miles east of Pretoria.

The day after arrival in their new base, at about 11 am, the sailors were surprised by the loud boom of a gun and a shell fell about 100 yards short of the wagons and tents. Great clouds of dust flew up and fragments of rock showered down on their heads. Several more shells exploded, but all fell short. They had been fired by a big gun which the Boers had mounted on a railway truck, but which had retired by the time the Naval Brigade had prepared their own guns to reply. Further attempts by the Boers to hit the naval camp were equally unsuccessful, but made life uncomfortable, and everybody was pleased when the order came to march out under cover of darkness and occupy concealed forward positions, as part of Roberts' overall plan to encircle the Boers and cut off their retreat.

Captain Wilson wrote: 'Accordingly, at 2.30 a.m. next morning, in inky darkness and cold unspeakable, we set off. The guns were bad enough to move by day, but when one could not see one's hand in front of one's face, the difficulties very nearly became impossibilities. We marched for three hours at the rate of nearly one mile per hour, and at 5.30 a.m. reached the ridge we were to occupy, and early in the morning commenced the action commonly known as Diamond Hill.'

The naval guns were still out of range when French and Broadwood threw their squadrons of Lancers and Household Cavalry against the Boer flanks, pushing them back, and Ian Hamilton, disobeying Roberts' orders, mounted an attack on Diamond Hill itself, with the Sussex Regiment, the Derbyshire Regiment and the City Imperial Volunteers. The next day Bearcroft's guns came within range. On field-carriages the 12-pounders had an effective range of 9,500 yards, and now they were at 7000.

But two dangers faced the British. First, they were low on ammunition, and second, the struggle between the cavalry and the Boers on the points of the Diamond Hill crescent seemed to be a stalemate. If the cavalry line were to break the British force could have found themselves surrounded and cut off in yet another siege. Then there was the victorious, for the moment, De Wet to think about, roaming free along the Orange River Colony rescue line. Any hope of help from the rump of the Natal Force could be instantly discounted. The massive army with which Buller had hammered his way northwards had melted away, leaving only holding forces in their wake, such as Halsey at Standerton and Burne in his storm-lashed eyrie at Gras Kop, with army detachments of the strength of a couple of companies. Even they were many miles away.

Bearcroft was ordered to concentrate his fire on the railway truck carrying the big gun. This was a difficult target to hit, as it was able to alter the range at whim, but equally it was difficult for the Boers to put it to full use when it had to be kept mobile, because that also had the effect of altering its own range. The naval guns were able to silence it effectively by damaging the intervening line, thereby preventing it from closing the range. Eventually, no doubt concerned that the line behind it would be damaged and the gun stranded, the Boers withdrew it eastwards to safety.

The Naval Brigade fired fifty-seven shells from the two guns that day, doing much damage to the Boer sangars, as well as to the railway line. The station master at Poort Station told them that one of their lyddite shells into one sangar had killed seven and wounded many more. Roberts himself took the trouble to pass by their tents next morning to congratulate them on their straight shooting, saying that it was their last lyddite shell which had 'cleared out the Boers altogether'.

Lieutenant Back's 12-pounders had gone into action at Diamond Hill alongside the 85th Battery, Royal Field Artillery, with the Warwickshires and Yorkshires on the flanks. Now a veteran of the fight for Pretoria, the teenage Cunningham wrote home to his mother after the battle of Diamond Hill. He could have been recording a Sunday School picnic:

Have been chasing Brother Boer out towards Middleburg, trying to round them up ... marched about eight miles and did absolutely nothing, though fairly heavy firing was going on all around us. We started again at six next morning, and marched till 10.30, when we came across a farm with oranges and any amount of forage. Finding the good lady's husband had been away six months fighting against us, we commandeered the forage for the mules and the oranges for ourselves. Then we started lunch and had not been sitting down ten minutes when a most inconsiderate Brigadier-General came up and ordered us to move on. I think he really ought to have considered the fact that we were at lunch.... We then came into action and fired between thirty and forty rounds.... Rifle shots and volleys and artillery were all banging away ... In the night, John Boer fled, leaving nothing behind ... I picked up a few bits of scrap iron that will look well in Lizzie's museum.

After Diamond Hill the Naval Brigade treked back with the guns to Koodoos-poort and then to Marks' Farm, about sixteen miles east of Pretoria, emplacing the guns in permanent positions there which covered the 'poort' in the hills. It was a restful place and the time they spent there was enjoyable. There was plenty of timber and corrugated iron to make comfortable huts. There was a fine stretch of level veldt for games of cricket. There were frequent rides on the stores train into Pretoria. Going in was downhill, which presented no problem, but on the way back it was often necessary for passengers to climb down from the ancient locomotive and walk up the steep bits.

And there was plenty of opportunity for game-shooting on the farm, which fairly abounded with guinea fowl. All these things combined to make for a pleasant interlude after the hardships they had endured. The only sour note was when Mr Marks found that the sailors had been shooting and eating his pet guinea fowls.

They stayed there for five weeks.

CHAPTER 27

GRANT'S GUNS CHASE DE WET

Grant's Guns had used their long stay at Heilbron to practise limbering up and training their oxen. It was therefore disappointing to get orders on 31 July, just after arriving in Krugersdorp, to load 'Little Bobs' and 'Sloper' on to a train with all their wagons and equipment, but to leave the oxen behind. Everything was aboard by 6 pm and they chugged off through the night to Kopjes Station, just south of the Heilbron branch line. There they were allotted some fresh oxen, but felt that they were a poor lot compared with the ones they had trained up only to leave at Krugersdorp.

On 2 August they marched 15 miles to Wonderpeusal and bivouacked alongside various army units. De Wet was holding a chain of kopjes across the Vaal River, and he soon opened fire on their camp, doing considerable damage to the tents and wagons of the Sherwood Foresters. The oxen were grazing peacefully in a meadow some distance in the rear, so, in order to bring the 4.7s into action quickly, they had to be manhandled at the double. With everybody on the drag-ropes, including some 'press-ganged' soldiers, they ploughed straight through an unfortunate farmer's field of mealies and on to the ridge. Fergusson found the range very smartly and burst a shrapnel shell directly on one of the Boer big guns. As escaped prisoner told them later that this had killed four of the crew.

Two nights later De Wet broke away, retreating towards Zeerust, and the British set off in pursuit. It was the beginning of a long and arduous chase.

The guns' carriages were showing signs of serious wear after all the rough treatment they had suffered in negotiating so many miles of rocky ground, muddy drifts, sandy deserts and dongas. Armourer's Mate Joe Tuck of HMS *Barossa* reported that the wheels of No 1 Gun, 'Little Bobs', were particularly weak. The web of the wheel was sheared at the point where it entered the boss for two or three inches. If shearing continued right round, the wheel would fall off. These two long-range guns were the trump cards in the British hand.

Lengthy discussions were held with the specialists from the Royal Engineers, Royal Artillery and Army Service Corps detachments with the column, and it was decided to screw bolts into the boss either side of the web to minimize lateral motion. Tuck borrowed taps and dies and ratchets from the Royal Artillery and inserted four bolts.

They marched on to Modderfontein – 15 miles – on 9 August, and then on to Lindique Drift, on the Vaal River, the next day. The road to the Drift was steep and very twisty, and the bed of the four-feet-deep Vaal was full of large stones. It was very difficult to steer the sick gun, and more alarm set in when they found that some of Tuck's bolts had worked loose and that the other wheel seemed to be wearing in a similar fashion.

On to Lonsberg – 19 miles. De Wet had burned the grass of the veldt ahead, a common trick of his, designed to deprive the British horses and oxen of grazing. But now the sailors were marching against a vicious headwind, maybe Force 6 or 7, and the clouds of dust, smoke and hot ash become intolerable. Their eyes were smarting and almost closed. Their eyelids and nostrils were cracked and bleeding. But they were not far behind De Wet now and they struggled on.

At their next bivouac the bluejackets had just rolled into their blankets for the night when they were woken by crackling smoke and flames. The Boers had torched the long grass again and the fire was really close on the windward side. The sailors tumbled up, still half-asleep, to try and fight the fire, but the wind swept it rapidly through the camp. By the time they had managed to get it under control the blaze had destroyed much of their bedding and leather tack. One of the ammunition wagons had started to burn and was only saved in the nick of time.

By now Joe Tuck was working through the night at each stop in his efforts to keep the guns mobile. All the bolts had sheared or drawn, and he was reduced to cannibalizing wagons for suitable bolts, or indeed anywhere else that they could be found, and then cutting a suitable thread on them. An angle-iron was made, after a fashion, by bending a bit of iron tyre in the cooking fire and then bolting it through the boss and wheel.

Commander Grant mentioned this 'indefatigable man', in his Letter of Proceedings, dated Krugersdorp, 28 August, 1900: 'I must bring to your notice the zeal and energy displayed during the march by Joseph Tuck, armourer's mate of HMS *Barossa*. It was due to his exertions that the guns could be taken along, every halt, day or night, being utilised by him, aided by the guns' crews, to repair, replace nuts etc'.

A pleasant surprise arrived on 11 August by way of a General Order complimenting Grant's Guns on their marching endurance and general conduct, and authorizing a double tot all round, but their delight was soon dampened when the final paragraph was read out: 'Reveille will sound at 2 am, and the force will march at 3 am'.

They duly marched at 3 am, as ordered, to Welverdiend, on the Klerksdorp line, where they arrived at 9.45 am to find themselves in company with several detachments of cavalry, mounted infantry and Smith-Dorrien's Brigades, which had been moved south from Pretoria to help hold the Kroonstad-Vaal River line.

According to Lieutenant Fergusson: 'No. 1 gun was now staggering like a drunken man, the wheels describing a sort of figure of eight in the air.'

It was clear that the 4.7 could not go on and it was decided to dispatch it to Pretoria, with the Gunner and a seven-man bluejacket escort, for proper repairs.

Then, when they crossed the freezing cold five-feet-deep Mooi River on 13 August, they found that No. 2 gun, 'Sloper', had developed the same problem, but the General insisted that the gun was brought on.

On to Schoolplatz – 15 miles – still very close behind De Wet, despite weary oxen and footsore bluejackets. They could hear the sound of Methuen's guns, 20 miles off, engaging De Wet, and they continually passed signs of him being hard-pressed in his flight, the road being littered with abandoned wagons and equipment, besides hundreds of dead horses and mules. Rumour had it that Methuen had De Wet cornered at Rietfontein. They had heard such stories umpteen times by now, but nevertheless they pressed on as hurriedly as the condition of No. 2 gun would permit. The rumours *had* been true, but they were true no longer. De Wet had managed to wriggle out of the trap and escape through Olifant's Nek.

On the afternoon of 17 August orders were received by heliograph to proceed to Krugersdorp, so back they went, having toiled unnecessarily for 27 miles. No. 2 gun wheel was nearly sheared all the way round by now, so Commander Grant reported to the General that he considered it to be in a dangerous condition and asked permission to place the gun on a wagon. This was agreed, provided that 'Sloper' could be unloaded, mounted and fired within one hour, if required. When put to the test, the sailors did it in seventeen minutes, which was a great relief to Grant, who said that the past few days had been like 'a bad dream', being constantly on the lookout for even the smallest rocks and holes in the road which could have put paid to the 4.7.

At Leeuwfontein the gun was packed on the wagon. The technical language in the report which described the method of doing this will be completely incomprehensible to anyone not fully initiated into the mysterious world of engineering: 'On arrival, the trail of the carriage was sunk about a foot. A wagon was emptied and backed over the trail with the wheels on either side of it. A purchase was hooked to a strop round the dessel-boom of the wagon, and to a pendant toggled through the gun; a few rollers on the floor of the wagon completed the arrangements, and the gun was drawn out of the cradle and on to the wagon without difficulty.'

19 August, on to Vlakfontein – 17 miles. The mounting, less heavy now that the wagon bore the gun, made good progress. In fact, the man steering reported that now she was 'a bit quick on the helm'.

Krugersdorp was reached on 22 August. They had marched an incredible distance of 250 miles in 15 days. And that over some rough terrain.

No 2 gun was placed with a local firm to have new bosses cast and wheels strengthened by having circular plates bolted and riveted over the fractured webs. Then they settled down to wait for 'Little Bobs' to come back from Pretoria.

By 29 August repairs to 'Sloper' were still not complete, so it was left in Krugersdorp with a guard of bluejackets and 280 rounds while they went off on trek again, taking 'Little Bobs' and 300 rounds with General Hart's column through heavy rainstorms and treacherously muddy rough roads to where the Boers were entrenched near the Johannesburg Waterworks.

A few shells dispersed the burghers and the sailors marched on to Jackfontein in pursuit, then Woolstadt, where they found the body of Theron, the Boer commander. Then they trudged on to Welverdiend and Klerksdaal. In an attempt to surround the town, General Hart split his column into three as they approached Potchefstroom, where the Boers were thought to be preparing to make a stand. The bluejackets had marched thirty-seven miles through the night. They had taken turns to ride on the wagons, but nevertheless they were desperately in need of sleep when they arrived at 8 o'clock in the morning.

Placing the naval gun in a position to command the town, Hart posted pickets all around it. Then he had his men, including the sailors, conduct a house-to-house search. Not many Boers escaped. There were many of their wounded in the town and eighty others were found in the search, who quickly surrendered, along with their arms and a large quantity of ammunition.

During this time a party of Boers drew up a big gun behind a crest about 4,000 yards away and began shelling Hart's camp, but Grant managed to locate their position accurately and dropped a lyddite shell right on top of it, first shot, and once more De Wet melted away.

CHAPTER 28

SQUEEZING THE LEMON

'That old pig Bearcroft' and his crews enjoyed Mr Mark's hospitality, and his guinea fowl, until 22 July, when the order came for them to set off again to help clear the Boers from the Delagoa Bay railway, all the way down to Komati Poort.

They broke camp and trekked off eastwards, passing Bronker's Spruit on the 24th, where they came across the unkempt graves of the English soldiers who had died there in the First Boer War nineteen years before. For all the urgency of their march, the bluejackets were given permission to linger at the spot for a while to repair and tidy up the little cemetery.

The next day was truly unpleasant. All day long they were on the march and all day long the wind howled and the rain lashed into their faces. Just short of their planned camping ground, towards dusk, one of the guns became stuck in a drift and it took them an hour to extricate it. The ground all around had become a sea of slurry and the kopjes had taken on the 'melting butterscotch fudge' look that was usual in such conditions. But everybody managed to change into dry clothes and crawl under their tarpaulins to sleep. Royal Marine Lieutenant Wilson recalled that he slept in the Officers' Mess wagon that night. The weather was so bad that even 'Bantam', Wilson's pet ox, who was very tame, knew his name and liked biscuits, slept under the wagon. The wind continued raging throughout the night, making such a noise that nobody heard Captain Bearcroft's shouts when his tent blew down in the early hours. Clad only in his shirt, all the Captain could do was to roll himself in the wet canvas and try to sleep.

It had been a truly terrible night, so much so that an officer and three men of the Argyll & Sutherland Highlanders actually died from exposure. But the next day was bright and, after spending the forenoon drying their clothes around enormous camp-fires, they marched off, making Brugspruit on Friday, 27 July. Here their camp was very comfortable, being sited near a colliery

201

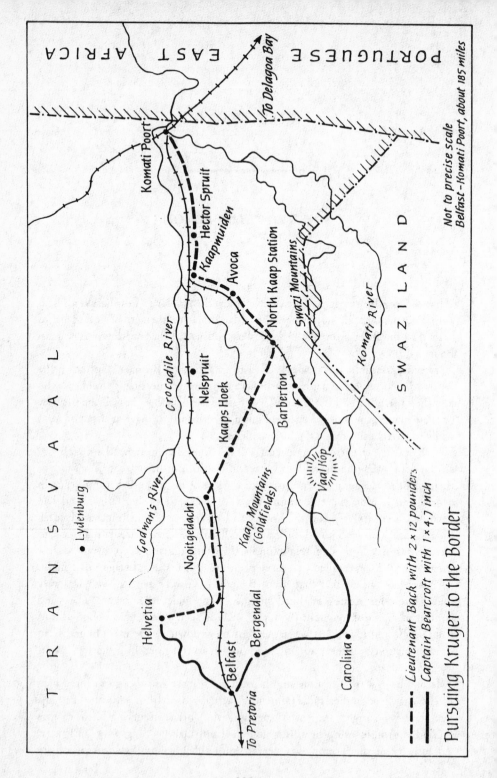

Pursuing Kruger to the Border

- - - Lieutenant Back with 2 × 12 pounders
——— Captain Bearcroft with 1 × 4.7 inch

Not to precise scale
Belfast – Komati Poort, about 185 miles

owned by a Mr Howard, who earlier in the war had been instrumental in assisting British officers to escape from the Model School in Pretoria, where Winston Churchill had been held.

The few days they spent here were very pleasant, the only incident of note being that one day some of the officers were out shooting buck when they were mistaken for a party of Boers by some Australian infantry and several bullets hummed past their ears before they were able to identify themselves, to the profuse apologies of their Antipodean colleagues.

There was a store about five miles away which had an ample supply of beer. Some contraband ammunition had been found at the store, however, and the owner was arrested and the establishment taken over by the Provost-Marshal. After such a long beerless existence, everybody considered the beer to be quite cheap, even at three shillings a pint, which was treble what it cost in England even fifty years later!

Friday, 3 August found them at Oliphant's River, and at Middelburg the next day. There was a store in Middelburg bearing the name of the absent proprietor, one J. Chamberlain. It had been completely ransacked by the Boers, presumably on account of the man's name!

The road out of Middelburg in the direction of Lydenburg was beautifully firm and flat, and made an excellent cricket pitch, although the outfield was difficult, being liberally dotted with anthills and boulders. Several matches were organized and attracted quite a number of spectators, the usual opposition being the Naval Brigade's current escorts, the Scots Guards.

Nearly three weeks went by before the order to move off was given. Everybody was delighted with this because there had been rumours that they were to be sent back to their ships. After all, the army up ahead seemed to be doing a good enough job without the long-range support of naval guns. In fact, they had not fired a single shot in anger since Diamond Hill, a lapse of nearly two and a half months. But it would have been cruelly disappointing not to be in at the finish, after the many hundreds of miles that they had trekked and sweated.

A gruelling pace was set for the next chase. At one time Lieutenant Back's 12-pounders were following hard on the heels of the cavalry, as if they were Horse Artillery. It was a strange sight to see the high-stepping mules trotting instead of plodding along, with the big gun and limber bouncing over the road behind them, and a couple of dozen or so barefoot sailors running alongside, taking turns every so often to jump on a gun-carriage or a wagon for a lift. Naturally such a pace could not be maintained indefinitely, especially when the weather broke and torrential rain drenched them for the umpteenth time. The road was quickly trampled into a sticky goo by the hundreds of feet, wheels and hooves that had already passed over it and the going became very heavy indeed.

They were closing on the town of Belfast on 24 August when the guns became stuck firmly in deep mud and the mules simply refused to pull their full weight. It was biting cold, but they soon got themselves warm by manhandling the guns into position on the low hills overlooking Belfast, which the Boers held in some force.

Field Marshal Lord Roberts arrived by train the next day from Pretoria, the line having been repaired by the Royal Engineers at each British advance. In the afternoon General Buller galloped in, followed shortly by General French. A top-level conference was conducted in a railway carriage and it was decided that Buller and French should push hard on the Boer flanks to slow down the enemy's retreat eastwards, and that Pole-Carew, with the Naval Brigade, should advance on the centre.

With much sweating and straining on the part of both mules and men, the naval guns were positioned on Monument Hill, the highest point in the Transvaal, which dominated the whole countryside to the east. This was not necessarily good tactics, because the Boers were able to sight their range from the monument itself, which resulted in a deluge of bullets and pom-pom fire desending on the naval gunners for the next two days.

Some of the enemy's tricks were becoming stale. They had been used repeatedly on countless occasions since the beginning of the war and were now quite transparent. The black powder trick was one of the oldest. The idea was to use smokeless powder with the main guns, but place one or two obsolete pieces using black powder elsewhere. The black powder made a lot of smoke when the gun was fired and the theory was that this would draw the enemy's fire and fool him into wasting his time by aiming at the wrong guns. Meanwhile, the guns using smokeless powder would not be spotted. That was the theory, but by now the British gunners had learned to ignore the misleading puffs of smoke and simply to stare resolutely through their telescopes trying to spot telltale signs of activity in other places.

In the middle of the forenoon next day the bluejackets' 4.7 crossed the railway, still under heavy sniper-fire from the Zarps. 'Long Tom' itself was now shelling the Marines' 4.7, but its shots were falling well to the rear. Slowly the British infantry pushed their way through the town until the Zarps formed the last pocket of resistance in their stronghold at Bergendal Farm. The British artillery plastered the farm with shells, the infantry pressed forward in a determined rush and the town of Belfast was taken.

The fight for Belfast was the last time that Bearcroft's guns would go into action ashore against the Boers. It was, therefore, particularly cruel luck on Royal Marine Lieutenant Wilson that he should be hit in the thigh after coming through so many actions all the way from Graspan, ten months before, without sustaining a scratch. Fortunately Fleet-Surgeon Porter was close by when Wilson was struck and he was soon bandaged up and placed in an ambulance wagon.

After Belfast the naval brigade was split into fragments. The Royal Marines'

4.7 was to remain dug in on Monument Hill, where it was to stay until they returned to Pretoria, when it was passed over to the army. Lieutenant Back, with the two 12-pounders, was to rejoin Pole-Carew. Bearcroft himself was to take the other 4.7 on a southward swing to Carolina, about twenty miles away.

Cunningham went off on his holidays again. His father had been appointed to the Royal Commission to go out to South Africa to report on medical affairs, and had arrived in Pretoria. Lord Roberts sent direct instructions for the boy to proceed on leave, and so, on 5 September, the Midshipman clambered aboard a goods truck for Pretoria to spend a comfortable week with his father in the luxury of a special train. Even in those days of blatant string-pulling through personal friendships, it was not surprising that Cunningham felt that the Roberts connection made him unpopular with Captain Bearcroft.

Bearcroft's gun was escorted by the Black Watch and Brabant's Horse. There was nothing particular to note about Carolina. It was a typical South African town, with two or three tin-roofed stores, a bank, a doctor, and a large church in a large square. And nothing much happened there. But the Boers were retreating all the way and they soon moved on to Barberton, a sixty-mile trek away in the middle of the De Kaap Goldfield, only fifty miles from the border. The only resistance was by way of an occasional skirmish, but otherwise the trip was uneventful. Going down a steep incline into Barberton several carts capsized and a wagon broke away and three oxen were badly injured in the cascade of heavily loaded vehicles. One had its horn torn off, one had a crushed foot and the third broke a leg.

In the town they found a company of Duke of Cambridge's Own Yeomanry, which they liberated, and in the railway sheds there were no less than fifty locomotives in various states of repair.

There was a considerable Scottish community in Barberton and Bearcroft's men enjoyed a genuinely warm welcome. The evenings were spent socializing and dancing to reels and flings. It is even recorded that 'some charming Dutch ladies assisted'.

Lieutenant Back's 12-pounder battery, who were having to make do without the services of Midshipman Cunningham pro tem, but nevertheless included Lieutenant Colquhoun of the Royal Victorian Navy, thirty-six bluejackets, six wagons and a water-cart, a colonial 'conductor', Mr Duggan, to look after the animals, twelve Cape 'boys', fifty-four oxen and fifty-eight mules, pushed on down the railway with Pole-Carew's 11th Division, towards the border with Mozambique, with the Boers continually retreating in front of them.

Immediately they left Belfast they came under heavy rifle and pom-pom fire from the rocky ridges ahead and Back's guns were hurried forward to support the 85th Field Battery, with whom they were good friends, having marched with them for hundreds of miles. But they were not able to help very much. The range was far too short and the naval 12-pounders simply could not be made to bear. All night long there was sporadic sniping, but in the morning they found that the Boer riflemen, true to style, had slipped away. But the Boers' big guns were still within range and at dawn they began to hammer the British forward positions with 6.2 inch shells.

The naval guns were moved up half a mile to assist the Royal Artillery's 5 inch howitzer battery in silencing this giant gun. This was an expensive operation, taking no less than forty-one rounds before the job was done, and this at a range of 9,000 yards, which required extreme elevation and damaged the improvised gun-carriages considerably.

In fact it was found that the wooden part of the carriage of one of the 12-pounders was 'sprung' close to the axle. Armourer's Mate Smithfield's skills were brought into play and within a few hours he had fitted a new carriage to the old wheels and axle, and remounted the gun. Lieutenant Back mentioned Smithfield in his dispatch, saying that he had 'repaired wheels, wagons, even railway trucks, and whether as armourer, blacksmith, wheelwright or carpenter, there was nothing he could not do, and do well.'

But the Boers looked like being difficult to shift, until heavy gunfire was heard booming around the mountains to the north-east. This was Buller, fighting his way to Machadodorp; this threatened the Boer rear and they slowly retired.

Pole-Carew continued his advance, pushing on to Helvetia the next day, where it was planned to rejoin Buller's column. 'A memorable march through the mountains,' Back wrote, 'clothed in mist, and along very steep and rocky roads cut out of the steep sides. Range after range had to be crossed, and it was a striking sight, when at the summit of one of them to see the road winding along the valleys and up the opposite mountains, covered, as far as the eye could reach, with the snake-like, crawling supply columns.'

They passed hundreds of broken-down wagons, all evidence of De la Rey's discomfiture, and literally herds of mules and horses, all lost and some badly injured, wandered aimlessly along the roads, causing chaos and obstructions. But the naval guns, with ten mules on each, and often assisted by the bluejackets and Coldstream Guard escort on drag-ropes, kept up a good pace and were never far behind the head of the column.

Back's 12-pounders were to fire their final shots at the Boers near Waterval Onder Station, when the cavalry up ahead came under fire from a pom-pom which was quickly silenced.

Pushing on eastwards towards Nooigedacht, they began to meet hundreds of liberated British prisoners of war trudging back up the line towards Pretoria and a good meal.

The Boers had destroyed the bridge at Godwan's River, which necessitated an annoying ten-mile detour to the south of the railway, and a very steep climb to Kaaps Hoek, a little settlement high in the mountains, which would otherwise probably have never seen the trappings of war passing through its remote setting. But the place offered an unforgettable panoramic view of all the operations to the east. To the north-east, in the Lydenburg Mountains, Buller's heliograph could be seen flashing its orders, whilst to the south-east, around Barberton, French's cavalry were winding their way through the passes in the Swazi Mountains, looking like a column of ants marching across a pineapple.

Then the descent came, down the other side of Kaaps Hoek. The check-chains and the drag-shoes were in use the whole time and it was very hard work to control the heavy guns and wagons. Once at the bottom, they were faced with almost impassable terrain on the way to Avoca and on to Kaapmuiden Junction. For much of the way there were difficult spruits and dongas, and for several miles they faced a wall of thick brush and the ground was covered with huge boulders. To make any headway at all they first had to cut an entirely new road through this tangle of virgin scrub.

At Kaapmuiden Junction there were many abandoned locomotives and other rolling stock. There were also whole truckloads of flour, but the Boers had contaminated it with paraffin and burned it. Some of the trucks were still in flames. In nine days Back's crews had toiled ninety miles over the worst terrain they had met throughout the war. Now there were only fifty-four miles to go to Komati Poort, but first they had to tackle the Crocodile Valley.

Back wrote; 'wide open valley, hot, stifling, and suggestive of malaria, covered with thorn, scrub and occasional bright yellow-fever trees. On each side were ranges of low-lying hills, their outlines blurred and indistinct in the stifling mirage – altogether a most undesirable country, and almost waterless.'

The Naval Brigade happened to be in the van and therefore got to do the heaviest work in clearing the thick thorn brush from the stony track, which was so badly overgrown that it seemed to have been unused for many years. Worse still, there were many spruits to cross and deep potholes to be filled with stones before the guns and wagons could pass, all very arduous under the broiling sun of the South African spring.

From Hector Spruit Station down to Komati Poort, twenty-six miles, the railway track was one long dump of abandoned stores, ammunition and black swarms of flies buzzing around the dozens of dead mules that had been left to rot in the sun. An enormous amount of rolling stock blocked the line, for a solid eight miles at one point, and many of the trucks were full of bags of sugar, coffee, mealies and flour, all contaminated and burning smokily.

But the saddest sight of all was a 'Long Tom', rendered useless by its erstwhile owners, with its crooked muzzle pointing drunkenly askance. This gun had caused so much pain and annoyance to the British, especially around Ladysmith. It had fought nobly for its cause. Perhaps it deserved a more dignified end.

Oom Paul Kruger, of course, had been in the rear of the retreating burghers ever since he had fled from Pretoria four months previously. Bidding farewell to his long-suffering wife in the little house on Church Street (they were never to meet again), he had set up a mobile seat of Government in a luxurious train carriage, attached to an engine with steam up twenty-four hours a day, on the Delagoa Line. But now he had been shunted up against the buffers at Komati Poort by Pole-Carew and had only two options at his disposal. Either he could surrender or he could flee again. He fled again, popping out of Transvaal into neutral Mozambique like a pip from a squeezed lemon, to be borne away from Lourenço Marques in a Dutch warship.

At last the Delagoa Line was in British hands. The supply of arms to Transvaal could now be completely blocked. But how much did they already have?

CHAPTER 29

WINDSWEPT AND WATCHING

Lieutenant Arthur Halsey, the Philomels and their 12-pounder were still on guard at Standerton, and Burne and his *Tartar* crew still on the towering windswept window ledge of Gras Kop, peering through their telescopes at the comings and goings below them for miles around. They watched Buller's army bulldoze its way past them, on its way up to Ermelo and on to the high dusty plains of south-east Transvaal, eventually to join up with Roberts' forces in the push to Komati Poort. They watched various bands of Boers playing cat and mouse with Buller. But most of all they did nothing. The nothingness itself was unhealthy enough, for both body and mind, but the weather conditions did little to help.

In his diary for Sunday, 12 August, Burne wrote;

> The gales of wind up here are something awful. This evening, as we were toasting the 'Grouse' at home, a furious blast blew down and split my tent, although fortunately we had a refuge in the mess-house which the Dorsets had made by digging a deep hole roofed over with tin; here we are fairly comfortable and have stocked this splendid apartment with Boer furniture, including a small organ. Our evenings with the South Lancashires in this mess-house have been as merry as we could make them, and our president, Major Adams, whom we all like, occasionally fires off a tune on the organ which he plays beautifully, such as it is. The Volunteers with us are to be seen at all times sitting on the side of the hill surveying the country through their binoculars and watching the movements of the enemy.

All through September they watched, and did nothing much else, except bury two of the *Tartar*'s bluejackets who had died of enteric. Indeed, the recorded figures to the end of October, 1900, showed that disease had accounted for no less than 6,270 British servicemen's lives, as opposed to 4,186 who had been killed by the Boers. The latter figure did not, of course, include the 149 who had suffered an accidental fate. Among these were 1589 Private R. West of the Sussex Regiment, who had fallen overboard from the transport SS *Pavonia*, without ever setting foot in South Africa, or 2583 Private J. Buckley of the King's Royal Rifles, who was run over by a train, or 75428 Sergeant F. Newman and 68315 Sergeant G. Bellamy of 'M' Battery Royal Horse Artillery, who were both struck by lightning, or poor Trooper Smart, of Steinecker's Horse, who was mauled to death by a lion at Komati Poort.

Burne, as anxious as any of his men to leave this dreadful place, busied himself with the preparation of his accounts. This involved much paperwork, and Burne, as a Gunnery man first and a clerk second, had let a considerable backlog build up. So he buckled down to it, recording, among a myriad other details, that he had lost seventeen oxen out of the original count of eighty-four. With the office work done, he would not need to tarry once the word arrived to depart.

To be fair, Burne had not been entirely idle throughout the long months he had languished at Gras Kop. He was a thinking sailor, not so much an inventor, in the Percy Scott mould, but a very observant one all the same. In the course of the campaign he had taken the trouble to jot down many useful thoughts as and when they had occurred to him, and now he had opportunity to compile them properly. The copious notes he made would be sufficient to warrant a book of their own. He explains about the gunnery problems caused by 'mirage' in a climate like South Africa's and the differences in range of shot and the problems of accurate fuse-setting caused by variation in altitudes above sea-level. He talks about the necessity to standardize the dimensions of wheels, tyres and drag-shoes. He explains how he has discovered that, by placing a few sandbags a little way behind the wheels of a field gun, one not only checks the recoil, but the gun almost runs itself out again ready for the next shot, which saves the gun crew untold sweat. He suggests that if a 'split' gun trail had been incorporated into Percy Scott's design for a gun mounting, this would have facilitated greater elevations. He talks about the new telescopic sights that arrived and were used at Spion Kop for the first time. The sights had crosswires that were too thick, in his opinion, so they took some cobwebs from a bush and stuck them on the glass, which worked beautifully! In a polite nudge to the Royal Artillery, he recommends that gun crews should always be allowed to travel light by slinging their rifles on the gun barrel and their water bottles and bags of provisions on the limber, saying that the carrying of these things by the men only exhausts them pointlessly, when at any time they may need all their energy to toil up a hill and bring the gun into action. He goes into the intricacies of night-firing, explaining the techniques he used at Spion Kop and Colenso. He talks at length about the various merits and demerits of different types of field glasses, water filters, tents, breeches, boots and miscellaneous headgear and clothing. He even recommends carrying a small mincing machine in case the only meat available on trek is something unchewable like ox meat.

CHAPTER 30

TIME TO GO HOME

It was nearly time for the Navy to go home. The war itself was to drag on until the middle of 1902, with De Wets, Smuts and others making whatever trouble they could for the British Army. But the role of the long-range naval guns was over. Grant's Guns, 'Little Bobs' and 'Sloper', rumbled out of Frederickstad on 19 September, and on to Witpootje, encountering many small bands of Boers en route. They fired seventeen rounds of 4.7 ammunition before breakfast and carried on firing all day whenever a target presented itself.

As everywhere else, the Boers were retreating all the time. But they were on home ground, with ample meals and soft beds provided at friendly farms along their way. The campaign was costing them little except time. They were playing mouse to an exasperated cat.

The column had just returned to Potchefstroom on 25 September, which De Wet had re-occupied but had left so hurriedly on the approach of the British that his men forgot to haul down their flag from its pole, when orders were received to return to Krugersdorp. Grant's orders were to hand over his guns to the Royal Garrison Artillery and return to Simonstown and their ships.

The Potchefstroom column had marched 310 miles in 20 days. They had fired 22 rounds of common shell, 64 shrapnel and 101 lyddite. Only one man had reported sick in that time. Roberts, through General Hart, wished Commander Grant good-bye, adding, 'Well assisted by your subordinates, you have overcome serious campaigning difficulties with a ponderous gun which has deservedly become the terror of the enemy.'

Commander Grant's final dispatch read:

I have much pleasure in reporting that the spirit, endurance and behaviour of the officers and men throughout the campaign has been beyond praise. Work, often under conditions of great hardship, requiring endurance and spirit to a very high degree, has been met with the greatest spirit and cheeriness, and the smartness, discipline and soldierly qualities displayed will, I am sure, be ever remembered to their credit and to that of the Naval Service. In no instance had Lieutenant Fergusson ever had to bring a man before me for any crime, neglect of duty, slackness, or any other offence whatsoever, and this for a period of nearly nine months. The marching powers displayed by the men have been to me a revelation.

For the record distances covered and days on the march by Grant's Guns were:-

Bloemfontein – Winburg	95 miles in 8 days
Winburg – Heilbron	127 miles in 8 days (consecutive)
Chasing De Wet	265 miles in 17 days
Potchefstroom Column	310 miles in 20 days
Total marched	797 miles in 53 days

They reached Simonstown on 7 October 1900, where the *Doris*, the *Monarch* and the little *Barossa* awaited them.

De Wet? Nobody ever caught him, and he was still making a nuisance of himself to the British when the time came to fight the First World War in 1914.

Both Bearcroft and Lieutenant Back had adventures on the railway on their way back to Pretoria to hand their guns over to the Royal Artillery. Bearcroft loaded his 4.7 and crew on to a train and left Barberton on 2 October. There were rumours that the Boers planned to ambush them between Brugspruit and Balmoral. The Captain had his bluejackets on board, plus a company of Buffs who were travelling with them. He commanded a railway ganger, whose loyalties were suspect, to precede the train on a workman's pump-handle trolley. The man proceeded cautiously, while the train followed on some yards behind at walking pace. After covering three miles in this fashion they came to the ganger's track-side cottage. Bearcroft stationed fifteen men and a Petty Officer at the cottage, and the ganger removed the trolley from the rails so that the train could move forward. After 150 yards there was a tremendous explosion which toppled the engine from the line. Luckily the only casualty was the fireman, who was hurled from the footplate into a ditch, incurring a sprained ankle.

For the rest of the night the track was guarded by bluejackets in pairs at intervals, and Bearcroft set the Marines on guard up ahead along with the Buffs. But the Boers did not intend to go quietly. They attacked again with rifles from behind some distant rocks in the morning, but Bearcroft had managed to get a 15-pound gun sent up with a railway crane to set the engine back on the rails during the night and he brought this into action to drive them off.

The train set off again towards Pretoria, but had only gone 200 yards when

213

there was another explosion. Luckily it was only the line that was damaged and the engine itself was unscathed. When the rails had been set back in order they continued on their way to Pretoria, where they were joined by Lieutenant Back from Komati Poort and the Marines with the other 4.7 from Belfast.

Cunningham? After spending his week's leave with his father, he set off to rejoin Lieutenant Back's battery. But first he had to find them. He knew that they would be somewhere between Pretoria and Komati Poort, so he teamed up with two army officers who were going the same way, Captain Bolton of the Irish Guards and Major Baden-Powell of the Scots Guards, the brother of the Mafeking hero and founder of the Boy Scouts. They travelled mainly by goods truck. There seemed to be no particular reason to hurry, and they made several stops, including one at a small hotel on the Crocodile River, where they found refreshing bathing in the now scorching weather. They took it in turns to mount guard with a loaded rifle while the other two swam, although it is not clear whether the guard kept watch for Boers or crocodiles. Perhaps it was both. With sixty or seventy miles to go to Komati Poort, they heard that the British had already reached that place. There really was no reason to hurry now, so they lingered another ten days in the company of some friendly Guards and Royal Engineers, who were part of Lord Kitchener's escort and who had a very comfortable mess. Eventually Cunningham rejoined Lieutenant Back at Komati Poort. They had bivouacked for a week in 'this sultry place', when the order came to proceed back to Pretoria.

The transport was handed over to the Royal Army Service Corps and the guns and ammunition were loaded on to a funny little train, composed of six oddly assorted trucks and a weird-looking captured engine. Then they waited for the word that the line had been cleared of all the débris.

Lieutenant Back took his leave of General Pole-Carew, under whose command his sailors had trekked hundreds of miles, on 1 October, and the 'crazy dilapidated engine' chugged off. It had chugged three miles when it came to a halt, having lost its head of steam. Here was a chance for the stoker-stretcher-bearers to show some of their professional skills. It was their first opportunity to be involved in anything requiring much skill for many months. After a certain amount of ear-tugging, head-scratching and chin-rubbing, they decided that the tubes needed sweeping. Some makeshift flue brushes were manufactured out of some branches and some lengths of telegraph wire, and the tubes swept clean. They chugged off again, but when the next uphill section loomed up, the engine halted again. The stokers had assured everybody on the train that there would be no further problems, and now all the soldiers on board, mainly Coldstream Guards, burst out laughing. At this the entire naval contingent, sailors, stokers, the lot, leapt from the train as one, shouting 'Shove her up, mates!' and they literally pushed the train up the hill.

As they approached Hector Spruit, the driver, who was half-drunk, saw another engine shunting in the station. He should have braked, but instead he opened the throttle wide and smashed into the other engine, telescoping several trucks and killing one of the passengers, a Royal Engineer. It took more than two hours to clear the line, with the now well-worn but never-failing drag-ropes being put to use one last time.

From Pretoria Reuter's cabled on 7 October: 'The Naval Brigade arrived here this morning on their way to Cape Town. The work of the men has been most arduous. It has included the dragging of huge guns mounted on carriages, hastily made at Simonstown, a distance of nearly 1,000 miles.' In the interests of accuracy the actual mileage was 1,038.

They reached Simonstown five days after the others, the assembled naval contingent having been inspected by Roberts prior to leaving Pretoria and addressed by the Field Marshal in the most valedictory terms. In Simonstown the Ladies of the Town entertained the men to breakfast and most of them proceeded to rejoin their ships.

Cunningham was given the option either to go back to the *Doris* or to proceed home. In the light of the recent authorized truancy that he had enjoyed, it was not surprising that he chose to avoid future involvement with 'that old pig Bearcroft', and he sailed for home a few days later in the transport *Lake Erie*. But first he paid a visit to the Dockyard Cashier to collect his back pay for the time he had been ashore. He was handed a bag containing a hundred gold sovereigns, of which he lost £25 at poker on the voyage home, which, he said later, was probably the most valuable lesson he learned from the war.

All that remained of the Royal Navy ashore in South Africa were the Tartars and Philomels, keeping their lonely vigils on the Transvaal-Natal border. They had been there since July and they were starting to wonder if it was possible that they had been forgotten. Then, on 11 October, a breathless Halsey galloped up from Standerton to tell Burne he had received a wire from Admiral Harris ordering him to prepare the remnants of the Natal Naval Brigade to return to Durban. This was indeed cause for celebration and they dined sumptuously that night on partridge and pigeon that Burne had bagged on a foray with his gun.

The following day, another surprise arrived from the Admiral in Simonstown: 'Burne appointed Royal Yacht, *Victoria & Albert*. He should proceed Durban, whence his passage will be arranged.'

Their eventual departure was delayed because the Boers had pulled up a mile and a half of railway track. Pending its repair, Burne took the opportunity to conclude a little deal with old Mr Scheeper, a local Boer farmer. He had had his eye on Scheeper's pet crane for some time, feeling that the bird would make a nice present, in a suitable cage, for the Governor of Natal, Sir Walter Hely-Hutchinson, to adorn his garden in Pietermaritzburg. The Governor had performed several acts of kindness to the Lieutenant, particularly during his periods of illness, and Burne was anxious to demonstrate his gratitude. Regardless of the fact that Burne and Scheeper were official enemies (indeed, the old man's son was away on active service with the Wakkerstroom commando), such were the niceties of the day that Briton and Boer negotiated an agreeable commercial arrangement. The bird changed hands, as well, it seems, as a certain amount of coffee and provisions, with Scheeper undertaking to manufacture a cage.

At long last, on 23 October, the naval guns were passed over to Lieutenant Campbell and Captain Shepheard of the Royal Artillery. That evening a grand farewell feast was held, with the Queen's Regiment entertaining the naval officers and Bethune's Horse treating the ratings. They were off next morning at 7 am to catch the down mail train at Sandspruit. It had been a close-run thing, because Rundle, French and Hildyard were reported to be surrounding the Boers in a tighter and tighter circle. And Gras Kop was at the centre of that circle, which meant that the burghers would soon need to attack the British positions on the summit in order to gain a defensive position for themselves. In fact, on that very morning they took a patrol of Bethune's Horse prisoner (the latter evidently still feeling the effects of their previous night's carousing with the bluejackets), and shot their horses and smashed their rifles before sending them back to their camp.

Burne's last recollection, as his wagons rolled down to catch the train, flying an absurdly long home-made paying-off pennant with a bunch of flowers on the end of it, was the sight of one of his beloved 12-pounders, now the property of the Royal Artillery, going into action at Parson's Farm and delivering four shells into the midst of a body of marauding Boers to scatter them.

The train clattered its way down to Durban. The Mayor and other dignitaries were on the platform to greet it and afterwards they marched through the streets lined with roaring crowds to an official reception and breakfast. They were dirty and scruffy after their long journey, but Burne felt enormously proud of his bluejackets, who 'looked splendid, hard as nails and sunburnt.'

The *Natal Advertiser* reported the day's proceedings:

Among the first of the 'handy men' who, with their 4.7 inch guns, went to the front were those of HM Ships *Philomel* and *Tartar*. Though in many of the reports HMS *Terrible*'s men got the credit for the work done, the duties were equally shared by the two other contingents from the cruisers. On October 29th 1899, twenty-nine men of the *Tartar* left Durban, and on November 11th thirty-three men and two officers of the *Philomel* were entrained to Chieveley. These men went forward to the relief of Ladysmith, and had to face many hardships and many a stiff fight.

216

Today, the last of them returned from the front. Out of the twenty-nine men of HMS *Tartar* that went forward, only eighteen returned; and out of thirty-three men and two officers of HMS *Philomel* twenty-three men and two officers came down. These losses speak eloquently of the tasks performed, and the hardships endured.

Of the few who could not answer the roll-call this morning, some have been killed in action, others died of disease, while a few have been invalided. After the men of the *Powerful*, the *Terrible* and the Naval Volunteers returned, the *Philomel* and *Tartar* contingents were kept at their posts, and even on their return they had trouble at Gras Kop and Sandspruit. The officers in charge were Lieutenant Halsey, Lieutenant Burne and Midshipman Ledgard.

Shortly after 8 o'clock this morning a crowd began to assemble at the Railway Station, awaiting arrival of the down mail-train. On the platform were: the Commandant, Colonel Morris, the Mayor (Mr J. Nicol), Commander Dundas of HMS *Philomel*, the Deputy Mayor, (Mr J. Ellis Brown), Lieutenant Belcombe, Mr W. Cooley, Surgeon Elliott, and Paymaster Pym. About 100 men of HMS *Philomel*, under Sub-Lieutenant Hobson, were drawn up in a double line outside the station. The train was a trifle late in arriving, but as soon as it drew up, the warriors were marched outside. A ringing cheer from the crowd of nearly 1,500 welcomed them as soon as they took up a position and were called to attention.

The Mayor addressed them, and on behalf of Durban, offered them a hearty welcome back. These men, he said, had been entrusted to go to the front to defend the Colony, and they had done it well. They were among the first in the field and were the last to leave, and he felt sure they had done their duty faithfully, honestly, and well. (Applause.) They might be relied upon to do that in any part of the world, wherever and whenever called upon. They were looked upon as the 'handy men', the men who had done the greatest portion of the work during the campaign. They and their guns saved the situation. Even when they were marching down, he understood that they had had some fighting. On behalf of Natal, he thanked them for what they had done through these trying times. (Applause.)

Lieutenant Halsey, replying, said that after forty-eight hours in the train it was difficult for them to take a reception like this. The men and officers of the Brigade had done their duty, and would do it again if called upon. (Applause.) They were glad that they had been able to do anything in the fighting line, and they thanked the Mayor for the kind welcome extended to them. He called for three hearty cheers for the Mayor.

217

The crowd joined in the response, and raised another for 'Our Boys'. Lieutenant Halsey called for cheers for the Naval Volunteers, who had helped the Brigade so ably during the war.

The concourse of people had now greatly increased, and the Post Office front was thronged. The Brigade was given the word to march, and cheers were raised again and again until the men turned out into West Street. Headed by the Durban Local Volunteers' Band, the *Philomel* and *Tartar* men marched along to the Drill Hall. They were followed by Captain Dundas' piper, two standard bearers, and their comrades of the *Philomel*. At the Drill Hall, arms were piled and the men again fell in, the band playing them along to the Princess Cafe, where they were entertained. The Mayor, the Commandant, Major Taylor, Mr J. Ellis Brown and Mr E. W. Evans received them. At the order of the Commandant, one khaki man sat between two white men, the comrades of the warriors being dressed in their white ducks. At the order of the Town Council, Mr Dunn had provided a most substantial breakfast, to which the men did full justice.

The Loyal Toast having been duly honoured, Colonel Morris proposed 'Our Guests', and said he did not know why the 'villain of Durban' should be called upon to take up this toast, or why the honour of proposing had been conferred on him. He begged to tell them, for the information of those poor fellows who had just come down from the front, that he was the 'villain of Durban'. (Laughter). He meant that if any of these chaps were out after 11 o'clock at night he would find for them nice accommodation in the Superintendent's cells. There was a long time between 9 a.m. and 11 p.m., and he trusted they would not get into trouble. The villain of the piece had to propose the health of these fellows who had come down from the front. (Cheers.)

Now, these Navy fellows, if they could do so well on land, how much better could they not do at sea? (Cheers.) They knew how Jack had fought in the old days of Trafalgar, St Vincent, and at other great battles, and if they had to fight again they might depend upon it that Jack the 'handy man' was just as good today as he was then. (Cheers.) Jack had proved himself a splendid fellow ashore, and he wondered what any of the landlubbers would do at sea. (Laughter.) The sea was a ripping good place to look at, but from his point of view he would rather be on land. (Laughter.) Anyway, Jack did not like the land; he preferred to be on the sea. Therefore when at home on the sea, Jack would do a hundred times better than he had on shore. (Cheers.) He recommended any people who thought of fighting them on sea to take care what they were going against. He did not believe that the British Navy was to be beaten here or hereafter – (cheers) – and he was positively certain, from what he saw of the Navy when they were at the front, that those who went to look at them would

218

say, 'No, we will not play the game with you on water.' He was positively certain they would all be Admirals in time. (Laughter.) That was only if they waited long enough (cheers), and if they did not come across the 'villain of Durban' they would be all right. He wished them all thundering good luck, and he was sure that every one of them would grow younger, because he did not believe that any naval man grew older. When they got their feet back on board again they would feel like chickens. He hoped they would see the dear old country soon. (Applause.) If they did not see it soon they would see it later on. (Laughter.) Now, if they came across an enemy at sea, he knew exactly what would happen, and what they would read in the papers – that the enemy had gone to the bottom of the sea. (Laughter.) He dared say the Navy would be able to respond to the toast. He did not know their capacities for talking, but Jack was never hard up for saying something when called upon to do so. Again he wished them jolly good luck. (Cheers.)

All save the guests rose, and led the Commandant's stentorian voice, sang 'For they are Jolly Good Fellows.'

Chief Petty Officer Munro returned thanks on behalf of his comrades and said that the reception had been quite unexpected. They had had very hard times and they had had very good times. They had done what they did willingly – (applause) – and they were ready to do the same thing again for Her Majesty and the Empire, and also to uphold the good old name of the Navy. (Cheers.) He advised the fellows to keep out of the clutches of the Commandant, for from what he saw of him he thought it would be better. (Laughter.) When nearly twelve months ago they landed at Durban, the people were a bit more excited than they were today.

Lieutenant Halsey asked the men to drink to the Mayor and Council of Durban. Everybody outside knew, he said, how kindly Durban was looked upon. Durban was one of the best places in the station – (applause) – and it was on account of the wonderful way everything was managed by the Mayor and Council. (Cheers.)

The toast was pledged with enthusiasm and the Mayor said they were proud to have them here, and to entertain them. Then men then fell in again in Field Street, and marched off to the Point, the Durban Light Infantry Band playing 'Just a little bit off the Top' as a march.

The *Philomel* and the hospital ship *Orcana* had been dressed for the occasion and a number of their comrades assembled at the Passenger Jetty and cheered them on arrival. They were afterwards conveyed to the cruisers.

Among the Navals who returned from the front this morning is a little canine hero, 'Jack' the terrier, which has shared their fortunes throughout the war. When they left Durban ten months ago a little fox terrier followed them. While at the front he never left them, although he was not particular with whom he fed or what kind of weather prevailed. The firing of a 4.7 gun did not discourage him and through the booming of big guns and the rattle of musketry he stuck by his adopters. Through every engagement he went and has come back bearing an honourable scar on the head – shot by a Mauser bullet. The men, needless to say, idolise the little hero, whose neck is decorated with a large blue ribbon from which is suspended a Transvaal Commemoration Medal.

Then it was time for both Philomels and Tartars to take their leave of each other. They had fought side by side for many a mile, and the memories of their joint adventures would stay with them for the rest of their lives. The *Philomel* was lying alongside awaiting her contingent from the Brigade and, after the usual round of back-slapping and hand-shaking and much 'see you in Pompey' type conversation, the Tartars, including Commander Dundas and Midshipman Ledgard, were discharged to the SS *Tantallon Castle* for passage to the Cape, where they would rejoin *Tartar*, which had been cruising around the South Atlantic, and was at that moment about to leave Sierra Leone to head back south.

Midshipman Cunningham was not the only member of the Naval Brigade aboard the steamer *Lake Erie*, as she slid up Plymouth Sound and boomed a deep-throated greeting to an English autumn. Far from it. There was a considerable number of others.

It will be remembered that Lambton and his Ladysmith Brigade from the *Powerful* had been entertained by Queen Victoria, Lloyds of London and the Mayor of Portsmouth. Captain Percy Scott and the Terribles had been received like Royalty in the Far East. Lieutenant Michael Hodges had been showered with flowers in Dorchester. All the Royal Marines in Chatham, whose colleagues had served the 4.7s 'Ich Dien' and 'Joe Chamberlain', from the *Monarch* and the *Doris*, over a 900-mile trek, were given a holiday to celebrate their return. And the Philomels and Tartars had been feted to unprecedented limits at the Princess Cafe in Durban.

But *The Times* reported on 13 November, 1900: 'The Devonport contingent of the Naval Brigade, which returned from South Africa in the steamship *Lake Erie* on Saturday, arrived at Devonport yesterday. Their arrival at Devonport was unexpected, and there was no attempt to give them a reception.'

The Silent Service had remembered to live up to its name.

POSTSCRIPT

The end of this book marks the start of many other interesting tales. Lambton eventually inherited a brewery – perhaps the ultimate sailor's dream – but only on condition that he changed his name to Meux. All three of his surviving Lieutenants, Halsey, Heneage, and Hodges, became Admirals. Captain Percy Scott carried on with his inventions and was called to organize the defence of London against the first-ever air raids in the First World War. Midshipman Sharp went on to command one of the Royal Navy's earliest submarines – the historic *Holland 2*. Midshipman Cunningham became Commander-in-Chief of the Mediterranean Fleet in the Second World War and later First Sea Lord. Lieutenant Back was in command of the ironically named battleship HMS *Natal* and was killed when she blew up in the First World War. Ogilvy was to die at the young age of 43 in 1909.

And the Boer War exploits of these officers and their hard-as-nails Brigades of khaki-clad bluejackets, the Field Gun Jack Tars, have been commemorated ever since 1907 in the famous Royal Navy Field Gun Competitions at the annual Royal Tournament. It has been called the toughest sport in the world, and is a spectacle the flavour of which may be imagined by those who have not seen it, from the words of one open-mouthed American visitor, 'Oh, Jesus! No, I don't believe it!'

But all that, as they say, is another story.

APPENDIX I

OFFICERS OF NAVAL BRIGADES.

Brigade landed to defend Stormberg.

H.M.S. 'Powerful.'

Com. A. P. Ethelston. [Killed Graspan.]
Lieut. F. J. Saunders, R.M.L.I.
Surgeon C. M. Beadnell.
Mid. T. C. Armstrong.
Mid. G. E. Lewin.

H.M.S. 'Doris.'

Major J. H. Plumbe, R.M.L.I. [Killed Graspan.]
Capt. A. E. Marchant, R.M.L.I.

Lieut. W. T. C. Jones, R.M.L.I. [Wounded Graspan.]
Lieut. G. W. McO. Campbell, R.N.
Fleet Surgeon J. Porter.
Sub.-Lieut. R. F. White.
Ass. Paymaster B. C. Allen.
Mid. C. A. E. Huddart. [Killed Graspan.]
Mid. T. F. J. L. Wardle.

H.M.S. 'Monarch.'

Lieut. F. W. Dean.
Lieut. Guy Senior, R.M.A. [Killed Graspan.]

First Brigade reinforced and placed under orders of Lord Methuen.

H.M.S. 'Doris.'

Capt. R. C. Prothero, R.N. (in command). [Wounded Graspan].
Lieut. the Hon. E. S. H. Boyle.

Gunner E. E. Lowe.
Mid. Egerton.
Mid. W. W. Sillem.
Mid. J. F. Houstoun.

Reinforcements after Graspan.

H.M.S. 'Philomel.'

Capt. J. E. Bearcroft (commanded Brigade till it was recalled).

H.M.S. 'Doris.'

Sub-Lieut. M. G. Newton.
Surgeon E. P. Mourilyan.

Gunner H. Ball.
Mid. Robertson. [Died Modder River, enteric.]
Mid. J. W. Rainier.
Mid. F. P. Saunders.

223

H.M.S. 'Monarch.'

Com. S. V. Y. de Horsey. [Wounded Pretoria].

Capt. R. H. Morgan, R.M.L.I.
Lieut. L. O. Wilson, R.M.L.I. [Wounded Belfast.]

Joined at Modder River.

Lieut.-Com. W. J. Colquhoun, Royal Victorian Navy.

H.M.S. 'Monarch.'

Lieut. E. J. K. Newman.

Lieut. W. S. Poë, R.M.A.
Lieut. G. I. Raikes, R.M.A.

H.M.S. 'Powerful.'

Major A. G. B. Urmston.

Grant's Guns.

H.M.S. 'Doris.'

Com. W. L. Grant.
Mid. G. H. Lang.
Mid. J. Menzies. [Died enteric.]

H.M.S. 'Barrosa.'

Lieut. J. A. Fergusson.

H.M.S. 'Monarch.'

Surgeon T. T. Jeans.
Gunner J. Cannon.

Joined at Paardeberg and Poplar Grove.

H.M.S. 'Doris.'

Major S. D. Peile, R.M.L.I.
Lieut. A. H. French, R.M.L.I.

Mid. A. B. Cunningham.
Mid. Lloyd. [Died enteric.]

Joined at Bloemfontein.

H.M.S. 'Monarch'

Lieut. E. P. C. Back, R.N.

H.M.S. 'Philomel.'

Paymaster W. B. Penny.

Joined at Pretoria.

H.M.S. 'Doris.'

Mid. B. M. Denison.

Total number of officers 46
Killed 4
Wounded 4
Invalided 19
Died 3

H.M.S. 'Forte.'

Captain E. P. Jones (in command).
Lieut. F. W. Melvill.
Lieut. G. P. E. Hunt.
Staff Surgeon F. J. Lilly.
Act. Leiut. J. M. Steel.
Gunner E. Holland.

H.M.S. 'Terrible.'

Com. A. H. Limpus.
Lieut. F. C. A. Ogilvy.
Lieut. S. R. S. Richards.
Lieut. J. S. Wilde.
Lieut. G. P. England.
Sub-Lieut. S. Newcome.
Surgeon E. C. Lomas.
Surgeon C. C. Macmillan.
Engineer J. F. Arthur.
Engineer A. E. J. Murray.
Ass. Eng. F. J. Roskruge.
Gunner J. Wright.
Gunner E. J. Cole.
Gunner E. Williams.
Mid. P. F. Willoughby.
Mid. R. T. Down.
Mid. R. B. C. Hutchinson.

Mid. A. C. Ackland.
Mid. A. E. Sherrin.
Mid. H. E. W. C. Whyte.
Mid. G. M. Skinner.
Mid. G. L. Hodson.
Mid. W. W. Hallwright.
Mid. H. S. W. Boldero.
Mid. J. A. G. Troup.

H.M.S. 'Tartar.'

Lieut. J. E. Drummond.
Lieut. H. W. James.
Staff Surgeon J. Hughes.

H.M.S. 'Philomel.'

Lieut. A. Halsey.
Lieut. C. R. N. Burne.
Lieut. A. Deas.
Lieut. F. A. Clutterbuck.
Mid. W. R. Ledgard.
Clerk W. T. Hollins.

Natal Naval Volunteers.

Lieut. Anderson (in command).
Lieut. Chiazzari.
Lieut. Barrett.

The Ladysmith Brigade consisted of 17 officers and 267 men, the names and ranks of the officers being as follows:

Captain the Hon. Hedworth Lambton (in command).
Lieut. F. G. Egerton. [Killed.]
Lieut. A. W. Heneage.
Lieut. L. Halsey.
Lieut. M. H. Hodges.
Fleet-Paymaster W. H. F. Kay. [Died, enteric.]
Surgeon J. G. Fowler.
Engineer E. H. Ellis.
Engineer C. C. Sheen.
Gunner W. Sims.
Midshipman J. R. Middleton.
Midshipman H. T. Hayes.
Midshipman R. C. Hamilton.
Midshipman the Hon. I. L. A. Carnegie.
Midshipman Alick Stokes.

Midshipman E. G. Chichester. ⎫
Midshipman C. R. Sharp.   ⎬ from H.M.S. 'Terrible.'

Lieut. E. C. Tyndale-Biscoe (late R.N.) and Lieut. E. Stabb, R.N.R. [died, enteric], joined the Brigade after arrival at Ladysmith.

The 267 men included the guns' crews, small-arm companies, 2 engine-room artificers, and 6 stokers as a gun-mounting party, 42 stokers as stretcher-bearers and ammunition carriers, 8 armourers, 2 cooks, 9 marine servants, and a ship's steward's boy, besides a ship's corporal and a sick-berth attendant, blacksmith, and carpenters.

The casualties among the officers and men of the Ladysmith Brigade were:

	Officers.	Men.
Killed or died of wounds	1	5
Died of disease	2	25
Wounded	1	4

APPENXDIX II

LIST OF OFFICERS AND MEN* BELONGING TO THE *TERRIBLE* WHO LANDED WITH THE NAVAL BRIGADE IN SOUTH AFRICA.

SOUTH AFRICA.

Captain Percy Scott, Commandant of Durban	Mr Laycock, clerk
	Mr Blanchflower, clerk
Assistant-Paymaster Cullinan, Secretary to Commandant	Chief Writer Elliott
	Second Writer Shepherd
	Petty Officer Porch

Commandant's Staff in Durban

DURBAN DEFENCE FORCE, AND RELIEF OF LADYSMITH CONTINGENT.

Captain E. P. Jones (*Forte*), commanding Naval Brigade	Surgeon Lomas, R.N.
	Engineer Arthur, R.N.
Commander Limpus (second in command of Naval Brigade)	Mr Cole, Gunner, R.N.
	Master-at-Arms Crowe
Midshipman Hutchinson (A.D.C. to Captain Jones)	Chief Gunnery Instructor Baldwin

Staff duties with naval headquarters under Captain Jones

No. 1 4.7-inch Gun.

Lieutenant England, R.N., in command	„ Sandry
Midshipman Sherrin	„ Elliott
Chief Petty Officer Bate (Capt. of Gun)	„ Murray
Petty Officer Honniball	„ Powell
„ Skinner	„ Dennis
Ldg. Seaman Grounds	„ Palmer
Seaman Weippart	„ Lindridge
„ Moloney	„ Lovelady
„ Kewell	„ Hicks
„ Starling	„ Brennan

* Exclusive of officers and men borne for passage to China. Officers commanding units of *Terrible*'s guns have their ships' names shown in brackets.

227

Seaman	Williams		"	Legg
"	Cotton		"	Nethercoat
"	Shepard		"	Kimber
"	Helman		"	Benn

No. 2 4.7-inch Gun.

Lieutenant Hunt (*Forte*) in command			"	Symes McLeod
Midshipman Troup			"	Pearce
Chief Petty Officer Stephens (Capt. of Gun)			"	Simmons
Petty Officer Dear			"	Howe
" Wright			"	Pope
Ldg. Seaman Gardner			"	Gardner
Seaman	Towers		"	Livermore
"	Grady		"	Carpenter
"	Burnham		"	Cotcher
"	Rood		"	Channen
"	Curtis		"	Plummer
"	Rowe		"	Salter
"	Tucker			

Miscellaneous, attached to 4.7 Battery.

Sick-berth Steward Stewart			Armourer Ellis	
Ldg. Stoker Clark			Carpenter's Mate Brown	
Stoker	Miles		Blacksmith Burnett	Special Duties
"	Clifton	Ambulance Section	Carpenter's Crew, Adams	
"	Skene		Ldg. Signalman Large	
"	Austin			
"	McGuire			
"	Morgan			

Lieutenant Richard's 12-pounder Unit (Two Guns).

Midshipman Down

(1)		(2)	
Ldg. Seaman Beatty (Capt. of Gun)		Sergeant Roper (Capt. of Gun)	
Seaman	Ashton	Lance-Corpl. Porteous	
"	Lintern	Private Mills	
"	Perkis	" Annetts	
"	Allison	" Stubbington	
"	Hurl	" Nowell	
"	Bird	" Gulliver	
"	Dennis	" Fazackerly	
"	Marsh	Shipwright McLeod	Special Duties
"	Sales	Armourer Murray	
		Petty Officer Jeffery	

228

Lieut. Wilde's 12-pounder Unit (Two Guns).
Midshipman Ackland

(1)		(2)	
Petty Officer	Metcalfe (Capt. of Gun)	Petty Officer	H. Mitchell (Capt. of Gun)
Seaman	Murphy	Seaman	Barrett
"	Warren	"	Roman
"	Stansmore	"	Stones
"	Fisher	"	Talbot
"	Jones	"	Cook
"	Alexander	"	Smith
"	Terry	"	Gurr
"	Lock	"	Pellett
"	Wilson	"	Harris
"	White	"	Hughes
		"	Maloney

Lieut. Burne's ('Philomel') 12-pounder Unit (Two Guns).
Midshipman White

(1)		(2)	
Petty Officer	Mitchell (Capt. of Gun)	Petty Officer	Mullis (Capt. of Gun)
Seaman	House	Seaman	Treharne
"	Shepherd	"	Elms
"	Ratcliffe	"	Gurney
"	Webber	"	Fegan
"	Tuck	"	Kirby
"	Moyse	"	Russell
"	Long	"	Patten
"	Phillips	"	Jones
Stoker	Dunstall	Stoker	Taylor

Lieut. Melville's ('Forte') 12-pounder Unit (Two Guns).
Mr Williams, Gunner, R.N.

(1)		(2)	
Petty Officer	Brimble (Capt. of Gun)	Petty Officer	Strudwick (Capt of Gun)
Ldg. Seamen	White	Seaman	Evans
Seaman	Dews	"	Harwood
"	Nightingale	"	Reading
"	Gould	"	Frood
"	Leniham	"	Alexander
"	Robertson	"	Dyer
"	Bonnick	"	Woodward
"	Judd	"	Caws
"	Cooke	"	Wiltshire
		Stoker	Sears

Lieut. Ogilvy's 12-pounder Battery (Four Guns).

Officers

Lieutenant Deas, R.N. (*Philomel*)	Midshipman Willoughby
Surgeon Macmillan, R.N.	,, Boldero
Mr Wright, Gunner	,, Hallwright
	,, Hodson

(1)	(2)
Petty Officer Venness (Capt. of Gun)	Petty Officer Taylor (Capt. of Gun at
,, Peckett	Colenso)
Seaman Ryall	,, Challoner (Capt. of Gun)
,, Randall	Seaman Dibden
,, Knight	,, Melbourne
,, Campling	,, Bradbury
,, Marjoran	,, Smith
,, Hayles	,, Thomas
Stoker King	,, Sawyers
,, Willey	,, Cox
	,, Newstead
	Stoker Aldworth

(3)	(4)
Petty Officer Ward (Capt. of Gun)	Petty Officer Symons (Capt. of Gun)
,, Hunt	,, Fitzgerald
Seaman Bobbett	Seaman Pledge
,, Ousley	,, Vosper
,, Webster	,, Rovery
,, Leach	,, Aylsbury
,, Courtney	,, Funnell
,, Edney	,, Davis
,, Haynes	,, Ball
Stoker Howard	Stoker Riddle

Miscellaneous, attached to Ogilvy's Battery.

Sick-Berth Steward Attree	⎫	Ldg. Signalman Brown	⎫
Stoker Ross		,, Shipwright Harvey	
,, Gouge	⎬ Ambulance	Armourer's Mate Ford	⎬ Special
,, Curtis	Section	Cooke's Mate Couzins	Duties
,, Bailey		Private (R.M.L.I.) Lessey	
,, Sterck		,, ,, Lovall	⎭
,, Yeomans	⎭		

Lieut. Drummond, 6-inch Gun.

Midshipman Skinner		Stoker	Hooker
Petty Officer Connor (Gunnery Instructor)		"	Johnson
"	Allen (Capt. of Gun)	"	Sheldon
"	Carey (Second of Gun)	"	White
Seaman	Rees	"	Sweeney
"	Orr	"	Belsey
"	Cole	"	Haberfield
"	Osbourne	"	Arnell
"	Smithen	"	Vickers
"	Reed	"	Knight
"	Lavers	"	Wilkins
"	Tuttle	"	Goldsmith
"	Shouler	"	Lane
"	Thomas	"	Stone
"	Toms	"	Weir
"	Shergold	"	French
"	Varnham	"	Eames
"	Bryant	"	Stevenson
"	Silver	"	Bishop
"	Stevens	"	Cooper
"	Elston	"	Foord
"	Harris	"	Burns
"	Ford	"	Evans
Ldg. Stoker	Cripps	"	Stevens
"	Parham	"	Maurice
Stoker	Murray	"	Woolley
		Armourer	Whitlock

Searchlight Train, with Ladysmith Relief Column.

Sub-Lieutenant Newcome, R.N.		Yeoman of Signals Arnold	
Engineer Murray, R.N.		Petty Officer Prince	
Artificer Jones		Stoker	Cox
		"	Aughton

Ammunition Guard at Frere.

Petty Officer Horner		Seaman	Hamon
Seaman	Hunter	"	Thomas

231

APPENDIX III

LIST OF DISTINCTIONS AWARDED FOR SERVICE WITH NAVAL BRIGADES IN THE SOUTH AFRICAN WAR.

COMPANIONS OF THE ORDER OF THE BATH.

Captain the Hon. Hedworth Lambton, R.N.
Captain E. P. Jones, R.N.
Captain R. C. Prothero, R.N.

Captain J. E. Bearcroft, R.N.
Major S. P. Peile, R.M.L.I.
Major A. E. Marchant, R.M.L.I.

COMPANIONS OF THE DISTINGUISHED SERVICE ORDER.

Lieutenant G. P. E. Hunt, R.N.
Captain W. T. C. Jones, R.M.L.I.
Surgeon E. C. Macmillan, R.N.
Staff-Surgeon E. C. Lomas, R.N.
Lieutenant W. J. Colquhoun, Victorian Navy.

Lieutenant N. W. Chiazzari, Natal Naval Volunteers.
Captain Leslie O. Wilson, R.M.L.I.
Captain F. J. Saunders, R.M.L.I.

CONSPICUOUS SERVICE CROSS.

Ernest E. Lowe, Gunner, R.N.
Joseph Wright, Gunner, R.N.
T. C. Armstrong, Midshipman, R.N.
T. F. J. L. Wardle, Midshipman, R.N.

R. B. C. Hutchinson, Midshipman, R.N.
C. A. E. Huddart, Midshipman, R.N.
[Killed Graspan.]

PROMOTIONS.

COMMANDERS TO BE CAPTAINS.

Commander A. H. Limpus, R.N.
Commander W. L. Grant, R.N.

Commander S. V. V. de Horsey, R.N.

LIEUTENANTS TO BE COMMANDERS.

Lieutenant F. G. Egerton (promoted after being mortally wounded).
Lieutenant F. C. A. Ogilvy.
    "   F. W. Dean.

Lieutenant Arthur Halsey.
    "   H. W. James.
    "   J. A. Fergusson.

Major A. G. B. Urmston, R.M.L.I., to be Brevet-Lieut. Col.
Captain A. E. Marchant, C.B., R.M.L.I., to be Major.
Lieutenant W. T. C. Jones, D.S.O., R.M.L.I., to be Captain.
Fleet-Surgeon J. Porter, R.N., to be Deputy Inspector-General of Hospitals and Fleets.
Staff-Surgeon F. J. Lilly, R.N., to be Fleet-Surgeon.
Surgeon C. M. Beadnell, R.N. ⎫
    "   E. C. Lomas, R.N. ⎬ to be Staff-Surgeons.
Assistant-Paymaster B. C. Allen, R.N., to be Paymaster.
Engineer E. H. Ellis, R.N. ⎫
    "   C. C. Sheen, R.N. ⎬ to be Chief Engineers.
Gunner W. Sims, R.N., to be Lieutenant, R.N.

NOTED FOR EARLY PROMOTION.

Lieutenant E. P. C. Back.
    "   J. E. Drummond.

Lieutenant C. R. N. Burne.
Surgeon J. G. Fowler.

The majority of the midshipmen were recommended for early promotion, on qualifying for the rank of Lieutenant.

A LIST OF PETTY OFFICERS, NON-COMMISSIONED OFFICERS AND MEN OF THE ROYAL NAVY AND MARINES SPECIALLY MENTIONED IN DESPATCHES.

LADYSMITH BRIGADE.

Captains of Guns.

H. W. C. Lee, P.O.I., Captain of 4.7 on Junction Hill.
P. T. Sisk, P.O.I.,   "   "   at Cove Redoubt.
A. C. Pratt, L.S.   " 12-pounder at Leicester Post.
A. G. Withers, P.O.I,   "   "   at Gordon Post.
S. E. Hemmings, L.S.   "   "   at Manchester Camp.

THE NATAL NAVAL BRIGADE.

Geo. Crowe, M.A.A.
Chief Petty Officers. – Thos. Baldwin, Wm. Bate, Ben. Stephens, Alex. A. Munro.
Petty Officers, 1st Class. – Pat. Cashman, T. Mitchell, J. Mulliss, J. Weatherhead, J. Venness, N. Symons, H. Harrison, J. Funnett.

Petty Officers, 2nd Class. – G. H. Epsley, E. A. Harvey, C. Challoner, T. Sargent. Leading Seaman W. H. Franklin.

Able Seamen. – P. Treherne, D. Shepherd, H. House, W. Jones, E. Cheeseman, D. Smith, J. Macdonald, G. Baldwin, J. Sawyer, H. Wright, T. Payne, F. Ryall, W. Wiltshire.

Ordinary Seamen. – A. E. Reading, H. Harwood, F. Tuck.

Chief Armourer J. Restall; Armourer Ellis; Armourer's Mate O. A. Hart; Armourer's Crew. Geo. Hooper.

Yeomen of Signals T. Ball, E. Waring, C. Patton.

Stokers G. Sears, W. Dunstall.

Natal Naval Volunteers. – Leading Seaman W. Antony; Thos. Druce, A.B.

CAPTAIN BEARCROFT'S BRIGADE.

Chief Petty Officer Jeremiah Brien.

Petty Officers, 1st Class. – W. J. Jago, F. S. Barrett, – Fuller, W. C. Browning, P. Tunnicliffe, T. W. Ashley, B. Murphy, J. Hunkin.

Leading Seamen. – A. E. James, E. E. Gray.

Able Seamen. – S. Delbridge, Pat. McCarthy, T. C. Davey, J. D. Sharp, Geo. Lobb, Chas. Crook, Wm Percival.

Armourer S. K. Colevill; Armourer's Mate A. Smithfield; Armourer's Crew, J. C. Hocking.

Yeoman of Signals C. Chapman; 2nd S.B. Steward W. J. Phillips.

Leading Stoker (2nd Class) D. J. Sandford.

Royal Marine Artillery. – Colour-Sergt. R. Boyd, Sergeant Gill, Lance-Sergeant E. Burroughs, Gunner H. Johnson, Bugler A. E. Trayfoot.

Royal Marine Light Infantry. – Sergeants D. Leach, Geo. Wheeler, and E. Churchman. Lance-Sergeant A. Woollacott. Lance-Corporals E. Rice and Hucking. Privates H. Freeman, J. Conway, C. Piper, J. Roades.

GRANT'S GUNS.

Petty Officers, 1st Class. – B. Murphy, R. Aitkin, I. Tabb, – Higgins, R. Hall. Leading Seaman – Gardiner. Able Seamen A. G. Clark, J. C. Hartnett, H. Widdicombe.

Armourer's Mate Joseph Tuck.

BIBLIOGRAPHY

Naval Brigades During the South African War, Jeans, Sampson Low, 1901.
With the Flag to Pretoria, Wilson, Harmsworth, 1901.
With the Naval Brigade in Natal, Burne, Edward Arnold, 1902.
The Commission of H.M.S. TERRIBLE, Crowe, Newnes, 1903.
Fifty Years in the Royal Navy, Scott, John Murray, 1919.
A Sailor's Odyssey, Cunningham, Hutchinson, 1951.
The Siege of Ladysmith, Gerald Sharp, McDonald & Janes, 1976.
A Dictionary of Battles, Young, New English Library, 1977.
The Boer War, Pakenham, Weidenfeld & Nicolson, 1979.
Ladysmith, Chisholm, Osprey, 1979.
Men of Destiny – CECIL RHODES, Plomer, Heron Books.
The Times *Review*
Who Was Who.

INDEX

Abdy, Major, 86, 87
Acton Homes, 91
Adams, Major, 209
Albrecht, Trooper, 87
Alexandra, Princess of Wales, 141
Allen, Assistant-Paymaster B.C. 28
Allen, Petty Officer, 126, 128
Almond's Nek, 179–181
Aloe Knoll, 94
Amery, Leo, 52
Anderton, Lieutenant, 66, 131
Argyll & Sutherland Highlanders, 14, 54, 55, 60, 120, 173, 201
Armstrong & Co., 120
Armstrong, Midshipman T. C., 28, 37, 39
Army Ordnance Corps, 13
Army Service Corps, 13, 198, 214
Ashley, Petty Officer, 39
Atkins, J. B., 52, 88, 94, 132
Austin, AB. Sidney, 35
Australasian, 26
Australian Mounted Infantry, 184, 203

Baboon Kop, 173
Back, Lieutenant E. P. C., 168, 191, 195, 203, 205, 206, 207, 21, 3, 214, 221
Baden-Powell, Colonel Robert S., 26
Baden-Powell, Major, 214
Baldwin, Chief Gunnery Instructor, 66, 80, 131
Ball, Gunner, 59
Balmoral, 213
'Bantam', pet ox, 201
Barber, Mr, Mayor of Windsor, 143
Barberton, 205, 207, 213
Barnes, Marine W., 35
Barossa H.M.S., 98, 99, 174, 197, 198, 213
Bate, Chief Petty Officer William, 66, 68, 70
Beadnell, Surgeon C. M., 28, 37, 39, 121
Bearcroft, Captain J. E., 39, 54, 59, 62, 76, 78, 99, 107, 116, 118, 152–154, 159, 160,

169–171, 173, 175, 185, 187, 191–195, 201, 204, 205, 213, 215
Beaton's Hotel & Store, 177
Belcher, Able Seaman, 163
Belcombe, Lieutenant, 217
Belfast, 203–205, 214
Bellamy, Sergeant G., 210
Belmont, 31–33, 39, 53, 55, 59, 60, 73, 107, 150, 155
Bennett, Marine Alfred, 35
Bergendal Farm, 204
Bethlehem, 25
Bethune's Horse, 216
Biggarsberg Hills, 6, 135, 161, 164
Bird, Petty Officer, 66
Black Watch, 14, 60, 61, 120, 173, 205
Boldero, Midshipman, 50, 72, 149
Bolton, Captain, 214
Border Mounted Rifles, 24
Border Regiment, 14
Botha, Christiaan, 167
Botha, General, 50, 52, 93, 94, 96, 97, 127–129, 133, 167, 172, 191–194
Botha's Pass, 16, 176–178, 181
Boyle, Lieutenant the Hon. E. S. H., 30, 34, 37
Boyle, Marine J., 35
Brabant's Horse, 173, 205
Brakfontein, 91, 100, 102, 106
Brazier Creagh, Major, 136, 189
Broadwood, General, 107, 159, 194
Brock, Petty Officer W., 163
Brocklehurst General, 189
Bronker's Spruit, 201
Brown, Marine A., 35
Brugspruit 201, 213
Buckley, Private J., 210
Buller, Gen. Sir Redvers, 7, 18, 26, 27, 29, 30, 49, 52, 57, 63, 65–70, 73–76, 80, 83, 85, 87–95, 97–100, 103–106, 124–127,

237

129–131, 133–136, 138, 139, 148, 150,
161, 164–167, 174, 176, 177, 179, 180,
181, 195, 204, 206, 207, 209
Bulwana, 24, 82, 86, 98, 125, 133, 135
Burger, General Schalk, 96
Burleigh, Bennet, *Daily Telegraph* 81
Burne, Lieutenant, 50, 66, 84, 90, 92, 96, 100,
104–105, 130, 132, 135, 136, 148,
163–167, 176, 177, 199, 181, 182, 189,
190, 195, 209
Bushman's Hoek, 30, 57

Caesar's Camp, 22, 24, 25, 86, 87, 123, 125
Cameronians, 14
Campbell, Lieutenant G. W. McO, 27, 37, 39,
216
Campling, Able Seaman, 69
Cannon, Gunner, 98
Cape Mounted Rifles, 13, 57, 58
Carey, Petty Officer, 126
Carleton, Colonel, 18, 19, 25
Carnegie, Midshipman the Hon. I. L. A., 15,
86, 125, 135
Casham, Leading Seaman Patrick, 132
Cemetery Hill, 22, 24
Chiazarri, Lieutenant, 66
Chichester, Midshipman E. G., 3, 4, 15, 19,
83, 142, 149
Chieveley, 52, 66, 70, 84, 87–90, 105, 106,
124, 127, 131, 216
Churchill, Winston, 25, 52, 88, 203
Cingolo, 127, 128
City Imperial Volunteers, 122, 185, 194
Clery, General, 52, 63, 102, 105, 161, 163,
179
Clutterbuck, Lieutenant, 50, 189, 190
Coke, General, 178, 189
Coldstream Guards, 14, 206, 214
Cole, Mr, gunner, 49, 66
Colenso, 7, 19, 63, 65, 66, 70, 73–76, 80, 88,
97, 106, 120, 125, 128, 130, 134–136, 139,
163, 189, 210
Colley, General Sir George, 4, 180, 182
Colquhoun, Lieutenant-Commander W. J., 168,
205
Columbian S.S., 139, 140
Colville, General, 173, 187, 193
Conan Doyle, Sir Arthur, 6
Connaught Rangers, 14, 68
Connor, Petty Officer, 126
Cooley, Mr W., 217
Cove Redoubt, 21, 22, 24, 43, 46, 47, 51, 87,
98, 124, 133
Crabbe, Colonel, 32
Crocodile River, 207, 214

Crofton, Colonel, 95
Cronje, General, 54, 59, 60, 79, 109, 116–118,
121, 122, 132, 135, 150, 151, 193
Cronje, Mrs, 121
Crowe, Master-at-Arms George, 4, 89, 92, 96,
131, 186
Cunningham, Midshipman Andrew Browne,
153, 154, 159, 168, 171, 175, 185, 187,
191, 193, 195, 206, 214, 215, 220, 221

De Aar, 29, 31, 57, 98
De Beers, 53, 117
de Horsey, Commander S. V. Y., 59, 81, 192
De Wet, Christiaan, 112, 116, 118, 120, 121,
151, 154, 156, 159, 167, 170, 173, 187,
188, 193, 194, 197–200, 212, 213
De Wet, Piet, 172
De Wet's Farm, 167
Dean, Lieutenant F. W., 28, 33, 34, 37, 39,
110, 116
Deas, Lieutenant, 50, 66, 70, 71
Delagoa Bay, 10, 11, 140, 163, 183
Delagoa Bay Railway, 63, 191, 193, 194, 201,
208
De la Rey, Aadrian, 59
De la Rey, General, 54, 55, 60, 173, 185, 193,
206
Derbyshire Militia, 187, 194
Devonshire Regiment, 24, 69, 84, 87, 105, 136,
179
Diamond Hill, 194–196, 203
Diamond Fields Artillery, 116, 155
Dick-Cunyngham, Colonel, 86
Dido H.M.S., 76
Digby-Jones, Lieutenant, 87
Dingaan's Day, 83
Doornkop, 184
Dorchester, England, 146, 147, 220
Doris H.M.S., 3, 8, 28, 30, 35, 36, 39, 53, 59,
98, 99, 109, 118, 122, 150, 152, 153, 160,
175, 213, 215, 220
Dorset Regiment, 14, 95, 178–180, 189, 209
Dragoon Guards, 14
Drakensberg Mountains, 27, 166, 176
Drew, Andrew A. W., 81
Drummond, Lieutenant, 50, 126
Duggan, Mr, conductor, 205
Duke of Cambridge's Own Yeomanry, 205
Dundas, Commander, 217, 220
Dundee, 6, 18, 55, 164, 165
Dundonald, Lord, 65, 66, 134
Dunn, Able Seaman, 124
Dunottar Castle, 17, 26, 52, 75, 76, 98
Durban Light Infantry Band, 218
Dyson, Colour-Sergeant, 34

East Kent Regiment (Buffs), 213
East London, 17, 30
East Surreys, 105, 177, 179, 180
Egerton, Lieutenant F. G., 15, 21, 40, 43, 133
Egerton, Midshipman, 30
Elandslaagte, 55, 161, 163–165, 181
Elliott, Surgeon, 217
Ellis Brown, Mr J., 217
Ellis, Engineer E. H., 15
Emly, Able Seaman J., 20, 41
England, Lieutenant, 49, 66, 80, 92, 100, 102, 103, 105, 109, 132
Enslin, 33, 36, 77, 109, 158
Epsley, Petty Officer, 66
Essex Regiment, 120
Estcourt, 19, 49, 52, 82, 125
Ethelston, Commander A. P., 8, 28–30, 34, 35, 37, 57, 153
Excellent, H.M.S., 7

Fergusson, Lieutenant, J. A., 98, 174, 188, 197, 199, 213
Fitzgerald, Petty Officer, 2
Ford, Leading Seaman W., 20, 41
Fort Wylie, 63, 66–71
Forte, H.M.S., 8, 49, 50, 65, 96, 129, 135, 165, 181, 182, 189
Fowler, Surgeon J. G., 15, 40, 43
Frederickstad, 212
French, General Sir John, 18, 19, 63, 106, 107, 109, 110–112, 116, 118, 155, 157, 161, 169, 183, 194, 204, 207, 216
French, Lieutenant A. H., 152, 154
Fuller, Petty Officer, 39

Gans Vlei Spruit, 178, 179
Gascon, 49
Gatacre, Lieutenant-General Sir William Forbes, 57, 58, 63
Glencoe, 6, 164–166, 181
Gloucester Regiment, 83
Gordon Highlanders, 14, 24, 84–86, 120, 121, 139, 182, 185
Gordon Hill, 20–22, 46
Gough, Colonel, 134
Gould, Able Seaman George Lewin, 149
Grant, Commander W. L., 98, 107, 111, 118, 119, 153, 188, 198–200, 212
Grant's Guns, 98, 109, 116, 151, 152, 158, 173–175, 187, 193, 197, 198, 212, 213
Gras Kop, 190, 195, 209, 210, 216, 217
Graspan, 33, 36, 38, 39, 53–55, 59, 73, 77, 142, 144, 150, 153, 204
Greagsby, Marine H., 35
Grenadier Guards, 14, 32, 143, 144, 193

Greylingstad, 190
Grimwood, Colonel, 18, 19
Grobelaar's Hill, 131
Gun Hill, 31, 66, 76, 80, 89, 105, 126, 127, 130, 131

'Hairy Mary', train, 80
Haldane, Captain, 52
Hall, Able Seaman, 3
Halsey, Lieutenant Arthur, 50, 51, 73, 83, 125, 176–178, 182, 189, 190, 195, 209, 215, 217–219
Halsey, Lieutenant Lionel, 15, 20, 21, 42, 46, 47, 51, 84, 85, 87, 123, 125, 133, 134, 139, 142, 163, 221
Hamilton, Colonel Ian, 18, 19, 24, 86
Hamilton, General Bruce, 138, 173, 185
Hamilton, Midshipman R. C., 15
Hannay's Mounted Infantry, 120
Harmes, Reverend, 82
Harris, Rear-Admiral Sir Robert, 6–8, 28, 30, 39, 59, 77, 139, 140, 153, 182, 215
Harrismith, 22, 25
Hart, Major-General, 63, 66, 102, 130, 132, 200, 212
Hatt, Fred, Boy Seaman, 2
Hawarden Castle, 49
Hayes, Midshipman H. T., 15
Hayles, Ordinary Seaman Frank, 68
Headley, Captain R. E., 181
Hector Spruit, 207, 214
Hector Spruit Station, 207
Heidelberg, 16, 25, 83, 86, 190
Heilbron, 174, 187, 188, 193, 197, 213
Helman, Able Seaman, 129
Helpmakaar Hill, 22, 24
Hely-Hutchinson, Sir Walter, 19, 215
Heneage, Lieutenant A. W., 15, 43, 133, 138, 142, 221
Highland Light Infantry, 173
Hildyard, Major-General, 63, 66, 102, 105, 127, 164, 165, 167, 181, 216
Hlangwane, 64, 127–131
Hobson, Sub-Lieutenant, 217
Hodges, Lieutenant M. H., 15, 20, 21, 43, 133, 140, 142, 146, 220, 221
Hodson, Midshipman, 50, 72, 149
Hollins, Mr, clerk, 50, 72
Honning Spruit, 172
Houston, Midshipman J. F., 30
Howard, Major-General F., 24, 86
Howard, Mr, 203
Howell, Alma Mary, 77
Huddart, Midshipman C. A. E., 28, 34–38, 150, 153

Hudson, Scott & Sons Ltd., 77
Hunt, Lieutenant, 50, 66, 80, 96, 100, 102,
  105, 132, 165, 181
Hurst, Able Seaman Henry, 35
Hussars, 18th, 13, 105, 189

Land, Midshipman G. H., 98
Lansdowne, War Secretary, 74, 76
Large, Signalman, 95
Ledgard, Midshipman, 50, 217, 220
Lee-Metford, rifles, 16, 58, 94, 133
Lees, Lieutenant, 133, 182
Leeuw Spruit Station, 188
Leicestershire Regiment, 13
Lewin, Midshipman G. E., 28
Life Guards, 14
Lilly, Staff-Surgeon, 50, 135, 166
Limpus, Commander, 27, 49, 50, 66, 76, 132
Lindique Drift, 198
Lismore Castle, 49
'Little Bobs', 4.7″ gun, 109, 152, 173, 187,
  197, 200, 212
Liverpool Regiment, 13, 24, 40
Lloyd, Midshipman Lionel, 152, 154, 158
Lloyd's of London, 146, 220
Lombard's Kop, 19, 24, 55
Long, Colonel, 66, 67, 70, 73, 129, 139
'Long Tom', Boer gun, 5, 6, 19–22, 24, 40,
  41, 47, 68, 82, 86, 87, 94, 102, 103, 111,
  125, 133, 135, 155, 173, 204, 207
Lonsberg, 198
Lookout Hill (also see Spion Kop), 91
Lourenço Marques, 10,208
Lowe, Gunner E. E., 30, 34, 37
Loyal North Lancashires, 31, 33
Lyddite, 7, 16, 41, 61, 62, 67, 68, 80, 82, 87,
  92, 102, 118–120, 124, 131, 132, 151, 152,
  173, 177, 179, 180, 195, 200, 212
Lyons, Messrs J., 82
Lyttelton, Major-General, 63, 66, 91, 92, 95,
  102, 103, 105, 138, 179, 182

Machadodorp, 206
Macmillan, Surgeon, 71
Mafeking, 26, 27, 55, 57, 63, 77, 106, 193,
  214, 222
Magersfontein, 58–60, 62, 65, 73, 79, 80, 99,
  106, 107, 110, 116, 118, 120, 121
Magicienne, H.M.S., 10
Majuba Hill, 4, 16, 121, 131, 134, 161, 166,
  167, 176, 180, 181
Manchester Regiment, 14, 24, 86, 87
Marchant, Captain A. E., 28, 34–36, 38, 39,
  175, 186
Maria S.S., 10

Marie des Anges, Mother, 124
Marine Light Infantry, Royal, 28, 35, 152, 169,
  193
Marks, Mr, 196, 201
Martin, Marine H., 35
Martini-Henry rifles, 60
Masters, Able Seaman, 42
Masterson, Lieutenant, 87
Mauritius, 2, 149
Mauser, rifles, 5, 18, 32, 34, 41, 46, 54, 55,
  60, 61, 67, 68, 70, 86, 91, 93, 94, 102, 112,
  119–121, 130, 131, 171, 173, 177, 179,
  185, 192, 220
McBride, Major John, 171
McDonald, General, 107, 173
Melville, Lieutenant, 129, 130
Menzies, Midshipman J., 98
Metcalfe, Marine J., 35
Metcalfe, Petty Officer, 66
Methuen, General Lord, 30–33, 38, 53–55,
  60–63, 78, 80, 88, 99, 107, 150, 188, 199
Meyer, General Lukas, 18
Middleburg, 16, 25, 195, 203
Middlesex Regiment, 14, 179
Middleton, Midshipman J. R., 15
Milner, Sir Alfred, 53
Milwaukee S.S., 122
Mitchell, Petty Officer H., 66
Mitchell, Petty Officer R., 66
Modderfontein, 198
Modder River, 31, 54, 55, 58–62, 76, 78–81,
  88, 99, 106, 107, 109–112, 116, 118–122,
  150–152, 156, 168
Modder River Station, 116
Modder Spruit, 19, 25
Monarch H.M.S., 3, 8, 28, 35, 39, 59, 81,
  99, 117, 150, 155, 156, 168, 191–193, 213,
  220
Monte Cristo, 63, 127–130
Monument Hill, 204, 205
Mooi River, 52, 199
Morgan, Captain R. H., 59
Morier, Sir Robert, 11
Morris, Colonel, Town Commandant of
  Durban, 148, 217, 218
Mount Alice, 90, 100, 101, 102, 124
Mount Prospect, 182
Mourilyan, Surgeon E. P., 59
Mullins, Captain, 51
Mullis, Petty Officer, 66
Munro, Chief Petty Officer, 167, 219
Munster Fusiliers, 14

Nail, Ordinary Seaman J., 20, 41
Natal Advertiser, 216

240

Natal Carbineers, 24, 84, 134
Natal Naval Volunteers, 21, 50, 66, 131, 134, 161, 182, 215
Natal Volunteers, 24
National-Zeitung, 5
Naval Hill, Bloemfontein, 159, 173
Newcastle, 6, 17, 22, 24, 166, 167, 181
Newcome, Sub-Lieutenant, 49, 51
Newman, Lieutenant E. J. K., 59
Newman, Sergeant F., 210
Newstead, Able Seaman, 69
Newton, Sub-Lieutenant M. G., 28, 59
Nicholson's Nek, 18, 24, 55
Nicol, Mr J., 217
North Lancashire Regiment, 13, 53
Northampton Regiment, 14, 31, 33
Northumberland Fusiliers, 14, 31, 33, 58

O'Neill's Farm, 167
Observation Hill, 22, 25, 86
Ogilvy, Lieutenant, 49, 66–70, 72, 76, 92, 96, 100–102, 104, 126, 128, 132, 133, 143, 148, 221
'Old Joey', 4.7" gun, 60
Oliphant's River, 203
One Tree Hill, 151, 152
Orange Free State, (Orange River Colony), 5, 10, 17, 29, 109, 110, 116, 151, 156–158, 166–168, 170, 172, 174, 178, 181, 187, 193, 195
Orange River, 17, 53, 62, 79, 169
Orcana. S.S., hospital ship, 219
Orlando H.M.S., 3, 149
Orotava, S.S., 142
Osborne, Royal Yacht, 2
Oxfordshire Light Infantry, 120

Paardeberg, 107, 117, 118, 120–122, 128, 132, 135, 150, 151, 158
Park, Colonel, 87
Parkinson, Able Seaman F., 163
Parson's Farm, 216
Paton, Stoker David, 138
Pavonia, S.S., 210
Payne, Able Seaman, 123
Peck, Sergeant, 51
Peile, Major S. D., 152–154
Penelope, H.M.S., 10
Penn Symons, General, 18, 26, 165
Penny, Paymaster W. B., 168
Pepworth Hill, 22, 24, 40
Perrin, Regimental Sergeant-Major Bill, 84
Philomel H.M.S., 39, 45, 50, 51, 70, 71, 84, 96, 132, 148, 163, 168, 182, 186, 216–220
Pietermaritzburg, 13, 19, 51, 63, 126, 215

Pieter's Hill, 131–133
Pieter's Station, 135
Pink, Mr, Mayor of Portsmouth, 142
Pitt, Private, 87
Plumbe, Major J. H., 28, 34–37, 150, 153
Poe, Lieutehnant W. S., 59
Pole-Carew, General, 55, 58, 59, 169, 171, 184, 204–206, 208, 214
Poort Station, 195
Poplar Grove, 150–152, 154, 158, 160
Porter, Fleet-Surgeon J., 28, 35, 37, 204
Potgeiter's Drift, 65, 88, 90, 96–98, 101
Powerful H.M.S., 1–3, 8, 10, 15, 28, 30, 35, 41, 44, 47, 49, 59, 85, 87, 124, 135, 137–143, 149, 153, 158, 217, 220
Pretoria, 11, 16, 17, 25, 27, 45, 52, 63, 150, 183, 191–196, 199, 200, 203–207, 213–215
Pretorius Drift, 90
Prince of Wales, 1, 46
Princess Cafe, Durban, 218, 220
'Princess Victoria', 4.7" gun, 44, 84, 85, 87, 133, 139, 145
Pringle, Mr., 68
Prinsloo, 173
Prothero, Captain R. C., 30, 31, 33, 34, 36, 37, 150, 154, 160
'Puffing Billy', Boer gun, 82
Pym, Paymaster, 217

Quagga's Hill, 179
Queen's Regiment, 216
Queenstown, 29, 30, 57, 63

Radford, Marine F., 35
Raikes, Lieutenant G. I., 59
Railway Hill, 131, 132
Rainier, Midshipman J. W., 59
Ralph, Julian, 74
Ramdam, 109–111
Reddersburg, 173
Reuter's, 8, 61, 78–80, 215
Rhenoster Valley, 187
Rhodes, Cecil, 26, 47, 53, 109, 153
Rhodes, Colonel Frank, 26, 45, 47, 84
Richards, Lieutenant, 49, 50, 66, 69
Riet, River, 58, 110, 111
Rietfontein, 199
Rifle Brigade, 24
Rifleman's Ridge, 25
Rifles 60th, 18
Roberts, Boatswain, 2
Roberts, Field-Marshal Lord (Bobs), 74, 75, 79, 98, 99, 106, 107, 109–112, 116–121, 126, 129, 138, 150–152, 154–158, 161, 166,

241

168–173, 183–185, 187, 191–195, 204, 205, 209, 212, 215
Robertson, Midshipman, 28, 59, 78
Robinson, Captain C. G., 3
Roper, Sergeant, 66, 69
Roskruge, Assistant Engineer, 49, 149
Roslin Castle, 26, 27, 49
Rossiya, 1
Royal Canadian Regiment, 112, 116, 120
Royal Dublin Fusiliers, 13, 24, 68, 73–75, 130, 136, 178, 179
Royal Army Medical Corps, 13
Royal Artillery, 8, 13, 20, 24, 33, 34, 38, 66–68, 70, 71, 86, 89, 92, 102, 107, 117, 119, 121, 133, 139, 155, 159, 161, 170, 173, 176, 179, 180, 184, 189, 192, 195, 198, 206, 210, 212, 213, 216
Royal Horse Artillery, 102, 105, 107, 203, 210
Royal Marine Artillery, 28, 143, 159
Royal Engineers, 13, 21, 33, 38, 40, 54, 59, 60, 85, 87, 92, 93, 101, 102, 104, 125, 173, 177, 181, 184, 187, 189, 198, 204, 214, 215
Royal Berkshire Regiment, 13, 29, 30, 57
Royal Horse Guards, 14
Royal Irish Fusiliers, 18, 24, 63
Royal Irish Rifles, 57, 58, 173
Royal Lancasters, 177
Royal West Surreys, 69
Royston, Colonel W., 24
Rundle, General, 173, 216

Salt River Junction, 28, 30
Sandspruit, 25, 182, 189, 190, 216, 217
Saunders, Midshipman F., 59
Saunders, Lieutenant, F. J., 28, 34, 37
Scheeper, Mr, 215, 216
Scots Guards, 32, 54, 137, 171, 203, 214
Scots Greys, 14, 110
Scott Turner, the Misses, 77
Scott, Captain Percy, 3, 5, 7, 8, 15, 27, 30, 49, 50, 51, 53, 54, 80, 126, 139, 148, 149, 210, 220, 221
Scott, Private, 87
Scottish Borderers, King's Own, 120
Seaforth Highlanders, 60, 61, 120, 173
Senior, Captain Guy, 28, 34, 36, 37
Sharp, Midshipman C. R., 3, 4, 15, 47, 82, 139, 140, 146, 149, 221
Sheen, Engineer C. C., 15, 41
Shepheard, Captain, 216
Sherwood Foresters, 197
Shooter's Hill, 69, 76
Shropshire Regiment, 120
Signal Hill, 100–102
Sillem, Midshipman W. W., 30, 34, 37, 38

Silverton, 194
Sim, Lieutenant-Colonel, 97
Simmer and Jack Mine, 184
Simons Bay, 2–4, 137, 139, 140
Simonstown, 3, 4, 8, 9, 15, 28, 30, 49, 57, 60, 111, 173, 212, 213, 215
Sims, Gunner W., 15, 20, 21, 85, 140, 142
Six Mile Spruit, 191
Skinner, Midshipman, 49, 126
'Sloper', 4.7" gun, 109, 152, 173, 187, 197, 199, 200, 212
Smart, Trooper, 210
Smithfield, Armourer's Mate, 206
Smuts, Jan, 173, 212
South African Light Horse, 31
South Lancashires, 177, 179, 190, 209
South Railway Jetty, 141, 143
Spion Kop (Lookout Hill), 88, 91–94, 96, 97, 100, 102, 103, 105, 106, 121, 124, 125, 127, 210
Spitz Kop, 177
Springfield, 88, 90, 105
Spytfontein, 54, 60, 62
St. Vincent, training ship, 142
Staats Field Artillery, 16
Stabb, Lieutenant, 42, 133
Standerton, 16, 190, 195, 209, 215
Steel, Lieutenant, 50, 52, 165, 181
Steevens, G. W., 41
Stephens, Chief Petty Officer, 66, 68, 80
Stewart, Major, 33, 54, 59
Steyn, President, 17, 60, 156, 157, 170
Stokes, Midshipman Alick, 15
Stormberg, 29, 30, 57, 58, 73, 106
Sussex Regiment, 194, 210
Symons, Petty Officer, 66

Tabanyama, 93
Talana, 18
Tantallon Castle, S.S., 220
Tartar H.M.S., 50, 52, 65, 66, 70, 71, 92, 97, 216, 217, 220
Taylor, Petty Officer, 66, 67
Taylor, Lieutenant, 35
Tchrengula, 18, 19, 25
Terrible H.M.S., 1–4, 7, 8, 15, 49, 51, 53, 65, 70, 81, 124, 126, 140, 148, 149, 193
Thorneycroft, Lieutenant-Colonel Alec, 92, 93, 95, 97
Thorneycroft's Mounted Infantry, 92
Tuck, Armourer's Mate Joe, 197, 198
Tugela, River, 6, 50, 63, 66, 67, 69, 82, 88, 90, 97, 100, 102, 105, 126–130, 139, 176
Tunbridge, Thomas, coxswain, 129
Tyndale-Biscoe, Lieutenant, 42, 133

Umgeni, 27, 28
Umlass Waterworks, 50
Urmston, Major A. G. B., 59, 142
Utrecht, 25, 166, 179, 181

Vaal River, 166, 171, 172, 197–199
Vaal Krantz, 100, 102, 104–106, 125, 126, 130

Van Wyk's Hill, 176, 178, 181
Venness, Petty Officer, 66, 67
Ventersburg, 25
Vereeniging, 172
Vet River, 169, 170
Victoria, Queen, 1, 16, 39, 76, 142, 145, 146, 148, 181, 220
Victory H.M.S., 141
Viljoen's Drift, 168, 172, 175, 186, 187
Volksrust, 179–182
Vredefort Road Station, 172, 187
Vryheid, 25

Wagon Hill, 22, 24, 25, 85–87, 125
Wakkerstroom, 16, 25, 182, 190, 216
Ward, Able Seaman Albert, 87
Ward, Colonel, 25, 123, 137
Ward, Petty Officer, 66
Wardle, Midshipman T. F. J. L., 28, 34, 37
Warren, Lieutenant-General Sir Charles, 88, 90–97, 103
Warwickshire Regiment, 14, 195
Waterval Drift, 111, 112, 119, 121, 151
Waterval Onder Station, 206
Wauchope, Major-General, 61
Webster, Able Seaman, 69
Welverdiend, 199, 200

Wepener, 173
West, Private R., 210
West Surreys, 179
Weston, 'Aggie', 77, 78
Wheeler, Stoker, 123
White, Sub-Lieutenant R. F., 28, 37
White, Lieutenant-General Sir George, 6–8, 18–22, 24–26, 65, 73, 82–87, 124, 136–138, 145
White, Able Seaman, 69
White, Midshipman, 49
Whyte, Midshipman, 84
Wilde, Lieutenant, 49, 50, 66, 130
Wilkes, Able Seaman J., 163
Willow Grange, 55
Wilson, Lieutenant (later Captain) L.O., 59, 169, 193, 194, 201, 204
Winburg, 25, 156, 173, 174, 213
Windsor Castle, 76, 142, 144, 145, 149
Witpootje, 212
Woodgate, General, 92, 93, 95
Wool's Drift, 16, 166, 167
Woolstadt, 200
Wright, Mr, gunner, 49, 66, 70, 71

Yellowboom Farm, 176, 178
Yorkshire Light Infantry, King's Own, 2, 13, 31, 33–35
Yorkshire, S.S., 49
Yule, Brigadier-General, 18

Zand River, 170
Zarps, 25, 192, 204
Zululand Expedition, 126, 148
Zwaart Kop, 100–102, 104

243

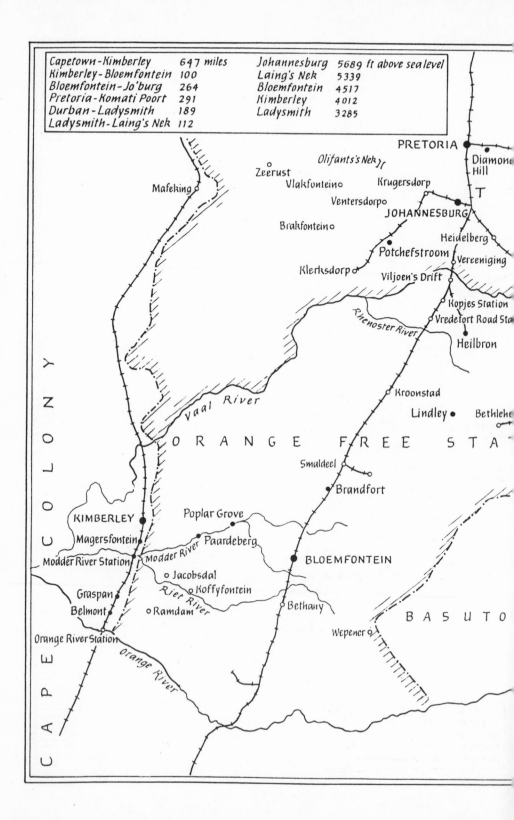

Capetown-Kimberley	647 miles	Johannesburg	5689 ft above sea level
Kimberley-Bloemfontein	100	Laing's Nek	5339
Bloemfontein-Jo'burg	264	Bloemfontein	4517
Pretoria-Komati Poort	291	Kimberley	4012
Durban-Ladysmith	189	Ladysmith	3285
Ladysmith-Laing's Nek	112		